*The Albert Schweitzer–Helene Bresslau Letters*

The Albert Schweitzer Library

Albert Schweitzer and Helene Bresslau, ca. 1911.
*Courtesy of the Albert Schweitzer Archive, Günsbach.*

THE
*Albert Schweitzer–Helene Bresslau*
LETTERS
*1902–1912*

*Edited by* Rhena Schweitzer Miller
*and* Gustav Woytt

*Translated from the German and Edited by* Antje Bultmann Lemke
*Assistant Editor,* Nancy Stewart

SYRACUSE UNIVERSITY PRESS

First Edition 2003
03  04  05  06  07  08      6  5  4  3  2  1

Originally published in German as *Albert Schweitzer–Helene Bresslau:
Die Jahre vor Lambarene, Briefe 1902–1912*, edited by Rhena Schweitzer Miller
and Gustav Woytt (Munich: C. H. Beck, 1992).

The paper used in this publication meets the minimum requirements of
American National Standard for Information Sciences—Permanence
of Paper for Printed Library Materials, ANSI Z39.48–1984.∞™

**Library of Congress Cataloging-in-Publication Data**
Schweitzer, Albert, 1875–1965.
    [Jahre vor Lambarene. English]
The Albert Schweitzer–Helene Bresslau letters, 1902–1912 /
    edited by
Rhena Schweitzer Miller and Gustav Woytt ; translated from the German
    and edited by Antje Bultmann Lemke with Nancy Stewart, assistant
    editor.— 1st ed.
p. cm.—(The Albert Schweitzer library)
Includes bibliographical references and index.
ISBN 0–8156–2994-X (alk. paper)
1. Schweitzer, Albert, 1875–1965—Correspondence. 2. Bresslau,
    Helene, 1879–1957—Correspondence. 3. Missionaries,
    Medical—Gabon—Lambaréné (Moyen-Ogooué)—Correspondence. 4.
    Theologians—Europe—Biography. 5. Musicians—Europe—Biography. I.
    Bresslau, Helene, 1879–1957. II. Schweitzer Miller, Rhena. III. Woytt,
    Gustav. IV. Lemke, Antje Bultmann. V. Stewart, Nancy. VI. Title. VII.
Series: Albert Schweitzer library (Syracuse, N.Y.)
CT1018.S45 A413 2003
610'.92—dc21
2002015509

*To Gustav Woytt*

**Rhena Schweitzer Miller,** daughter and only child of Helene and Albert Schweitzer, has written many articles about her father's life and participates in Albert Schweitzer organizations worldwide.

**Gustay Woytt** was the son of Schweitzer's sister, Adele, and a close family friend who assisted Schweitzer with his writings and translations.

**Antje Bultmann Lemke** is professor emerita of Syracuse University and director emerita of the Schweitzer Fellowship. She is the translator of Albert Schweitzer's *Out of My Life and Thought: An Autobiography.*

**Nancy Stewart** has a nursing background. She spent a year in Nigeria with her husband, who was helping to establish a medical school.

# CONTENTS

# ILLUSTRATIONS

# PREFACE

*I*t verges on the miraculous that a selection from the correspondence between my parents, Helene and Albert Schweitzer, from 1901 to 1912, can be published.

In 1957, after the death of my mother, I had to move out very hastily from the house in Königsfeld in the Black Forest that my father had had built before he returned to Africa in 1924. All that I could do was to pack everything that appeared important to me as best I could into trunks and boxes, which were put into storage in various places in Switzerland for many years. I then spent ten years in Africa and later moved to the United States. From time to time, while visiting in Switzerland, I would rummage around in the boxes and trunks, but I never had much time for it. I did not even think of searching for any correspondence between my parents because I seemed to remember that my mother once told me that she had burned all my father's letters. Thus, I was absolutely astonished when I found these letters a few years ago. I probably had misunderstood my mother. This correspondence contains far fewer letters from her than from my father, so she probably meant that she had destroyed a portion of her own letters.

To my great surprise, I found that both my father and my mother wrote a large part, about two-thirds, of their correspondence in French. My father was probably following the tradition of cultivated Alsatian families, who spoke in Alsatian dialect but wrote their letters in French. My mother, who came from an old German family, spoke excellent French, which often earned her my father's praise. She probably used this language to fit in with the custom of the country and to please my father.

For me, these letters were a revelation. I had known my parents only as older people because my father was forty-four and my mother forty when I was born. In addition, they both were rather reserved people, and while I was growing up, my father spent most of his time in Africa. In these letters, I got to know my parents as young people, with their idealism, their struggles, and their strong will, which made it possible for them to achieve their goal of going to Africa together in spite of all obstacles.

These letters are the only personal testimony of the relationship between Helene Bresslau and Albert Schweitzer in the years before they journeyed out into the African forest. In quick succession, the writers express their thoughts and feelings without restraint, and in reading their words we can follow along as two extraordinary personalities find their way to one another over the course of a decade. In his wedding sermon for Elly Knapp and Theodor Heuss, my father said, "The great happiness of this moment is not that two human beings inwardly vow to one another, 'We want to live for one another,' but it means, 'We want to live with each other for something.' " The same is true to an even higher degree of the couple Helene Bresslau and Albert Schweitzer. It was the common task that united them.

These letters also throw a new light on my father's intellectual development and the slow ripening of his decision to go to Africa. The young man who knew what he wanted but not how it could be attained became the man of action who knew his path.

We come to know his manifold areas of interest and can follow the development of the important books he wrote during these years. He reports on the preaching activity that was so important to him but that has not yet received adequate consideration. He is intensively occupied with the problem of how Jesus' message can be brought home to modern humanity. Music, too, is important to him, as indicated by his rendition of the works of Bach, his activities for the preservation of old organs and for the creation of new ones with beautiful tone. Later, medicine is added to the list of his interests. Amazingly, my father and my mother rarely mention this study of a completely new subject and the experience of contact with sick human beings; my mother writes only a little about her nursing experiences. Still less do my parents appear to have reflected on the black people in whose midst they would live. Academic activity is seldom mentioned. It is the realization of his promise "to enter on a path of immediate service as a human being" that is close to my father's heart.

Since his time in Lambaréné, my father has become world famous. My mother, although his life's partner and an irreplaceable colleague in the first period of activity in their jungle hospital, has existed in his shadow from that time. Only a few people know what part she had in his development and what a significant role she played in his younger years. She was an important woman in her own right. Much has been written about my father, but these letters bear witness to the influence my mother had on his life. That is why making this correspondence accessible to the public is a project particularly dear to my heart. Out of the 460 letters exchanged between my parents from 1902 to 1912, those of purely local interest and those with redundancies—that is, letters for holidays—have been omitted. Ellipses enclosed within square brackets ([ . . . ]) indicate editorial omissions within the letters. All other ellipses throughout the letters are part of my parents' writing style.

For the first publication of this book in German, I would like to give heartfelt thanks to Dr. Ingrid Lent, who lovingly saw this correspondence through the press, and to my cousin Gustav Woytt, without whose help this edition would never have come about.

For the English edition, I am indebted to Antje Bultmann Lemke, with whom I made the selections and who lovingly translated the chosen letters with the assistance of Ann Martin, Kurt Bergel, and Kitty Bergel. Nancy Stewart also gave invaluable help with the manuscript. My deepest gratitude goes to them all.

Rhena Schweitzer Miller

# INTRODUCTION

## Albert Schweitzer

*O*n his father's side, Albert Schweitzer came from a family of schoolmasters: his grandfather, his great-grandfather, and his great-great-grandfather were village schoolmasters in Lower Alsace. His grandfather, Philipp, was the first to know French; his diary is written alternately in German and French. When Napoleon III acceded to the throne in 1852, Philipp asked to be released from his teaching position and started up a grocery business in Pfaffenhofen—not in order to earn more money, as his great-grandchild Jean-Paul Sartre writes,[1] but because, as a convinced republican, he did not wish to swear the civil service oath to the emperor. From 1875 to 1886, he was the mayor of this little Lower Alsatian town; it should be noted that because the German administration had taken precedence over the French laws, the mayors were not elected, but rather appointed by the German government.

Of the three sons born from Philipp's marriage with Marie Louise Gerst, the two elder, Auguste and Charles, moved to France before 1870; both of them lived in Paris, Auguste as a wealthy merchant, Charles as a German teacher who reformed the teaching of German in France and was Jean-Paul Sartre's grandfather. These two paternal uncles brought Albert Schweitzer to Paris early in his life.

The youngest son, Louis Théophile, born on March 21, 1846, in Pfaffenhofen, studied theology, was the vicar for Pastor Johann Jakob Schillinger in Mühlbach in the Münsteral Valley, and then was parish administrator and teacher for the small Protestant congregation in Kaysers-

---

1. In *Les mots* (The words) (Paris: Gallimard, 1964), 5.

berg (Upper Alsace). In 1872, he married Adele Schillinger, the Mühlbach pastor's daughter, who was born on October 1, 1842. One of Adele's half-brothers, Albert Schillinger, had been the pastor of St. Nicholas's Church in Strasbourg. In 1872, he died as a consequence of the deprivations suffered during the siege of Strasbourg. Adele called her first son Albert after him.

The Schillingers were from Albishausen in Wurttemberg; the Schweitzers had not emigrated from the Toggenburg region to Alsace after the Thirty Years' War, as Albert Schweitzer later assumed, but came from Frankfurt am Main.

Whereas Louis Schweitzer had a cheerful, humorous temperament, Adele was rather strict, sometimes passionate; she was very interested in political events. She had inherited this character from her father, whom family tradition reported as strict and sometimes subject to fits of temper. His grandson describes him as having a masterful nature. Albert inherited this nature, along with a tendency toward outbursts of temper; one of his female coworkers in Lambaréné called him "the master" in her letters.

Louis and Adele's marriage produced five children. The two eldest, Luise and Albert, were born in Kaysersberg; the three younger ones, Adele, Marguerite, and Paul, in Günsbach in the Münsteral Valley. Their father had been called as pastor of this congregation in 1875, and he served it until his death in 1925. Albert was born on January 14, 1875, in the house with the little tower at the upper end of Kaysersberg. The wine turned out particularly well that year; Schweitzer was always proud of the fact that he had been born in a good year for wine and in the town of the Münster preacher Geiler von Kaysersberg. He grew up in Günsbach, which he always regarded as his home. He spent a very happy childhood there, as he himself tells us; there was not even a generational conflict with his parents—his father became his "best friend."

Schweitzer tells us about his school days in Günsbach, Münster, and Mühlhausen in his memoirs[1] and in his autobiography.[2] He was neither a model pupil nor the class valedictorian; nevertheless, he did well in his Abitur[3] in 1893.

---

1. Albert Schweitzer, Out of My Childhood and Youth (Syracuse, N.Y.: Syracuse Univ. Press, 1977), 21–23.

2. Albert Schweitzer, Out of My Life and Thought, translated by C. T. Campion (1933; rpt., New York: Henry Holt, 1990), 2.

3. University qualifying exam.

The Schweitzer family, 1889. Albert is standing between his parents. *Courtesy of the Albert Schweitzer Archive, Günsbach.*

A decisive factor in his development as an organist was an extended stay in Paris following his *Abitur*. His uncle Auguste, who lived there, was first an employee and then a partner in the Harth Company, which was in the import-export trade. He had married Mathilde Hertle, his employer's sister-in-law, who was born on January 29, 1850, in Saar-Union, a little town in northern Alsace. This marriage remained childless for a long time, so Mathilde turned her love to her brother-in-law Louis's children. She decisively influenced and encouraged Schweitzer's development.

She paid for Schweitzer's first organ lessons with Charles Marie Widor, the famous composer and organist at the church of St. Sulpice, the home of the organ built by Cavaillé-Coll. Widor also was from Alsace; his father had been an organ builder in Rufach. Schweitzer had been so well prepared by his Mühlhausen organ teacher, Eugen Münch, that Widor accepted him as a pupil, even though otherwise he taught only members of the organ class at the Paris Conservatory. The teacher-student relationship soon grew into a lasting friendship. Widor showed Schweitzer how to make his technique more profound, and Schweitzer, in turn, led his teacher to a better understanding of the chorale preludes of Bach by translating the German chorale texts and showing him how Bach's tone painting reflects the contents of the text.

Without his aunt Mathilde's initiative, Schweitzer would not have become the organist he is acknowledged to be. She was the first to recognize and encourage the young man's great gifts; she spoke words of encouragement to him when he stood in need of them and predicted a great future for him. She died on February 18, 1902, probably from cancer. At the beginning of his correspondence with Helene Bresslau, Schweitzer is still completely under the influence of her death; he shows an almost adulatory devotion to the memory of "the one who is resting in the Père Lachaise," the famous Paris cemetery.

After the *Abitur*, Schweitzer attended the University of Strasbourg. His main subject was theology, but he also studied philosophy and musicology. Like almost all theological students, he lived in the St. Wilhelm student residence on the Thomasstaden. After the early death of his Mühlhausen organ teacher, Eugen Münch, he also took over the organ part in the performances of Bach's cantatas and passions that Eugen's brother, Ernst Münch, was conducting in St. Wilhelm's Church. At the time, this church was considered one of the most significant nurseries of the rising Bach cult. Thus, Schweitzer had the opportunity to become engaged with the practical problems of rendering Bach's works as well.

The Kaiser Wilhelm University in Strasbourg, founded after 1870, was flourishing in the 1890s. The mostly young professors, including the Protestant theological faculty, sought to realize the ideal of a modern university. Their most significant teacher was the New Testament scholar Heinrich Julius Holtzmann, originator of a new Marcan hypothesis of the evangelist's work. The entire faculty had a decidedly liberal character, which was in keeping with Schweitzer's origins because both his father and his deceased uncle Albert Schillinger were convinced supporters of this theological orientation.

Schweitzer, already at the beginning of a second year of study, during a fall maneuver in which he participated as part of his year of service, was visited by doubts about the correctness of the picture of Jesus prevalent at the time. Reading the tenth and eleventh chapters of the Gospel of Matthew led him to the realization that Jesus believed in the late Jewish conception of the imminent end of the world and of the dawning of the supernatural

Kingdom of God, and that His activity could be understood only under this assumption. He laid out this theory of "consistent eschatology" in detail in his later works.

After the state theological examination, at the instigation of Professor Theobald Ziegler, Schweitzer decided to take a doctorate in philosophy. The topic he chose for his dissertation was Kant's religious philosophy.

He spent the winter semester 1898–90 in Paris; he lived in a room at 20 rue de la Sorbonne. Besides his intensive study of Kant, he worked on the organ with Widor, who was now teaching him free of charge, and on the piano with J. Philipp and Marie Jaëll-Trautman, the latter a student of Liszt. Owing to her method, he became master of his fingers even without time-consuming practice. He was able to give his last concert at the age of seventy-nine at the organ of St. Thomas's Church in Strasbourg.

This second Paris stay was just as formative for Schweitzer as the first had been. At Widor's insistence, in 1902 he began to write an essay about the nature of Bach's art for the organ students of the Paris Conservatory. This essay grew into a book, which appeared in 1905.

His relationship with his aunt Mathilde deepened; she spoke encouraging words to him about his work, even later, when he presented his theory of consistent eschatology in a sketch of the life of Jesus.

Then there was his friendship with Adele Herrenschmidt. The two lines Schweitzer devotes to her in his autobiography give no clue to the role she played in his life.[1] She was born on February 14, 1845, in Paris, but, like his aunt Mathilde, she came from Saar-Union, where her parents ran a tannery. First in Neuilly, then in Paris, she directed a finishing school for girls from other countries who wanted to learn French. Schweitzer introduced her pupils to the musical language of Wagner. She spent the summer in the Grimmialp spa hotel in the highlands of Bern, and from 1901 to 1909 Schweitzer also spent a few weeks with her on the Grimmialp every summer, except that of 1907. At that time, he was in the habit of designating his intimate acquaintances by nicknames, giving Adele Herrenschmidt the name "Tata."

It was there that large portions of the essay in French on Bach, the research on the life of Jesus, and the German edition of *J. S. Bach* in 1906 came into being.

---

1. Schweitzer, *Out of My Life and Thought*, 98.

*Introduction*

He spent the summer semester of 1899 in Berlin. Hardly any Alsatian students, much less theological ones, strayed into the imperial capital at that time. If the theologians did visit a different German faculty, the liberals went to Tübingen, the orthodox to Erlangen, and Paris was still closer to Strasbourg than Berlin was.

According to his own testimony, Schweitzer spent more time on music than on theology or philosophy. The Colmar district superintendent, Friedrich Curtius,[1] had recommended him to his stepmother, the widow of the Hellenist Ernst Curtius, who had excavated Olympia. In her house, Schweitzer came to know the academic world of Berlin; there he suddenly realized that he and his contemporaries were living in an age of epigones. In his autobiography, written thirty years later, he rates the intellectual life of Berlin higher than that of the metropolis of Paris, but in his correspondence with Helene Bresslau, he does not even mention Berlin, whereas he mentions his circle of acquaintances in Paris; the reevaluation took place in retrospect.

In the summer of 1899, Schweitzer took his degree in Strasbourg with a dissertation on Kant's religious philosophy. It was his second work to appear in print; a French obituary of his Mühlhausen organ teacher Eugen Münch had appeared anonymously a year earlier.

Now at last Schweitzer returned to theology. He conceived the plan of treating both the life of Jesus and the faith of primitive Christianity in connection with the problem of the Lord's Supper. Of the three projected treatises, only two appeared: *The Problem of the Last Supper* (1901) and *The Secret of the Messiahship and the Secret of the Passion: A Sketch of the Life of Jesus* (1901). In the latter book, dedicated to his father, he first presented the idea of consistent eschatology that already had been occupying him for six years. It also served as the dissertation for his appointment as privatdozent[2] at the University of Strasbourg in March 1902; his inaugural lecture was on the concept of the Logos in the Gospel of John.

His career as a university teacher seemed to be laid out for him.

His correspondence with Helene Bresslau began at the same time. How had the acquaintance come about?

Back in Kaysersberg, the Schweitzers had become friends with the dis-

1. 1851–1933.
2. Assistant professor.

trict judge (he was also called a justice of the peace, as in the French era), Richard Haas, and his wife. Both came from Kaiserslautern. The German administration appointed lawyers from the Palatinate and the Rhineland for vacant judgeships in Alsace if no suitable Alsatian candidate presented himself; in those areas, the French Civil Code from the Napoleonic era was still in force, so these lawyers were immediately familiar with the law of the land in Alsace.

Frau Haas describes this friendship in her as yet unpublished memoirs. The two women gave birth to their first children almost simultaneously. Their friendship survived the separation when first Pastor Schweitzer was called to Günsbach and later Judge Haas was transferred to Metz.

After the early death of her husband, the widow Haas moved to Strasbourg with her three children, Elsa, Lina, and Fritz. When Albert Schweitzer and his sister Adele were also staying in Strasbourg in the 1890s, he as a student and she at a boarding school, the friendship was renewed in the second generation.

Fritz Haas attended the gymnasium[1] at the cathedral. There he became friends with his classmate Ernst Bresslau, son of Harry Bresslau, who was a professor of medieval history at the University of Strasbourg. When Fritz's sister Lina married Willibald Conrad, a member of the Board of Works, on August 6, 1898, Ernst Bresslau and his sister Helene were invited by one and Albert Schweitzer by the other; Schweitzer escorted Helene to the table. An opportunity to become better acquainted was provided by the Cycling Club. Fritz Haas tells of its inception in his unpublished memoirs, written after 1935:

> The Cycling Club was more than its sporting-enthusiast name suggested. The cycling was as it were only the excuse conjured up to legitimate our meetings, and the longer it went on the less it was [our] exclusive purpose. In those days, one simply needed a means of doing away with the conventional barriers when hemmed in [with regard to] the free social dealings between the two sexes, and she [Helene] found it in cycling.
> The thought arose at a party at the Bresslau's, to which my sister, Elly Knapp and I had been invited. . . . It was probably his[2] sister[3] who made

1. Classical high school.
2. Ernst Bresslau.
3. Helene Bresslau.

the suggestion of drawing Albert Schweitzer into the group; being closer
to him must have been her secret wish, ever since she first became acquainted with him at my sister's wedding.


In her book of reminiscences, *View from the Cathedral Tower* (written in
1934), Elly Heuss-Knapp also tells of the Cycling Club, of the trips to the
Rhine forest near Strasbourg or to the Odilienberg. She names additional
members: the art historian Polaczek, the deputy Leoni. "The most important one—that was always clear to us—was Albert Schweitzer."

Schweitzer, too, devotes a longish paragraph to the bicycle in his reminiscences of his youth: "Today's young people can scarcely imagine what
the rise of the bicycle meant for us. A previously undreamed-of opportunity
to go out into nature was opened up for us. I exploited it freely and joyfully."
But he does not say a word about the Cycling Club, either here or in his
autobiography.

Fritz Haas marvels "that this very busy man found something satisfying
in our circle, which was certainly animated but really rather innocuous."
The young girls must have exercised their natural attraction on the twenty-
five-year-old Schweitzer. Beyond that, he experienced in their company
the results of a different, freer upbringing; they had other things on their
minds than only marriage, children, and cooking; they were actively interested in social and political problems. Among his circle of acquaintances in
Paris, and probably in Alsace as well, the tradition of an almost conventual
upbringing common in Catholic countries was still prevalent. The daughter of a good house always was brought up with governesses, had no professional training, and was never permitted to go out alone, particularly with
young men. In his socially critical study written in 1919, *Why It Is So Difficult to Assemble a Good Choir in Paris*, Albert Schweitzer points out the
harmful consequences of such an upbringing.

In 1902, when this correspondence begins and the acquaintance becomes a friendship, Schweitzer, at the age of just twenty-seven, was a privatdozent on the Protestant theological faculty, a vicar of St. Nicholas's
Church in Strasbourg, and organist for the Bach concerts of the St. Wilhelm choir; in addition, he was working on a book about Bach that he had
undertaken, at Widor's urging, to write in French for French organists and
music lovers.

The historian Friedrich Meinecke, who was professor of recent history in Strasbourg from 1901 to 1906, writes in his memoirs, composed after 1943, about Privatdozent Schweitzer, whom he encountered in the faculty common room:

> I do not wish to be too free with the word "genius" which I just used for Dehio, but I must also apply it to one of the youngest Strasbourg dozenten at the time, one of the few Alsatians. When I first came to know him in the common room, I was immediately captivated by his handsome appearance, his glowing countenance, his confident movements. He is a privatdozent in theology, I was told, who is not treated well by his senior professors because he has a somewhat restless spirit. For he not only pursues Early Christian studies in his field, but burns his candle at both ends, plays the organ excellently, and is working on a book about Bach. My wife and I were later moved with gratitude by listening to his organ playing in the little church of St. Wilhelm on the Schiffleutstaden. A circle of younger friends was devoted to him, but even here one was somewhat put off by hearing that he had given up his career in theology and had now begun studying medicine as a third field in order to be able to go out to the blacks one day as a doctor. That was Albert Schweitzer, whose name is spoken with awe today wherever people are concerned with the highest ethical spirit of sacrifice in their own lives and with the deepest questions of civilization.[1]

Gustav Woytt

## Helene Bresslau

In the curriculum vitae my mother had to write in 1910 to be admitted to the Frankfurt nursing examination, she states:

> I, Helene Marianne Bresslau, was born in Berlin on January 25th, 1879, the daughter of university professor Dr. Harry Bresslau, and am a member of the Church of the Augsburg Confession. At the age of six, I was accepted into the ninth form of the Queen Charlotte's School and transferred from it to the Girls' High School when my father took up an appointment at the University of Strasbourg at Easter in 1890. After

---

1. *Strasbourg, Freiburg, Berlin, 1901–1919: Erinnerungen von Friedrich Meinecke* (Stuttgart: K. F. Koehler, ca. 1949), 25–26.

completing school and teacher training, I passed the state test for teaching at girls' high schools in December of 1896 and then devoted myself to musical studies, in the course of which I attended the city's music conservatory for two years beginning in September of 1897. I spent the winter of 1899/1890 in Italy with my parents, which inspired me to turn my attention to art history and to attend lectures at my home university during the following five semesters. In the autumn of 1902, I went to England, where I worked as a teacher and instructor and at the same time had my attention directed to a consideration of social questions and conditions.

On January 1st, 1904, I joined the Protestant Deaconess' Society in order to complete a course in nursing and was assigned to the nursing school at Stettin, from which I was obliged to return home on April 1st after three months of instruction. On April 1st, 1905, I began working for the Strasbourg municipal administration as municipal inspector of orphans and worked uninterruptedly for four years in this position. But this activity made me increasingly eager to fill in the gaps in my knowledge of nursing.

On April 1st, 1909, I resigned my position, devoted the summer months to recreation on a journey through Russia and Finland, and on October 1st, 1909, I enrolled as a student in the nursing school of the Protestant Deaconess' Society in Frankfurt in the city hospital to prepare myself for taking the state test.


My mother was of Jewish parentage. Her father, Harry Bresslau, was born in Dannenberg on March 22, 1848, son of the banker and brickworks' owner Abraham Heinrich Bresslau and his wife Marianne, née Heinemann. In 1857, his parents moved to Uelzen, where my grandfather had his early education. In 1860, he entered the Gymnasium Johanneum in Lüneburg. Early on he showed particular interest in the subject of history, which later developed into his professional goal. In 1866, fortune dealt his family a heavy blow. His father left the city under cover of night after his bank had failed and fled to America, where he became an employee of a New York State newspaper. He continued to live there until 1886 and never returned to Europe. His wife, who was already sickly, never recovered from this blow. She died in 1870. Harry Bresslau, now the head of the family, had been a college student since 1866. His sister Betty went to England as a governess; his brother Stefan became an apprentice in a banking house in Lüneburg; and the two youngest were taken in by one of his mother's sisters until my grandfather was able to take them into his home after his marriage in 1874.

His father's disappearance and his difficult family circumstances weighed heavily on my grandfather, but he completed his studies and became a senior assistant teacher at the Andreas Realgymnasium in Berlin and a lecturer in history at the university. In 1890, he was appointed a professor at the University of Strasbourg and worked there as an assistant professor of medieval history. He lived and worked in Strasbourg until he was expelled by the French in 1918. His main area of research was medieval imperial documents. He attached particular importance to his collaboration on the *Monumenta Germaniae Historica,* to whose central board of directors he belonged for more than thirty-eight years, beginning in 1888. For thirty-seven years, he was the director of publications; from 1889 to 1903, he was also the editor of the *New Archive.* In 1903, he experienced the bitter disappointment of not being chosen as chairman of the central committee of the *Monumenta Germaniae Historica,* as he justifiably had anticipated. Perhaps he had not been appointed because he was Jewish. He felt this setback as a serious affront and immediately stepped down as editor of the *New Archive.* In 1916, he volunteered to write the history of the *Monumenta Germaniae Historica.* He was able to send off the finished manuscript to Berlin before his expulsion from Alsace on December 1, 1918. That my grandparents had to leave Strasbourg was humiliating for them, especially because they had to carry their own heavy hand luggage over the Rhine Bridge.

They moved to Heidelberg, where my grandfather continued his collaboration on the *Monumenta Germaniae Historica* and was also active in the Alsatian Scientific Society. He was able to complete his manual of paleography before he died on October 27, 1926. It became a standard work and was still in print in 1957. P. Kehr said in his obituary notice that my grandfather, in his Strasbourg days, was cheerful and lovable, receptive and adaptable, but also aware of his abilities. He was considered an excellent teacher with a large number of students. They were devoted to him, and many became his friends. But his Jewishness caused many difficulties for him, which gave him pain. The historian Friedrich Meinecke writes in his reminiscences that as a privatdozent my grandfather once went to Leopold von Ranke,[1] then an old man, and complained about the setback he was

1. 1795–1886, German historian.

suffering in his career. Ranke is said to have answered, "But, Bresslau, you should go over; after all, you are a historical Christian, too."

But my grandfather did not convert. He did leave the Jewish community and had his children, my mother and her two brothers, baptized and given a Christian education. In the Berlin anti-Semitism conflict, he firmly supported the Judaism Party, but in his home the Sabbath was not celebrated, nor were any Jewish holidays. What that must have meant for my grandmother is something I asked myself much later, when she was already dead, and I regret never having spoken with her about it.

I was seven years old when my grandfather died. I hardly knew him. My grandmother reached a ripe old age, living long enough to experience the Hitler era and the beginning of the Second World War. I can recall the celebration of my grandparents' golden wedding anniversary, when there was a great family gathering, and my grandmother wore a small golden wreath in her hair, which was still dark brown. She was born in 1854 as Caroline Isay and was a twenty-year-old girl living in Trier when my twenty-six-year-old grandfather married her. They set up housekeeping in Berlin and took the place of parents for my grandfather's younger sister and brother, Clara and Ludwig. When my mother was born in 1879, her brother Ernst was already two years old, and a second brother, Hermann, followed her in 1883. Hermann became a teacher and died young, at thirty, during an operation; Ernst studied medicine and natural sciences, became a well-known zoologist, and was a professor at the University of Cologne, where he supervised the growth of the newly founded zoological institute. In 1934, he immigrated to Brazil with his family and died there quite unexpectedly in 1935.

Unfortunately, I know nothing about my mother's first eleven years in Berlin. She never spoke of them. She spent a happy childhood and youth in Strasbourg, regretting only that she was not permitted to learn Latin and Greek like her brothers. One of the friends she made at the Lindner Girls' High School, the school for the daughters of upper-class Germans, was Elly Knapp, who later married Theodor Heuss[1] and to whom she remained attached throughout her life. There she passed the state test for teaching at girls' high schools but never applied for a position at a school because she believed that she would not be able to be equally fair to all the pupils and was afraid that she would favor the more intelligent ones. That is why she

---

1. 1884–1963, first president of West Germany after World War II.

practiced the teaching profession only in the private domain. Early on she became aware of her responsibility for the poor and the disadvantaged. This social perspective led her to begin work as an inspector of orphans in the city of Strasbourg and inspired her to found a home for low-income mothers, most of them single mothers, which moved her beyond the conventions of her class and time.

A special experience was a visit to Italy in 1899–1900 with her parents, during which my grandfather searched for medieval documents and my mother enjoyed the nature and art of the south. A chest filled with art books and art magazines in her house in Königsfeld stood as testimony to this period.

Her family home was the hospitable house of a professor to which students came and went for dinners and parties. It was expected of her that she should play the role of daughter of the house. That cannot have come easily to her. She had no interest in superficial conversation, which both she and her father felt to be a waste of time. She also had different interests than those a daughter of a good house took for granted at that time. Her parents probably worried about her, but they granted her freedom in her decisions and in her way of life.

My parents met at a wedding in 1898. I heard from my mother that she was so bold as to criticize my father's German, which had an Alsatian tinge. He accepted the criticism, and she became his assistant in proofreading the manuscripts of his books. His sermons impressed her deeply. She was devout from the bottom of her heart, and for her, as for him, religion was a necessity. Both felt that they could not live primarily for themselves and their own interests, but that they were responsible for other human beings in need of help. My father tried in vain for several years to be allowed to take in orphaned boys before he finally found the road to Africa, and my mother had managed to have the refuge built for infants and their mothers. For my father, it was the call of Jesus that he had to follow and that led him into the African jungle; for my mother, it was the call of the heart to support him in his undertaking.

Many certainly viewed with critical eyes their long years of friendship without an engagement. My mother's fondness for travel, which took her even to Russia—by the standards of the day an adventurous undertaking for a young woman of thirty—was felt to be unusual. She enjoyed her excursions with the Cycling Club and its extended circle of friends, including my father. She was athletic in other ways, too, and was one of the first female skiers. A fall while skiing caused a spinal injury that brought her suffering throughout her life and that led to chronic sleeplessness. My father was greatly concerned about her "dear back" and about the tuberculosis that took her to Königsfeld in the Black Forest for a cure; after the years in Lambaréné, she spent most of her time there. Her illnesses meant additional concerns for my father at a time when he was taking on himself the great strain of completing his medical studies along with his activity as pastor and privatdozent, his concert tours, and the writing of his books, mostly at night. That he still found time to write to my mother so frequently— sometimes almost every day—is difficult to grasp. But she was his confidante, the woman to whom he could open his heart, and a fixed pole in his life of constant movement.

To give up his freedom and to marry was not easy for my father, but at that time it was the only possible way for my mother to accompany him to Africa.

For my parents, shared labor in the service of others was the basis of their marriage, which was celebrated on June 18, 1912, in the parsonage at Günsbach. The wreath and veil were handed to my mother by her sisters-in-law, Luise and Maggie Bresslau, with the following poem:

> By ancient custom's law, long understood,
> The veil is set upon the happy bride
> By the companions of her maidenhood,
> And parting words between them oft are sighed.—
> But here no words of parting do they say,
> Those maiden comrades, drooping presciently—
> No! we, the women, welcome thee today;
> O sister, we have waited long for thee!
> A woman's life of help and love thou know'st,
> Has tended others, lightening their pain,
> For woman's nature has thou, more than most;
> Come, sister, come! And join our festive train,
> Which in the bliss and toil of earth is bearing
> The holy secret of our human life
> With timid gesture—and with prideful daring,
> Varied as is the burden of a wife.
> Now may thy human life be well completed,

Now wholly grasp a woman's destiny!
And here, by us, thy loving sisters, greeted,
Take the white veil and wreath of greenery.

My mother said "Yes" to her woman's destiny. It led her to experience the great adventure of her life in the African jungle at the side of the man she loved. It broke her health, though, so that she could no longer stand by him in his work in the later years as she would have liked, and she had to make the sacrifice of letting others do what she wanted so much to go on doing herself.

Rhena Schweitzer Miller

*The Albert Schweitzer–Helene Bresslau Letters*

# *1901*

## 1. A. S.

Strasbourg, Thomasstift
March 2, 1901

[Fräulein Helene Bresslau
Ruprechtsauer Allee 45
Strasbourg i./E.]

Dear Miss Bresslau,

Please excuse me for not answering sooner after you fulfilled your two-year-old promise so kindly. I am delighted with the book.[1] I began reading last Sunday evening and finished in the wintry woods of Günsbach. It is entirely after my taste. I find in it deep and natural, practical feeling combined with a plastic view and ideal sense of history. This greatness of thought is lacking in most moderns. Thus, I express my gratitude not only for the fact that you fulfilled your obligation so kindly and "conscientiously," but also because you introduced me to a book that gives me great pleasure. I now look forward to reading other works of this man.

For this card, I wrote three drafts late at night so the sentence structure might meet with your approval. Awake or asleep, I worry about my untidy style—with little hope that it will improve. Please accept my heartfelt thanks and my kind regards.

Albert Schweitzer

---

1. Conrad Ferdinand Meyer, *Hutten's Letzte Tage* (1870; rpt., Berlin: Knaur, 1933).

# *1 9 0 2*

On March 9, 1902, Albert Schweitzer received his qualification as lecturer in the Department of Theology at the University of Strasbourg. The subject of his first lecture was the Logos concept in the Gospel of John.

**2. A. S.**

Strasbourg
Regenbogengasse 15
Sunday, March 9, 1902

Dear Miss Bresslau,

What a pity, on Tuesday I have my confirmation classes, and you understand that a week prior to the confirmation I cannot cancel the class for an excursion. Duty comes first. I am also so tired and so behind with my work (last week I was not able to do anything) that I have to abstain from any major event. Thank you so much for letting me know about it. It is impossible. An afternoon excursion, however, would be most welcome if you can arrange one with Elsa, also for next week and the week after. At that time, I perhaps might make the acquaintance of your friend.

Bon voyage for Tuesday.

With kind regards.
Albert Schweitzer

## 3. H. B.

[Strasbourg]
May 5/6, 1902

My Friend,

You made me feel good, but you have also hurt me; therefore, I would like to continue our discussion. Actually, I would like to thank you because I have advanced through our exchange quite a bit. You are probably correct in your views about development, as far as we think of it as a slow, gradual becoming. I believe that everything that lies in us is dark, and we are not conscious of it until a word or an event coming from the outside suddenly brings it to our consciousness or puts it into a new light. In this way, rather by spurts, we advance a step and recognize it only afterward. This is what happened to me.

I often asked myself in the past: "Are all these thousands of girls who are destined to be happy so much better than I am?"—and while I am aware of my faults, I think that I am not really a bad person. And further: "Why does God put this boundless desire for happiness into our hearts if he denies us fulfillment?" One is inclined to feel only then that much, perhaps the best, can come to fruition—and one wants to rebel against being excluded from this fulfillment! That was my struggle and the end of my philosophy: If we only can attain fulfillment through harmonious unfolding of our powers—and must not this be our goal?—How else can we accomplish what we are meant to accomplish?—What happens if it is denied us?

You, too, must know the struggle of that part in us that is so filled with longing. How else could you have understood the silent cry of the cherry trees in Günsbach? Or did you always know that your path to life would pass by the closed gate of happiness? You see, my friend, this is the new insight that you gave me yesterday: Here is not the end; here the road only divides, and your path leads ahead; it goes farther, wherever it may lead; what matters is the "moving ahead," the way beyond that I was not able to find. And now this seems so simple and clear to me, so reassuring. And yet I never would have found this on my own; I wanted to convert you to my theory, which seemed so much kinder and brighter, yet it only led me to despair. You must not believe that what I told you yesterday made me helpless; that is overcome and buried—if it were not so, I could not have told you. It was only the indirect cause; it left me so little resistance that any agitation caused me physical pain, and every thought of my rudderless drifting upset me.

To be sure, I do not yet know my way—it is so much easier for a man whose profession gives him direction—will you help me to find mine? "Why would we have friends if we did not need them?" I always despised that phrase, but there is some truth in it. A young woman is dependent upon her talents, and if she does not have any special ones, she is in a predicament. Perhaps in this case, too, I might receive sudden help, as happened yesterday.

My friend, don't be angry with me that I tell you all of this. I feel as if these renunciations contain a hidden trait of sympathy between us. And leave this just as those of our discussions that are of no concern to any third person. If you want to tell me anything before we meet again, just write—if you send it with the morning mail, it will reach me directly—my parents know about our friendship. They know as much as they have to so that they don't draw wrong conclusions.

This is not a breach of trust; what our friendship is, what it means to us, is between us alone. A young woman has to account for her ways differently than a man who is independent.

You will understand, my friend, won't you: In addition to this, our friendship will remain a well-kept secret with my parents.

So again: I thank you!

Always in good friendship.
Helene Bresslau

## 4. A. S.

Saturday, July 19, 1902
9:00 in the evening

Now I have done my duty for tomorrow and can come to you to thank you for your words, which I read on my way to the university and which moved me so deeply. I had no way of knowing that yesterday, when I came home, sat in my armchair, and closed my eyes with the single thought not to think about anything, that just at that time you thought of me, that you wrote to bring me joy today; so I was egotistical, not you.

I should not have shown you that I was so sad, but I could not help it. I lacked the energy to make the effort to hide my feelings. I was so downcast, and the future seemed so utterly hopeless. And now you came this morning, and you lifted this hopelessness from me, so the blue sky was smiling for me, too. How can I thank you? I don't want you to reproach yourself—no. You are not the cause of my restlessness; neither am I; it is the movement of the needle of the compass until it finds the pole. We will find it. I ask too much of you; yet in spite of my anxieties, what you give me makes me happy. Your lines reveal the noble soul of a woman and a willingness for self-sacrifice that is given only to women. That is a precious gift for him who receives it, more precious than anything in this world because it is uplifting; it ennobles. Is it not the greatest and deepest truth in the encounter of two humans that they ennoble each other? I do not want you to look up to me because all I have is given to me by women and especially by the one to whom I was closest.[1] And what I missed in this loneliness I felt for the first time again today: the fresh breath, a woman who—perhaps with pain and sacrifice—wants to be there for me. For this, I thank you. I know that we will find the right path.

In deep gratitude I hold your hand.

Your friend,
A. S.

## 5. A. S.

[Günsbach]
Monday morning
September 7/8, 1902

I am sitting on my rock and reading Schleiermacher's beautiful lectures on religion. My rock lies above the valley—a small wilderness surrounded by vines: honeysuckle and blackberries fight for first place; blue sloes and red rosehips tell about the beauty of last spring. Now the modest fall flowers are still in bloom, and dry grass blades shiver in the east wind. Everything is enveloped in a blue, gossamer veil out of which the distant mountain chain shows like a silhouette. They are mowing in the meadows, and the fragrance of the hay invigorates the air up here. Late butterflies look for fluttering companions; trees appear in harsh outlines on the bare fields, as if

1. His aunt Mathilde Schweitzer, who had died in Paris on February 18, 1902.

Günsbach. *Courtesy of the Albert Schweitzer Archive, Günsbach.*

they painted the skeletons of bodies that are still filled with lush vitality. But I see everything in its splendor.

Now, however, I have to turn to my work, although I would love to dream in this invigorating autumnal atmosphere.

Now the blanket has to be folded, and I am going home.

**6. A. S.**

[Günsbach]
Thursday morning on my rock
September 18, 1902

Now Nature gives in. Two days it fought and wrestled against its aging. Rain and storm, wild clouds that raced gloomily in the sky accompany the wild pain with which the soul of Nature rises so passionately—An overnight peace has come. Nature now smiles in bright sunshine, like someone who has overcome, and the raindrops shine in the grape leaves like tears of past sorrows. Now the faded flowers and bare meadows do not hurt anymore. Shiny rosehips and dark sloes decorate Nature as if it were blossoming again. It puts brilliant jewelry on its dark and serious robe.— How beautiful and moving this is. This is how women struggle until they accept their fate, and then comes fall, smiling, when all charms and richness, which they hide inside, unfold—knowing through struggles and tears. And perhaps this last fall sunshine will help one of those who is still able to cry and laugh with Nature—

I have to tear myself away from here and begin to work on a sermon because I promised my father to substitute for him next Sunday.—The dog lies next to me, looks over my shoulder, and yawns.

**7. A. S.**

Again in Günsbach
October 9, 1902, on the rock

What a parting!—The cows graze in the dark green fields. A blue mist hovers above. Everything looks subdued; the mountains are shrouded. Out of this blue, translucent sea, you can hear the sound of the cowbells, from far and near, unreal in its rhythm and harmony—I feel like reading in a storybook—a red ladybug runs over my paper.—The brown blades of autumn—yet early tomorrow morning I have to leave for Paris—Much is difficult and some things are even more so than I imagined—

This last quiet hour of parting—a fear I cannot suppress. The path of duty as a higher destiny of our existence is difficult. One has to fight and struggle for the hours of pure happiness, of rising above this world—but they are so beautiful—I have read aloud the *Apology of Socrates* at Saar-

Union.[1] We all were moved—and I felt that I understand this human being, *understand him totally.*—

Now I pick the last flowers beside this rock for the grave at Père Lachaise[2]—a small bouquet, unpretentious among the luxuriant flower arrangements by which her grave will be adorned—but it carries the peace and pain of autumn, the rays of the setting sun and wondrous memory. At night, fragrant dreams of past happiness and abiding love rise from the fading blossoms. Good-bye fields, good-bye woods, good-bye mountains. I thank you.

**8. A. S.**

> October 11, 1902
> Between Troyes and Paris
> On the express train 4:30 P.M.

One can vaguely feel Paris in the distance. The sun is setting on the horizon, and the trees with their golden leaves cast long shadows (in the last sunlight). I read the letters of St. Ignatius in Greek, but the saint would not be pleased with me if he had known how much Nature distracted me. Is it strength or weakness to live in such a mystical union with Nature, to feel the effects of its smile and its tears deeply in one's soul—I have seen about a hundred pictures by Millet[3]—it felt as if he and I had looked at everything together.—

Paris—Paris

**9. A. S.**

> October 17, 1902
> Thursday evening
> On train to Strasbourg

Such long silence! Do you know what happened: The poor Leon Ehretsmann[4] died. I was asked to speak at his grave, and I was glad to do it,

---

1. Saar-Union, in Alsace, was the place where his aunt Mathilde's sister lived.
2. The cemetery in Paris where Aunt Mathilde was buried.
3. Jean-François Millet (1814–1875), a French realist painter.
4. Schweitzer's brother-in-law.

but because of this I lost three days of work, which I have to make up now. What an effort!—

My nights were short; I usually went to bed at two or three in the morning, and if you were sitting next to me now, you would not approve of my appearance. Today I labored all day long for the move; I prepared everything that goes from Günsbach to Strasbourg.

The evening twilight slowly disguises the gray mountains. I had to depart without having seen my rock again because of the bad weather. That was very sad—yes, everything was gray.

During the trip to the funeral at Colmar, I asked myself: How would it be if you were taken away so suddenly?—Once more I would want to see the people who shared in my life, and I would want to say a last word of goodbye and of gratitude—

What would I say to you?—

## 10. A. S.

[Strasbourg]
October, 1902

My thanks, from the bottom of my heart: I was so moved by the story that I trembled[1]—and that it was translated for me by someone who knows everything, yes: knows everything, and therefore knew of the effect it would have.—That has encouraged me—I feel the community of thought with the one who sat at her table and translated it in the evening hours to give something to me! Now I am so happy that I said everything, although it was hard to reveal my innermost thoughts and to share something that had been my own possession exclusively, as I was fighting for it again and again. And now you *help* me—you help me in that special way—and I am happy to say: "She has *the right* to speak to you about this because she has understood it completely! Understood that you *must* act as you do." I thank you—I will need your spiritual support for my life; that became so clear to me while I read—to have somebody again who may speak to me like *this!* The little manuscript is a precious gem for me, and when I face difficult times, I will read it and draw strength from it—I thank you for every-

1. Unknown story.

thing.—That somebody speaks with my soul in this way—that I have not experienced for a long time.—

## 11. H. B.

5 The Drive, Hove[1]
October 24, 1902

Let me just thank you—I cannot say more because too many tears interfere.

Afternoon:—Don't be afraid that I might talk with anyone; there is not a soul I could reach to whom I could say how I feel. This morning I was able to steal five minutes to run to the ocean, to my beloved, wild, fighting sea! It was so still and peaceful, and the sun cast a long, gleaming streak of light over the water, a radiating ribbon from the south to me. Above the rock on which I sat, the waves flowed from the left and from the right, those coming pushing the others back to reach the other side, always repeating the movement, yet always different. I tried to find some law for their movement, but I could not find it—perhaps I did not have enough time!—

Adieu

## 12. A. S.

Paris, Sunday evening,
October 26, 1902
After the Colonne concert

I was with some friends at the Châtelet to attend the Colonne concert. Brahms's Second Symphony was played! I sat at the back of the balcony and closed my eyes—I saw the ocean; I sat at the shore, and the waves came and went, and in the distance was a streak of light—that was not music, that was a dream! The dream of a little letter of this morning that I almost know by heart.—And when the concert was over, my dream vanished in the noise of the applause, but the ray of sun remained and was reflected in my face because someone who had looked at me asked: "What did you see when your eyes were closed? You seemed so strange, so far away from every-

---

1. For two months, Helene was a teacher in Brighton, England.

thing?"—I did not answer. The remainder of the concert was insignificant, tinkling at the piano. Pensively, I walked home.

Good night—

## 13. A. S.

[Strasbourg]
Monday evening, November 3, 1902
Returned from Antwerp

At home—I celebrated this first evening at home as if it were a Sunday evening. Now I am at home again for a long winter filled with work. My lamp was turned on at my desk, and the clock was ticking. But I sat at the easy chair, next to it, with closed eyes and folded hands—memories came like old friends, and they had the fragrance of delicious frankincense. *Home*—I heard this word for the first time at the seminary on a November evening when she[1] spoke it. The rain pounded against the window, and the fire in the stove drew flickering ghosts on the wall. "That is your home," she said, "and now you feel at home here because we have been here to-gether."—

Oh, how happy I was at that home, under the trees of the seminary when I wrote my sketch of the life of Jesus. And how I had to struggle until I felt at home in this room. It was a year ago!—Now, however, I feel at home here, too. A little homesickness in my deepest heart—but it is almost my home. It was a serious time for me, here in these close quarters. The time of my greatest loss here on earth, where a part of me leaves, the time of being torn out of my familiar surroundings, the time of work because of duty and not because of joyful enthusiasm. And yet—as this is the past, I feel that it helped me to move ahead because my earlier life was too enjoyable.

My lips moved quietly, and I thanked God that he let me find the deep-est meaning of life, that he showed me what it is, how it is, in the realm of the spirit as truth and ideal. Now winter may come; I am at home, happily at home. At home with those who understand me, who share my thoughts, even if all of them do not know *everything*. To all those who have given me something spiritual, I want to become worthy; I want to thank them that they help me because it is so easy to walk at the height when others carry us.

1. Aunt Mathilde.

In front of me is a short verse from November 2, 1899, which she sent me when I returned from Berlin to the seminary:

> Toujours plus haut que ce soit de toute la vie
> La devise sainte et bénie:
> Toujours plus haut.[1]

The great bell of the cathedral rings ten o'clock! *At home!*

## 14. A. S.

[Strasbourg]
Saturday,
November 15, 1902, evening

I finished everything, and now I am *all alone. All alone*—that is glorious. I turned off the lamp, and I followed the flickering of the fire in the stove, and the sound of the church bells penetrated the November dusk. It is Saturday evening.

Then I went over to the piano and played Beethoven's sonata for the fortepiano! That is nothing to perform for others, no—one has to be alone because one can rejoice, laugh, cry, and weep—. Oh, this heavenly exuberance—and then this dreamy, blissful world that wafts through these transparent chords—and I was by myself—and it was glorious, glorious. Is that selfish? Well—I don't care; it may be so—no, we were two, Beethoven and I.—How I thank you that you let me have a glimpse into your world—in your beautiful, pain-torn, sun-drenched, peacefully dying world. How many have thanked you? How many will thank you? You great prophet of overcoming and of struggle for joyful serenity!

## 15. A. S.

[Strasbourg]
Monday, November 24, 1902

My sister marries again—and now I can return to my home; I can live again under the trees of the seminary in the atmosphere of the old

---

1. "Always higher. May that be the motto for your whole life."

monastery.—No, I dream—I dream, yet it is so—. But the one who cried with me, who comforted me when I had to move, she is not here now to share my joy.

Will I find everything as I left it? No disappointment? I will be stronger than the disappointment; I want to be there, to work there, and have some influence on the students—there is my life, my future. I think that once I am at the seminary, everything will be easier; I will not have to struggle all the time in order to fulfill my duty, to be faithful.

I recently spoke with somebody who mentioned the *Ethics* by Paulsen.[1] The book contains a sentence, so he said, that is especially beautiful: When individual people who are called do not follow their conscience and their absolute personal sense of duty, the world suffers. (The original phrase is more beautiful.) I felt that this word, accidentally mentioned, was a word of comfort for me!

I am happy—But if something should interfere and they did not want me at the seminary!—

## 16. A. S.

[Strasbourg]
Monday, December 1, 1902

Events topple over each other—we buried Lucius,[2] who died suddenly. One less upright character in the world. Tonight I met Holtzmann[3] at the Stadenstrasse. I am not to take any additional steps to move into my new room at the seminary—Anrich[4] will take the place of Lucius. He will have to leave his position at the seminary, so there will be a vacancy—and they count on me. It gives me a headache—is it not a dream? This is the place where I want to fulfill my life. To move with the April sun back to the seminary, and as its director! I cannot really feel any joy, yet I don't know why. Yes—if my dead confidante[5] were still alive—"You will return there at some point," she told me on her deathbed—oh, if she could only be happy with

1. Friedrich Paulsen, *System der Ethik* (1899).
2. Paul Ernst Lucius (1852–1902), professor of church history.
3. Heinrich Julius Holtzmann (1832–1910), a New Testament professor.
4. Gustav Adolf Anrich, director of the seminary.
5. Aunt Mathilde.

me.—Everything always comes too quickly, and at the same time it comes too *late*; I have grown so tired, so joyless in exile, and I consumed myself with grief. I was too homesick, too sad—and what will happen now? There is my dream—to educate ministers and to be in daily contact with them, not just an office-pastor relation, but a human-pastor-idealist exchange.— Will I be able to do that? There are times when I am afraid of my future; it all seems so difficult.

The full position is, however, not yet assured. I will be able to believe it only on April 1st, when I will take over.

(*Please keep all this to yourself*)

## 17. A. S.

[Strasbourg]
Sunday evening
Last Advent 1902 [December 21, 1902]

I am so tired and yet so quietly happy—alone on the last Sunday of Advent. All alone in the house. Why am I that way, that I have an inner fear of all humans, even those who are close to me, afraid that they take my solitude away from me? There are only a few people to whom I have given the right to share in my thoughts, with whom to have dialogues. But with those few I feel so rich.

Fragrance of the Christmas tree—dreams—Paris, 20 rue de Sorbonne—where Kant was lying open on my table and the fire was singing in the fireplace. Kant gave me deep comfort; it was like reading a Christmas story. On December 23, 1898, I wrote, "At home," and here is what I read:

"*Duty!* Sublime and mighty name that embraces nothing charming or insinuating, but requires submission, and yet does not seek to move the will by threatening anything that would arouse natural aversion or terror in the mind but only holds forth a law that of itself finds entry into the mind, and yet gains reluctant reverence (though not always obedience), a law before which all inclinations are dumb, even though they secretly work against it; what origin is there worthy of you, and where is to be found the root of your noble descent which proudly rejects all kinship with the inclinations, descent from which is the indispensable condition of that worth which human beings alone can give themselves?

"It can be nothing less than what elevates a human being above himself (as part of the sensible world), what connects him with an order of things that only the understanding can think and that at the same time has under it the whole sensible world and with it the empirically determinable existence of human beings in time and the whole of all ends (which is alone suitable to such unconditional practical laws as the moral). It is nothing other than *personality,* that is, freedom and independence from the whole of nature, regarded nevertheless as also a capacity of a being subject to special laws—namely pure practical laws given by its own reason, so that a person as belonging to the sensible world is subject to his own personality insofar as he also belongs to the intelligible world; for it is then not to be wondered at that a human being, as belonging to both worlds, must regard his own nature in reference to his second and highest vocation only with reverence, and its laws with the highest respect." [1]

Whenever I take this book into my hands, it opens by itself to this section; here I find my innermost thoughts, and because I found these words at Christmas, they always fill me with the spirit of Christmas.—I copy these words for the second time, for someone who is allowed to share my innermost thoughts—the other rests at the Père Lachaise cemetery: she knew this passage by heart. If only I could continue to read Kant—sometimes I feel as if I were the first who really deeply understands him—"the disciple who loved his master." No, he is not a pedant, only on the surface. I love him as my Christmas friend, as my great educator, as my comforter. One feels removed from the world when one reads this passage!

Now knock at the doors of others on Christmas Eve, become their Christmas friend, and tell them as you came to me in distant solitude—that they are remembered.

## 18. A. S.

[Strasbourg]
Christmas Eve 1902
Alone—with myself

All alone—I was in Günsbach in the wonderful sun-filled woods and had to return tonight because I have to give the Christmas sermon tomorrow morning.

---

1. Translation from Immanuel Kant, *Critique of Practical Reason*, edited by Mary Gregor (1788; Cambridge: Cambridge University Press, 1997, rpt. 1999), 73–74.

So I sit by myself, put my head on my hand, let the thoughts wander wherever they want.—

How can a human achieve such change? What is that power of personality? The more I reflect upon it, the more it grows to enormous proportions—this mother could not foresee what kind of a son she had.—

Here we cannot comprehend anything—. And yet this deep humanity that kept him always modern, through which he anticipated the thoughts and pains of our times! And being nonreflective in everything he says: there is no rumination, no moving back and forth between arguments and counterarguments; everything stands there as spoken out of a delightful reminiscence of his soul. Divine Plato: this characterization of deep wisdom coming from the reminiscences of the soul fits also! But Christ is so powerful that He confronts us and says: I want you, you must—

—I read Christmas songs, "From Heaven above, I come to you"—Oh, how beautiful—Now my heart feels refreshed—. The fire died down in the stove—. It has been a sublime, quiet Christmas Eve—as if I hear a large clock ticking slowly and steadily (I don't know why I have this feeling), as if one cannot hear, in this holy night, the beats of seconds of world history.

How wonderful it is if one can say: I am happy, completely happy.

# *1903*

## 19. A. S.

[Strasbourg] Tuesday evening
March 3, 1903, At my place

[Miss Helene Bresslau, c/o Mrs. Shaw
10 Noreton Gardens, London W. S.]

For a long fifteen minutes, I sat in my chair, and my thoughts chased each other in my head and took away my breath. I just heard that the commission of the seminary voted unanimously for my appointment as director of studies for Oct. 1! This is a great turning point in my life, and *only you* understand completely what this appointment means for me. *The other one*, who knew it before you did, could not see the fulfillment of this dream that she dreamt for me. I still see her before me, exhausted on the couch, how she took my hand into her thin, transparent hands and said: "One day you will move there, this I tell you."

You alone understand everything. In these last weeks, I could not express anything because my soul was too restless, and I fought that inner struggle to remain "serene." Unfortunately, Nowack[1] had already pulled the faculty members of the seminary into this matter and presented a plan according to which I was supposed to occupy two small rooms at the seminary and not the large apartment of the director; in addition, a small "bachelor's" salary so I would not be able to marry because they did not want a married director. You know that I have "friends" among the faculty members who were thrilled to see me "put on ice." I had to accept the challenge and fight for my rights, to insist that they give me the apartment—and they

---

1. As head of the seminary, Wilhelm Nowack (1850–1928) was Schweitzer's superior. They were involved in disputes until Schweitzer left in 1906.

17

all assumed the reason was that I had plans to marry! If they could know how wrong they are and *why* I made the apartment a condition for my acceptance! You know and understand that without more space I cannot realize the plans for my future. Thus, I had an outer and inner struggle: superficially to insist on my rights and inwardly not to fall prey to their malicious politics. It was difficult—because I had to carry this load all by myself. Now it is all done with. The commission accepted all my conditions, and only the approval of the Thomas Chapter has to be added. On the outside, I was always calm, but inside I suffered greatly. I was always afraid to become mean and bitter. What will people say? They will congratulate me more or less honestly. They will say an instructor has had really good luck and gotten a fine position. The mixture of joy and fear with which I view this event you alone understand. This now seems to be the path that opens: educator of future ministers! How beautiful to plant seeds for good thoughts and noble aspirations in their hearts and to be effective through them. It is overwhelming; it takes my breath away. And then: It is the path to duty that opens up, the great duty that I almost wanted to reject, that I fought, to be defeated every time in the end and to find the only happiness in this duty. Now everything lies before me—I only have to follow my path. How many sleepless nights because of this duty, because it carries quite a burden, and "Paris" is a much greater sacrifice than I thought. I have used the last reserves of my energy in order to do my current work. But now all these struggles will be over, I see clearly. I follow my duty—without it, no happiness, no self-respect. I believe that I will be very happy.

It feels so good to have somebody to whom I can tell all this, who understands, who knows how to admonish and to reassure. What motivated you to select this friend? He gives almost nothing, yet demands everything from you. He is not a cheerful friend, the kind you should have, but a serious one, with a certain happy sadness. And you must cheer him up, so he will be able to pursue his course—

It is late, my head is buzzing. You are the first to whom I speak about my good luck—because you have the right and feel the need. It has been good that we can talk with each other.

Good evening.

A. S.

Please forgive me that I write in French; I cannot help it. You will not hold it against me.

## 20. A. S.

[Strasbourg]
Tuesday, May 12, 1903
3:45 in the morning

The first chapter of the third section of *The Last Supper*[1] is finished—I don't feel tired and believe that it turned out well. For more than eight years, it has occupied my thoughts, and now I will give it the final shape. I was afraid that I would never regain the buoyancy of mind with which I began my studies on the life of Jesus; now, however, I think that it will come back. I cannot write such lovely sheets as I sent them at that time, in the morning to Paris, to tell "how I am coming along," and I cannot receive the precious letters that admonished and at the same time reassured me—but I want to remain the same in spite of it. Would you like to participate in the joy I feel at the completion of this final chapter? Remain for me what you are—in order to find the right path, one has to be guided, encouraged, also admired and scolded. Why did you not come into this world as my aunt, or why can I not encounter you as a young woman, for whom I am the older person, and whom I met by chance during a meal? Why are you not twenty years older than I am? That would be more fitting with your gray hair—that causes me worry.

May I copy something for you that I received in Berlin from my aunt in 1899? It is a newspaper clipping:

"It is not by coincidence when two harmonizing souls meet. Living at different places, they did not know each other the day before; it is their kinship, their spiritual affinity that brought them together."—

This is true for us also. Good evening, no, good morning: not backward, but forward we must go.

A.

1. Albert Schweitzer, *Das Abendmahl im Zusammenhang mit dem Leben Jesu und der Geschichte des Urchristentums* (The Last Supper in connection with the life of Jesus and the history of the early Christianity), vol. 1, *Das Abendmahlsproblem auf Grund der wissenchaftlichen Forschung des 19. Jahrhunderts und der historischen Berichte* (The problem of the Last Supper based on the scientific research of the nineteenth century) (Tübingen: J. C. B. Mohr, Paul Siebeck, 1901).

**21. A. S.**

about "Jesus and the Wealthy"
2:00 A.M., June 23, 1903

I completely revised my article for the *Kirchenbote:*[1] "Jesus and the Wealthy." This is the second night I have spent with it. To be truthful is frightening because one never knows where one ends. I don't yet have the breath to articulate the essential things. I do have the feeling that every word I have written is true.—

Before I began to write, I sat in my armchair with closed eyes and was in my thoughts with you. Can I accept all that you give me? All this richness? The thought haunts me, and I think of it frequently. Today I carefully in-spected my new place at the seminary: I was moved, quite happy and yet sad.—How will it go?—And yet, you see, I never could have written this ar-ticle without the certainty that I act according to my "duty," which you know—

Good night, you are probably asleep.
A.

**22. A. S.**

[Strasbourg]
Saturday morning, 10:30
July 4, 1903

I have come home from my lecture and will begin to write my little ser-mon for tomorrow afternoon. But I am not in the mood for it: I am too sad, too indifferent, to have higher thoughts. Come, take the armchair, move it toward the table, and we will talk to each other—how good it would be if you could chat with me a little. You don't mind that I am wearing an old jacket? It is a little worn at the sleeves, and one button is missing.—

All week I had a fever, already on Sunday evening when I visited you; that's why I was so taciturn. I was awfully thirsty, and then I had to take quinine. That makes the head tired. And when I came home yesterday, I found a letter telling about a boy from my confirmation class of last year

1. *Church Messenger*, the newsletter for Alsatian churches.

who had to have his leg amputated. He is a nice fellow who liked me very much. Why does all this happen? During his illness, I visited him several times and tried to comfort him, but to see him in this desperate condition drives me to despair.

You don't answer me, but you look at me with your kind glance. Is it still true that you are happy when you fall asleep and when you wake up? I have thought about both of us frequently in these days. Always that question: Do I not ruin your life? Your path would be straight if I had not met you, or at least if I had acted with my usual indifference. You certainly would have found a home and a family, all that—and now I think that I have led you astray, and everything I accept from you is stolen from your happiness. That discourages me. I see you leaving for Russia; I know the grief this causes your parents—and if I did not exist, you would remain here; I know this because it is not your destiny to roam and struggle in this world, but to be a true woman in the circle of her family. Sometimes I could cry— what is the solution? And then again, I tell myself: Did she not tell you that she is happy, do believe it—and I force myself to believe it, but I ask myself whether this fire may not die down, and then only a dim memory will remain in your heart, and your life will be cold. If you only knew how much I admire you! I never have been able to tell you. If you only knew how the esteem you show me helps me on my way, how your affection raises me up. It and your deep love are a source of strength; I want my whole life, including that of my thought to be completely open before you, and I do not want you to experience any disappointment—but you pay for this too dearly. You idealize me, I know this, and that adds to my strength; your affection warms my heart,—but you, what do you get out of this? Letters, enjoyable triumphs, moments of deep happiness—and then a great emptiness.

Don't say anything; this is the way it is. We must not talk—

Give me both your hands—we are at the Rhine, I imagine—the smell of the hay—, just as at that time when I revealed the secret of my life to you. You were so happy to be the sister of my thoughts, and I felt miserable because I had opened myself up so completely. But then I did not regret it— now I feel relieved in the knowledge that you, such an honest and noble soul, know my innermost thoughts, and to talk about them with somebody is a great, good fortune for me. And even when I worry about you—it is not only in sadness.

God bless you. Each of us will go our way, and you will find happiness.

What kind? That is not the essential point. But tell me often that you are happy—I must hear that—.

Noon—for more than one and one-half hours I have been talking with you. I feel as if I woke up. But I feel better now.

Thank you.

A. S.

I will now write my sermon.

P.S. To look for a text, I opened my New Testament, and my eye fell on the second letter of Paul to Timothy 2:5, "And if a man strives for mastery, he is not crowned, except he *competes according to the rules.*"[1]


## 23. A. S.

Sunday afternoon, Sept. 6, 1903
at my table, Günsbach


My dear companion,

What a strong sun! I closed the shutters, yet it is light enough to write because the light comes stubbornly through the cracks and puts white spots on walls and curtains. How indiscreet! But, after all, nothing is hidden from the sun; it was always our friend—so it may come in. I put the armchair next to the table. So now we can talk with each other; no, first a second of silence to listen to the fountain. How wonderful that you know everything and that you sat at this table.

I would like to talk with you, my dear companion. About what? I don't know, but I want to feel close to you. I finished "Our Book"[2]—you could have written all these letters, all, without an exception—; I often thought that I had already read what I was reading—then I remembered our conversations. Your soul has much in common with that of the writer. May God preserve the nobility of your beautiful being forever.

I trembled when I read the sentence in which she says that a man owes what he has seen, felt, and thought to another being who has awakened what had been slumbering in him. Lucky, those who meet those who are

---

1. Schweitzer's emphasis. This translation is from the *New Oxford Annotated Bible*.
2. Elisabeth von Heyking (1861–1925), *Letters Which Never Reached Their Destination* (1902).

destined to awaken that which slumbers in them. What did we say when we parted: I thank you. "I thank you"—that was our parting word, and that will remain our word of "nonseparation." Is it not a blessing that we can say to each other, as we have done: I thank you?—

I now believe that nothing can tarnish our friendship. I am quite excited. I feel that I am moving toward the great moment, but I also feel that in that happiness will be a sharp pain. You know from the most intimate of my letters, caused by the last "storm," that I had an affection about which I did not speak and which I have not completely overcome—I know that I will conquer it, but it is very hard. I read Nietzsche: *Beyond Good and Evil*— this great and beautiful call to life, to acceptance of life; I hear miraculous strange harmonies that would be mine, too, if my duty would leave me time. My duty—why can't I shake it off? After this distress, however, I feel peace again,—not the sweet, passive peace, the confinement of the chained dog, but the proud peace of action. I know that my activity as I want to develop it with the renunciation of conventional happiness is necessary, not for myself, but for our time, and it will prove its merit only through renunciation. I feel that I do not deceive myself, that it is not some will o' the wisp idea that leads me astray; it is that *quietest* calm, the peace of a torn soul—you know that I hate St. Augustine; it is not the peace of a pious man: I am not pious. If I should come to the conclusion tomorrow that there is no God and no immortality, and that morality is only an invention of society—that would not touch me at all. The equilibrium of my inner life and the knowledge of my duty would not be shaken in the least. I would laugh heartily and say: "So what? The party will go on." That fills me with serene pride. My father beat me because I always made such a cross face. I could not smile because laughing about something amusing, as people do, is to me like plunking away on the piano—while standing—as Elsa[1] does it. But a "genuine" laugh, that is something different: that means to play the whole piece with beautiful, great chords; it is not laughing "heartily," but *from the heart*; it is the bliss of being and of acting that awakened in me; it is the laughter above the gray clouds that move along the mountains; *this laughter—it is the peak of great seriousness; it is higher than seriousness itself—*

It is strange, I can hear the words of Jesus better because I hear that

---

1. Elsa Haas (1873–1940) was a longtime friend.

great joy with which He proclaimed them. Some of this laughter is in *Beyond Good and Evil*, this new testament of the pride of human nature, which was supposed to be killed. In Nietzsche was something of the spirit of Christ; to say this is a sacrilege. It is, however, true; in the end, only the blasphemous is true. But he lacked action; for this reason, his "pride" paced inside a cage like a captured lion; instead of coming out of his cave to attack his prey, he tore himself to pieces in the end. But he was noble, this man. Had he lived twenty centuries earlier, he could have become St. Paul—

I am getting off the right way—if you would give away my secret!—But you understand this honesty beyond words. Let us open the shutters: The birds play so innocently in the linden tree. The world has not changed since the days of Christ. These are the young who flap their wings and wait for their mother to come back to feed them. Let us not say anymore—your good hand—that is right—let us see.

I love Sunday afternoons.—

## 24. A. S.

[Strasbourg]
At the seminary
September 25, 1903, 9:00 in the evening

Here I am, at my new table, in the study of my own apartment—the first lines I write here are for you. I have the feeling that you, without knowing that I moved today—must share my great joy.

How did I move here? Last evening I had supper with some friends in town; afterward I slowly walked up the stairs to my apartment. At the threshold to the entrance, I closed my eyes and waited for a few seconds— then I went inside: The room was dark, but a glimmer came from the street, and in the soft light I could recognize everything—vaguely. This is how life lies ahead of me, the life I will spend in these rooms—dark, yet brightened by a gentle, distant light—so be it—may God guide and bless me.—I would like to know what it is—this God whom I implore—does He exist?—What is the spirit that forces me to follow my path—I who am not naïve, but critical, not "humble" but "proud"—what do I know? Let us go on—the spirit that speaks to me is a *reality*, the only supernatural reality that really exists for me—the rest is only a symbol, based on the only reality: *I believe because*

*I act*—action is, for me, the essential reality—and while I act, I will be both humble and proud—truthful as cutting steel.

*To be humble*—not only to have the *right and the strength* to be truthful—that is what I want—to proclaim the whole truth and to confirm it with my life, to gain strength from it—for this alone I sacrifice the happiness of life. You may tell me that this is a *self-delusion*—whatever: *I live from it,* I suffer with it, I cry, I laugh about it, I am *happy* about it. And as long as a few women of noble spirit support me with their fair sympathy, I can go my way alone./

Be content and be quiet—
Higher and higher—
The peace of God, *which surpasses all understanding,*
Shall keep your hearts and minds through Jesus Christ.—

**25. A. S.**

[Strasbourg]
Tuesday evening
October 27, 1903

The first letter from my desk at the seminary. I suspected and knew for some time that one day you, too, would search for "your life," "your happiness," but when you told me about it so calmly last evening in the twilight of your room, I was moved—and since then I only ask myself, "Did I have the right to divert her from the path on which she surely would have found her happiness as the others have?" Did I have the right to take you, without your own realization, on this steep path that I have to climb? Believe me, I did not want it, and I still do not want it; even now I wish that you would find the happiness of having a family; even now I wish that you would find fulfillment as a woman, that some day you would have your own children, that as wife and mother you would do so much good—yes, I want this—yet I have lost the right to urge you. To believe that the other happiness would not fulfill you would be against your dignity.

You appeared to me great and strong, and I was proud to see you as "my equal"; I was unable to express everything I thought—and then I was afraid when I told myself that you have gone so far because of me. There is now something so serene and so beautiful in you (even your looks have changed)—do you know how much you give me? How easy it is to walk the good and straight path, to reach "higher," if one is supported as I am through you—! If you could know how freely and deeply I breathe in this air—and how grateful I am to you. You are such a wonderful woman [ . . . ]

How will it be when we meet again in ten years? Will we have "achieved" something?

## 26. H. B.

[Strasbourg]
Saturday morning
October 31, 1903

My friend,
My dear friend,

It is raining—no chance to meet alone. I will try to write in the few in-between minutes what I had intended to say. There is nothing to worry about between us—that has become impossible by now; how beautiful, how very beautiful it is to know this!—

Yet I do not like it that there is so much that has not been said—and then I am tormented by the thought that it caused you such anxiety that I want to go my way. Tomorrow you will give me the two sheets and a word about what I am telling you now, all right?

(This letter began in a happy mood—because of lack of opportunity to write, it remains an unfinished parting note. I add it as a sign of my change of mood.)

## 27. A. S.

[Strasbourg]
Saturday morning
October 31, 1903

It is raining—no doubt: Our place will remain empty.[1] But I will devote most of the day to you. Work has not yet started seriously, and I feel the

---

1. On March 22, 1902, Albert Schweitzer and Helene Bresslau had the decisive exchange about their future at a place on the bank of the Rhine. They celebrated this day every year.

need to speak with you. Tomorrow night you will have these sheets, and you will read them on the train. Warm Strasbourg will recede in the November fog. Thus, I will accompany you for the longest time, farther than your parents and your friends, and I will speak with you when the voices of the others cannot reach you anymore. Even on paper, when there are other people, I can never speak with you freely. Last night I went home in a sad mood because I always fear that people take the liberty to talk about you and me, to suspect a little affair—but then when I am alone with you, alone in my room when I call you in my thoughts, then I can talk with you without inhibition. Last night, as I lay my head on my pillow, I thought of you and told myself how beautiful it would be if you could transfer our place faraway, somewhere in the world into an unknown country; there we would meet again—only once—without bothering about people or time—and we would be ourselves: We would observe the sun, the trees, we would talk for years, be silent for hours—how beautiful that would be. But don't we have this, this being by ourselves, when we imagine each other close together? Yes, you are here, on my wastepaper basket with the cover, between my armchair and the window, in that comfortable corner: that, from now on, is your place here. The one who now rests at Père Lachaise cemetery used to sit on this basket (one has to sit very still or it "makes music")—You have the right to sit there. I give it to you. But do not talk, watch how the leaves, one after another, fall from the big tree. They fight: They would like to hold on to every branch they touch, but without mercy they continue to fall, and their inescapable fate draws them to the earth. The poor leaves! Do you see: another—again another, and always another one.

*II*

Here I am again: I must speak with you in more detail. Listen carefully. I blame myself for not trying hard enough to disengage you from me. How often I tell myself: "If you were to succeed in playing a less important part in her life and thought, yet maintain some relationship with her, she would look for affection somewhere else and find someone who can make her completely happy. But no, you write her letters, you open your innermost self to her, you share your thoughts with her—how can she search for true happiness anywhere else? Do you believe that one can live unpunished in such intimacy? She also knows about your struggle because of another

one—and yet this intimacy is a bond that unites your life even stronger—
how can one sow wheat in a field on which such beautiful red clover is
growing? And who will deliver you from the accusation that you have
taken possession of her and that you have taken everything she can give,
without having the courage and the right to accept her totally, to make her
your own? Yes, it is exactly that: I harvest in a field that is not mine. And if
she does not find her happiness as a woman, this rich happiness without
conflicts, then you are the cause. Without you, who knows? She would now
have her family, her child—and you will detain her on and on. One day she
will tell you; without bitterness she will say: 'You led me the wrong way. I
was a woman. I had the right to enjoy the happiness of a woman. Because of
you I looked for another kind of happiness, a sublime one, that is true, and
I engaged all my energy. I have experienced indescribable moments of bliss,
but in spite of this I went the wrong way because it is not my own, natural
way. Everything I had to give to the world, I could have given as a mother,
as head of a home; I could have gone beyond that circle and done much
good, but now I am uprooted: I cannot apply my gifts; I remained a dilettante in spite of my best intentions.' "—And if you speak to me like this
some day, not reproachfully, gently and without bitterness, what will I answer? You cannot deliver me from my self-accusations—

—You will read this surrounded by the noises of the train that takes you
far away; I know this is not a trip to "get away," but a trip to your *destiny*, the
trip that will decide your whole life. My concern is with you.

*III*

The leaves are still falling—

I did not want to discourage you or humiliate you (please do not be
bothered by the word "dilettante"). In the intimacy of our exchanges,
words have only an approximate value, the value of symbols. You understand everything I wanted to tell you, everything I had to tell you, all my
concerns—and the undivided pride I feel for you. Because you are a great,
noble soul.

I will be totally frank: I do know that when you are married, I will not
have the right to take this place in your thoughts, to write you letters like
this one. I know that this will be a loss for me, but that is nothing compared
to the happiness for which you must search. We have both arrived at a

point of intimacy that makes any explanation unnecessary. You will remain for me what you are: I will come to find the warmth at your hearth, and, as a "complete" woman, you will be more for me than you are now. The thought that you are "a marriageable young woman" (don't laugh, I am serious) always covers the ideal that you personify for me, I mean an independent woman and a friend, and who often spoils everything for me, my naturalness, my spontaneity.

And the road you want to go—do you know what that is? To be alone in this world—to become an "old maid," to want to be independent yet not be able to be! And you value social life—you do not stand above it; you will not dissociate yourself from it, to wall yourself in some occupation—my great, great friend—I worry so much about you. Forgive me—; but I wanted to be totally honest. Don't say I humiliate you. I am with you on your train, and I only ask: Think about it.

*Saturday evening, October 31, 1903*

I have my "home"; I have my duty, which stands clearly before me—You wander around and do not yet see where you will be, what you will do; that is the difference between you and me—.

My dear friend—will you ever find it? I don't dare to read my pages from this morning again—what will you say when you read them?

I wanted to be totally honest—you will find in them the admiration I feel for you—and my fears—my great fears. These are thoughts that demand an answer—please let me have one.

## 28. A. S.

Sunday morning
November 1, 1903

I think that I don't have to tell you anything else. Only that I hold you in high esteem and that I admire you. I do not have the courage to tell you what you mean in my life and all that you have become for me; you are my friend if ever a woman was the friend of a man. Why do I tell you this? You see it in the openness with which I speak to you in my letters. Why do I tell you this? I am always afraid to tie you too closely to me and to block your road to happiness. But tell me—have you become richer with me, have you become somebody? You also have found happiness; the horizon of your life has changed, it has become brighter,—please tell me; I know it, but I want to hear it from you. Is it true that I have given you the true concept of life? Do you feel that I awakened a chord that slumbered in you, but that nobody had been able to bring to life? And is the happiness I brought you something precious to you? Tell me and look deeply into my eyes.

You, too, have given me much; you have forced me to open up; you have torn my thoughts out of me; you told me with pride: "I have a right to know them"—when I was lonely and sad, you came to me, and you gave me everything a woman can give that is noble and beautiful, not without struggle, but without egoism; you were woman; we drowned the little professor's daughter in the Rhine—You have given me great support: the esteem and the affection of a noble person who watches over you everywhere, to the depth of your thoughts, and who does not permit you to falter because one always thinks: What would she say? Would I still be worthy of speaking to her as I do, of looking into her eyes, of accepting her respect and friendship?—Every noble woman is something of a guardian angel. You came to me when I was alone, when the first guardian angel[1] had left me. I fought against you; I did not want you to take her place, out of respect for you, and not to awaken the jealousy of the dead because you were a German; you were only a marriageable young lady—you conquered me, you overwhelmed me, and I was forced to make space for you in my thinking and in my life. And only now do I wholly perceive the woman in you—and because I know you differently from the others, who see only the young lady, I cannot act naturally in company; I want to keep it a secret, at all cost, that I know you, for fear that someone might interfere with our friendship.—

And now you search for your path: I do not have the right to hold you back: "We bring each other bad luck," that is true, not in its petit bourgeois meaning, but in the great sense that we draw each other into our own fate. I do not know whether, without you, I had the strength to continue my fight, whether I would have become unfaithful to my calling. But you were there; you held on to the best in me; and if I had become weak, I would have lost your respect and more than that: I would have humiliated you, I would have deceived you.—And I am the one who caused you to turn from the right path: I plead with you once more: wait, hold on to the thought to

1. Aunt Mathilde.

pursue your happiness as woman; believe me, it is your fate to have a family. Give yourself two more years—I plead with you with all my heart—but I plead without the right to hold you back. Is it me who brought you into the hustle and bustle of the intellectual world in which one progresses because one must, because one cannot stand still?—Go straight ahead—toward the sun—if our life has significance only for us, what does it matter whether it has been "happy" or "unhappy" measured by the events? The only true value is the one we give it; that is its real and eternal value.

May God bless and protect you.

I think of you with pride and concern—but I know that whatever happens will be "good."—[1]

## 29. A. S.

[Strasbourg]
Monday morning
November 2, 1903

You leave—and I cannot hold you back. Last evening when I saw you at the stairs with Elly,[2] both looking into emptiness—both so sad—I had to tell myself: I would have to say only one word, and everything would be different, but I do not have the right to say it—I don't have this right, and you know it. But to let you depart, to let you go into this world shrouded in mist—And when will I see you again? Promise me one thing: If you meet somebody with whom you might share your life and who asks you to accompany him: do not refuse; do not refuse./.

Tell me to go back to my work, command me; otherwise, I will spend the whole morning watching the leaves falling from the trees. In one hour, you will open the travel letters.[3]

1. Helene began her nurses' training at Stettin in 1904.

2. Elly Knapp, friend from the Cycling Club, later married Theodor Heuss (see p. xxvi).

3. Schweitzer had written the letters from October 31 to November 2, 1903, prior to Helene's departure for Berlin.

**30. H. B.**

> Berlin W. Keithstr. 6 first floor
> Adr. Miss Johanna Engel[1]
> November 8, 1903

My friend,

Thank you for everything, thank you for being so completely open. But don't ask for an answer from me—I cannot write; let us leave it as you wish: You speak to me and I am there, I listen to you. Burn this card and do not worry about me—you see many things very differently from what they really are. I do not want to hurt you, you know that—you must be *refreshed, enjoy your work, and be happy*. The first condition for this is: Stop your struggles, I want it. You must be at one with yourself. I trust that you do not misunderstand me.

**31. A. S.**

> [Strasbourg]
> Thursday evening
> November 26, 1903

Is it true? Tonight you are in the orphanage to find out whether this will be your "path"? Your friend[2] told me this afternoon (without my having asked for you) that you wanted information about this institution. She did not know what this news meant to me: I was moved. What a coincidence: tomorrow I take the first steps to find out about "my boys"—.

I worried about you during the last days, but now I am completely at ease. Why? I do not know. But I smile when I think of you. Good night. It is one o'clock in the morning. I tell myself that you will not write to me until you have a better picture: For this reason, you have not answered my letters.

I feel as if this whole life is an immense dream: People around me do not understand me anymore; they suspect something that they do not know; they cannot understand that I feel removed and especially why I

---

1. Johanna Engel (1867–1942), a cousin of Helene Bresslau's father and a painter. She committed suicide in 1942 when she was to be sent to Theresienstadt.
2. Elly Knapp.

don't care about my "career" as professor! As if that would be my goal, the career of a professor!—No, I want to *"live,"* live my life—you understand me! Listen to the wind in the big tree, our friend./.

## 32. A. S.

[Strasbourg]
Thursday evening
December 3, 1903

The time has come. A few days ago I saw the director of the orphanage, Dr. Schwander,[1] and I told him that he should let me know if he needed a place for two boys, eight to twelve years, because I knew somebody who wanted to take them. Of course, I did not tell him that I am this somebody. He will look and report to me. I was shaking when I put my hand to his doorknob, and for a moment I hesitated: "You can still go back, think carefully," I told myself—yet I calmly walked in.

Now it can become reality any day now. I wait. For several days, I was very excited. At the same time, I was sad. Now my plans, which I guarded for years like a treasure, will become public. That is painful: I always suffer when I give up a piece of myself; when I brought the manuscript of my life of Jesus[2] to the post office, it was also a moment of sadness—

Now everything moves ahead, toward fulfillment. Tonight I had one hour by myself, and I felt a deep happiness. It was a perfect Advent atmosphere. How mysterious is happiness!

1. Dr. Rudolf Schwander was the mayor of Strasbourg and head of the Office of Social Services. This first attempt did not lead to any result, and all further appeals had no success.

2. *The Quest of the Historical Jesus*, published in 1906. As Delbert R. Hillers explains in his foreword to the 1968 edition of this book, *Quest* was known by a number of titles: "The various German titles of Schweitzer's book, in successive editions, 'From Reimarus to Wrede' and 'History of Research on the Life of Jesus' are flat and unrevealing or misleading, suggesting that the work is only an ordered review of a century of scholarship, the kind of thing that is almost invariably very dull. It was evidently during the process of translation into English (by W. Montgomery) that a phrase, picked from the book itself, yielded an English title that is both accurate and more evocative, the key word being *quest*, calling to mind the Grail and other adventurous pursuits" (*The Quest of the Historical Jesus: A Critical Study of Its Progress from Reimarus to Wrede* [Baltimore and London: Johns Hopkins Univ. Press, in association with the Albert Schweitzer Institute, 1998], p. xi).

It came to me while I looked in vain for ideas for my Advent sermon: Suddenly thoughts flowed toward me, and I only had to open my hand to take hold of them—.

How are you? Why did you not send me a brief answer to my large parcel of letters? Tomorrow morning I will take these pages to the post office, I decided today. Please send me a brief answer *immediately* to tell me how you are; I must know. What was your impression of the orphanage? Will it be the right occupation for you? I think that you will have a lot to tell me. I have the *right* to know how you are.—

If, by chance, you should find an orphaned boy who needs a home, please let me know. If possible, I would like to take him in. *Please search* (without mentioning my name). That would be wonderful if my first boy could come through you.—What will it be?—Please give me your address for Christmas./.

### 33. H. B.

[Berlin]
December 17, 1903

I wanted to send you a greeting for Christmas, but perhaps you are not at Strasbourg at Christmas. So I write now. And I thank you for everything—but please do not ask for an answer from me. You are right; there are a few things I have to tell you, but I *cannot* write, and you know exactly: Our friendship does not depend upon a letter. Talk with me when you feel the need and never doubt: I am always there to listen to you and, when I can, to help you. I *want* you to be *strong* and *happy,* and that is what you must be, and you have all reason to be so. You should never worry about me, never.

On January 1st, I begin my three-month course in nursing at the city hospital at Stettin; until then I am here. That is all that is confirmed so far.

The person who has been the most for me while I am here is a sixty-five-year-old lady with a young heart. Her name is Mathilde.

—All the best. Farewell—

**34. A. S.**

At the seminary
Tuesday evening
December 23 [22], 1903

It's me. I write you a brief word that will reach you at Christmas so that you know where you can search for me on that evening when our thoughts will meet. Although I do not have to preach during the holidays, I am staying here to enjoy the solitude; I have such a desire to be by myself, to gather my thoughts. So I will be at home in my study because here, not in my private apartment, I feel at home. In the afternoon, I will wrap some packages for children of poor families I know.—I have been dreaming that I would not be alone in my large apartment during the holidays, but the course of real life is slower than that of dreams. That often grieves me; I would like to get out of this worry and the waiting to have the discussions with my family behind me, discussions that will without doubt inflame when I present the fait accompli. It is exhausting to swim between reality and dream. I know that my parents are sad that I do not spend the holidays with them, but I cannot do it: I belong to the poor for whom I can do a little good. But these are thoughts one cannot voice.

I have written two articles for the *Kirchenbote*, and I have preached every Sunday with great joy. The sermons were in some ways "incomplete"; I did not go to the full depth of my thinking because I would not have been understood. Is it not amazing that this great figure dominates us all and keeps us in chains? Sometimes I think of a revolt, as at "our Sunday afternoon" at Günsbach. Yes, He gives us energy, but He also takes some from us! He has taken away our personality; from free humans He turned us into slaves! How many fine talents has He suppressed—and He has created miserable human beings who might have been great characters without Him. That is blasphemy, if you wish, but He has the greatness to bear blasphemy—and you understand what is meant by blasphemy. Think of all the childish sermons that are preached about the "Christ child" today. He certainly did not want them; yet He has caused them. I don't have a clear picture of what I will preach on Sunday.

At the seminary, all goes well; I spend a great deal of time with two students in whom I have observed a negative development, and I try to guide them toward self-respect though work. Will I succeed?—

Have you received everything I sent your way: (1) a package with letters for the journey, (2) sheets that I sent to Berlin, (3) a short letter?

The Bach manuscript is progressing. I worked on it all day, in spite of a fever attack that left me tired. I felt it coming and forgot to take some quinine, which would have prevented it.

Thank you for your letter. It arrived at the right moment. I was afraid that I had hurt you without knowing it and that that had caused your silence. Those unfounded fears I also had several times with my aunt. It is strange. I am always in the grip of some kind of sad resignation, and I tell myself that one should be able to manage also without friends! Yet, at the first sign of life, all fears evaporate. Now that I know, it should not happen again.—

This has become a long letter, and yet some things I wanted to tell you are still missing. I, too, want to thank you for everything—I only have to close my eyes to see the bright sun that we saw one day together—and I am blinded. It supports and guides me, this sun.

Thank you for everything—also that you wrote whole pages in French. I was moved by that.

I don't know where to look for you during the holidays: Will you have a moment for yourself? Whatever: Happy holidays. Tonight I received the little novel of Gorki./. and I put everything away to read—because it came from you, and in addition it is very moving. Send me once in a while a sign of life of that kind./.

## 35. A. S.

At the seminary<br>December 31, 1903

Soon the clock will strike—the last moments and my last thoughts of this year belong to you because you share the largest part of my inner being.—Just now the bell of the cathedral rang midnight. So now we are in the new year. May God bless and protect you and may He guide you to recognize the path that will lead you to happiness. The whole past hour I was lying stretched out with closed eyes on the armchair in my study. I try to find whether there is another path than the one I see before me: No, I must follow it and be content with the friendship of the souls that give me some rays of sunshine without ever having a fire in my hearth and without ever being able to dream about happiness with anybody else. So I will follow my road. My beloved, my great friend: Thank you for everything you are for me and for the great affection you bestow on me. This affection encourages and supports me, and I thank you for that as the most precious in my whole existence in this past year. Keep this nobility of your soul alive and let me, now and then, believe that I was the one who awakened the good and the beauty in your being—then it will be easier for me to tell myself that I am also the one who happened to be on your road.

I imagine that you sit right at the bay window, a hand above your eyes. I take it gently to kiss, my great friend./.

# *1904*

*Helene Bresslau began her nurse's training at Stettin in 1904.*

**36. H. B.**

Stettin, January 13, 1904
City Hospital

My friend,

I had intended to write you a long letter—it is impossible! Thus only these few lines that will bring you all my best wishes for tomorrow.[1] Do you remember how last year another letter and I were the only ones who congratulated you on your birthday? I write in a hurry because I am at the women's surgical floor where I currently work, and I use the two minutes of rest I have in between feeding a patient and our own meal. I intended to take this afternoon off (we always have one free afternoon a week), but there is so much to do that I have to stay. We work from six o'clock in the morning to eight in the evening.—One feels pretty tired in the evening. But in spite of it, one loves the work; only once in a while thoughts come to mind that one probably should not pursue. I have a large room with old women—for most of them I wish a peaceful, quick death, and I think that it is almost immoral to keep them alive for a life that brings them only suffering.

I think of you so much; I wonder whether you are still alone. Please write me as frequently as possible, would you do that? And send me the *Kirchenbote*—in the isolation of the hospital I hear nothing about what is

1. Schweitzer's birthday.

38

going on in the world. But I learn much, very much. The other night I intended to write you, but I was too tired, and tonight we have *"Pastor's Hour"* (!) until ten o'clock. If you would like to, you can address your letters to "Sister Helene Bresslau" or to *Miss*, it does not matter. My name here is Sister Helene. I will remain until April 1st.

Somebody calls me; today we have major *operations*. I enjoy being in the room where the wounds are dressed; it is very interesting, but the other day when I had to be in the operating theater for the first time, I felt very ill.

Good-bye, my friend, tomorrow I will be with you in my thoughts, and with that the year you begin will be a happy and blessed one.

Please answer soon.

God bless you!

## 37. A. S.

> At the seminary
> Tuesday evening,
> January 19, 1904

Can you imagine that I would miss the opportunity to call you "Sister Helene"? Oh no. Good evening, Sister Helene. Take the armchair; wait a moment—I will move it closer to the table, now sit down, Sister Helene. Are you comfortable, Sister Helene? And now I am here for you, let us have a long conversation. Excuse me for one moment; I have to stoke the fire, so we will not get cold. And now give me your good hand, Sister Helene.

On the 14th I was at Hausbergen; my sister's boy was baptized, and the weather was horrible, by the way. When I returned in the evening, I found eight letters. Because I was very tired, I lay down immediately and read the letters, one after the other. Guess which one I opened first and read several times before I took up another one! Can you guess? Just admit that you know exactly that it was yours. Then I put my head on the pillow, put both my hands over my eyes (a position I learned from you), and surrendered myself to the feeling of bliss. Yes, it was bliss. How wonderful it is to have somebody who has the right to wish you a happy birthday and puts so many thoughts into this one wish. I forget that I want you to detach yourself from me and tell you that I went to sleep happy as a child. Since that time I have often reread your letter, and I always feel as if everything is now easy, when I see you in the distance with your simple and noble thoughts and with your

Letter from Helene Bresslau, 1904. *From the Albert Schweitzer Papers, courtesy of the Department of Special Collections, Syracuse University Library.*

soul that has grown through much struggle. I thank you with all my heart—
your friendship is at this moment the most precious possession I have in my
life.

Do you know that, until today, I fought a battle with myself? Tomorrow
a great celebration will take place in Paris, at the occasion of my uncle's
nomination as a member of the Legion of Honor. All friends and family will
be there, and I had planned, with Madame Harth, my aunt's sister, to arrive
as a surprise; but today I sent her a telegram to tell her that I cannot come.
Now, after the decision has been made, I am not nervous anymore. One
must have courage, do you agree?

I am still by myself. You know that I asked Dr. Schwander to let me
know when there are abandoned boys or orphans because I know somebody
who would like to raise them. None has been found so far. I also wrote to a
minister in a workers' settlement at Mühlhausen and made him the same
offer; no answer so far. I also have decided to put an advertisement in a
newspaper and to let nature take its course. Once in a while, when I think
of the difficulties such a project will cause, I tell myself: "You can still with-
draw; look, there is no necessity; you just pursue a fantasy."—But then, immediately, I regain my clear vision and know that this is my calling, that I
must follow this path, in spite of everything. And the good spirit returns,
and then I feel as if you look at me and speak with me. What good fortune
that I spoke with you about everything and that you now understand me
and can make everything easier—Sister Helene. Oh yes, you are my sister,
my good sister, and you share my lofty thoughts. As soon as I am not alone
anymore, I will let you know with just a short note. I have to interrupt for a
moment—I have to catch my breath because I have spoken with you without interruption, without knowing where to begin and where to end.

I know that I have forgotten the most important things about which I
intended to write. That is the reason I take up the pen again. My last sermons exhausted me.—I have, if that is possible, put too much of my heart
into them. I send you the last one from last Sunday and two from last summer. Next time you will get the Advent sermons. Tell me your opinion
about the article in the *Kirchenbote*, my dear critic. I am very happy at the
seminary. The students show great sympathy toward me and accept my authority without any difficulty. I even was able to take back a student who
had been dismissed last year and to keep another one who also has been in
trouble. I care for them as a father, try to point them in the right direction

by encouraging them to work. One of them just interrupted us. He did not see you—are you invisible to the others? I see you very clearly in the arm-chair.

I did not write you any letters—I was not able to, I was too tired. But on New Year's Eve I spoke with you. Here is the short page.—

I am concluding now, Sister Helene. Are you happy in your work? Sometimes I imagine that I walk between your patients' beds, and I would like to take a quick glance at your hall. I recently visited your parents and had a good conversation with your mother. Did you know that Dr. Lenel[1] comes to my church? He was there last Sunday. I notice that he has a gen-uine fondness for me, and I feel great sympathy toward him. He has a heart of gold.

God bless you, Sister Helene.

Thank you for writing to me in French: I know why you did it: to take increasingly the place of the one who died. You write admirably. Would we ever have thought that one day we would exchange our thoughts in French? You remember that I declined when you first offered it?

## 38. A. S.

[Strasbourg]
January 30, 1904

For me, pagan thoughts coexist with the Christian, and I am not able to separate them. In all of us, there is something pagan, something proud and grand that Christ did not know and that does not go well with Chris-tianity and with the ideas of Christ. Have you noticed that in His parables He never mentions woods as we know them, as dark, mysterious, impene-trable, as they correspond to the equally dark, equally mysterious, and equally impenetrable character of us, people of the northern countries? Whenever I am in the woods, as soon as I hear their melodies, there awak-ens something that slumbers deep in my heart, something pagan, yet reli-gious, some feeling of pride and energy, of harshness and haughtiness that I cannot define.

What would have become of the Germanic religion without Chris-tianity if it had developed independently, entirely on the force of its own

1. Dr. Walter Lenel, a scholar and friend of Schweitzer and Helene.

thought? Would it have been better for us to have this noble religion rather than this foreign religion of the Great One from Nazareth, which has some touch of decadence, from broken pride of His nation? Yes, everybody loves his neighbor as he loves himself, makes sacrifices for him, yet deep down he despises him and does not want to let him share his innermost life, so that it may not be desecrated. There are people whom I love only because I have allowed myself to detest them: It took me a long time to realize this and to recognize that everything else would be a lie and cowardice.

Recently, when I looked through old papers, I found a thought jotted down casually: "The great thinkers conquered the world; yes, but how many other thinkers have they killed, who is aware of that?" Thinkers who might have served us well! The great ones have crushed and destroyed those—and now we have a religion—and mindlessness, and all that is great and true in this world dies—from religion or from nonthinking. / Can you comprehend this?

**39. H. B.**

Stettin, City Hospital
February 2, 1904
In my room

You are surprised that I answer so late—but you know how little time I have, and I thought that you would not always expect an answer from me in order to write again, my friend? How much I enjoyed your long letter—that I do not have to tell you. You see, I received thirty letters and cards for my birthday; as answers I send little "Thank You" cards that go quite quickly, and one can produce half a dozen in a few free minutes while on duty. Would you like such a card? I write letters only to my parents; in the evening, I am too tired.

You ask me of my opinion about the articles in the *Kirchenbote*. But no, I am too dumb right now; I have nothing on my mind but my patients. And I only read what is sent to me, and even that I cannot finish. I did read one of your sermons and the *Kirchenbote*; among those, "Jesus and the Wise Men" I like best. In it, I recognize you, my friend, and you know that I almost think like you. In it, you are yourself: arrogant and humble—and slightly paradoxical. Are you annoyed that I tell you that? But you know how I mean it. And sometimes I have the impression that you know exactly if and how you have gone a little too far. And I feel that you are right; only through exaggeration can we shake the spirits when we force them into contradiction (while I write this word "contradiction," I am not sure whether it exists; I don't have a dictionary—please don't laugh at me!) When I write in French, I do so without even thinking about it,—it comes naturally, just as it was natural when I spoke French with you, but I realize that I make many mistakes.—You must excuse me!

I am very, very happy here, and I don't even suffer anymore from the physical exhaustion as I did in the beginning. But I would not like to stay here, however, even if I had the permission my parents—which I would never receive—. And why not? Because I am too egotistical, too much of an individual, and because I do not want to give up my life as an individual and sacrifice it for the rest of my life. Here our work absorbs us completely—physically and mentally.—

I was interrupted, and now I have barely a quarter of an hour to conclude this letter. I have been very happy here because I have almost always been alone in my room. The sister whom I share it with had night duty, so in the four weeks since I arrived, I have always been alone in the evening and at night, and she had the room during the day. Tomorrow she leaves. Who will be my next roommate? I am afraid because I have been used to always having a room to myself. Here everything changes, and very fast. On my floor, I have changed my hall already. In the former, I saw three of my patients dying, severe cases, whose death I had hoped for because of their great suffering. Then young people came, and the hall lost its character as a *museum room*—that was quite a change. And now I have two halls with young women, in one: nice, well-behaved ones; in the other: girls from another world, the kind everyone tries to hide from "well brought up" young women. All in all, thirty patients (more than one-half of the whole floor); they are, however, not seriously ill, and most of them can get up, and they help willingly, so I have less work, at least less heavy and less unpleasant than with my twelve old women. I like it there very much. I do a little of what the pastor spoke the other day (but can you imagine: not *because* he spoke of it!): physician of the soul, inner mission—and I believe that I don't do it entirely in his way! The "Pastor's Hour"—you are entirely correct in what you think about it. He is an "honorable servant of God," entirely honey and water—but very shallow water!—You can imagine that, on those evenings, I would rather go to bed! Because that is impossible, I keep myself busy with a collection of howlers.[1]—If you are interested, I will send you some. We have other classes, too—medical theory with two of our doctors—they are much more interesting.

My friend, play music, much music, also for me! You don't know how I long for it—that would be another reason why I could not spend the rest of my life in a hospital—for the first time in four months I played a little today—how to find time for such things?

Good night my friend.

Thank you, special thanks for the short note from New Year's Eve!

## 40. A. S.

[Strasbourg]
February 4, 1904
Nighttime

I received your letter today. Your words are the most precious gift I can receive—I feel totally enveloped in a world of purity and sympathy—. I read them often, your good words, even when I already know them by heart.—

But don't you know that I try to detach you from me? Apparently my approach is clumsy: I, indeed, want to detach you from me so you can attach yourself to somebody else. How can I achieve that?—

You now know the world that people like to hide from a well-bred young woman—you know the most miserable and horrible conditions on earth—you know how criminal men are—for every creature who has been hurt, there is a man who will have to stand judgment in eternity. Oh, what degradation of nature, what abysmal sadness, how much desperation underneath noisy gaiety.—

We will never be able to liberate the world from this.—

Good night.

---

1. Publishers' humorous blunders.

**41. A. S.**

Friday, February 5, 1904

So you write me in French—quite naturally. And you think that I would laugh at you because you may use an awkward expression?—First of all, there are none; you express yourself very charmingly, and if it were so, I would not see it because I hear you speak while I read your words.

So you need your "individual" life. I understand you, and just because of that I want you to marry. Then you will have your individual life and can pass on all the good that is in you. But every so often your thirst for an "individual" life frightens me—if one day you are faced with a requirement that challenges your individual life—what will you do? God bless you—

**42. A. S.**

Saturday, February 6, 1904

We preach about texts—prescribed texts—so we do not have to tell our own thoughts, and in the end we have run away from our own thoughts, so we no longer realize that we can preach only what is based on our own thoughts. That this is not taught us in our pastoral training I will hold against the professors forever. They shaped us into skillful practitioners but did not want us to strive for something higher.

[ . . . ]

**43. A. S.**

March 15, 1904

Atheism—could it not be a religion, too? The most beautiful and the most difficult, the religion that will follow the religion of Christ. Did He not say when He faced death, "My God, my God, why have you forsaken me?" So He died as an atheist?

Who has the courage to pursue this thought?

March 15, 1904. Meditation
on the train,
in the darkness of night.

## 44. A. S.

[Theological Seminary, Collegium Wilhelmitanum]
March 25, 1904

Have you thought of the anniversary of our friendship? Two years of deep friendship! Do you still remember how we walked back from our excursion to the flood dam with our bicycles while I spoke with you?—.

Now the weather is the same as it was then: the long waiting for spring. Yet, all the same, it is beautiful, this holding back, this timidity of our northern nature—Italian spring is not for me; it is too beautiful; it does not know these small, chilly flowers under bushes, which alternately weep and laugh, depending upon wind or sun. I went to Günsbach for a day (a week ago Wednesday) and spent the early spring day completely carefree. We were at our rock, the dog and I, and at the spot where we sat when my father told us the story we stopped. And I saw you, leaning against the small rock.—

Thank you for your letter: You don't tell much, but I see that you are happy with your work. You will hardly get a page this time (none!): The completion of the *Bach*[1] takes every second, and I collapse from fatigue.

The *Bach* will be a good book. There is, however, only one third of my soul in it. This philosophizing about art never satisfied me. I will be glad when my strength and my thoughts will not be absorbed anymore by a project that is only "interesting," but not my life.

In spite of my efforts, I have not yet found any boys—but I know that I will find some—after Easter.

You are with me often—and I confide my best thoughts in you, and your good eyes drive away all bad ones.—

Look at the buds on the big tree—Sister Helene—(for the last time)

Your friend A.

Two o'clock in the morning. It is late at night: I reviewed and reworked the first half of a chapter of my *Bach*. Now I will close it and take it to the mailbox.

---

1. *J. S. Bach, le musicien-poète*, first published in French, 1905.

I enjoy talking with you in my letters; my head is brimming with thoughts.

Good night.

## 45. A. S.

[Strasbourg]
Thursday morning
April 21, 1904

I cannot write: The shadows and the lights of the leaves on the big tree dance on the paper. It does not help when I move the table back; the tree follows me with its caresses, as if it wanted to tell me: "Why have you been away for so long?" Look: They also dance on this little sheet, its shadows, its lights: it sends you its greetings. Your words, your good glances, they remind me of the caresses of this big tree. But I have to miss it for a long time. But I have had them, and the memories will be with me forever.

I am writing a sermon for Sunday morning: "See, I am with you, every day till the end of the world," and I speak of those who help us because they are with us with their thoughts, the living and the dead, those close and those far away! You know that I could not say this as clearly without you.

Now, my great tree, I cannot be mad at you because you distract me. I will look at your dancing leaves and think about somebody who is far, far away—and yet so close. But I will not tell you the name; you do not have to know everything.

## 46: A. S.

[Strasbourg]
Sunday morning
May 1, 1904

The leaves have grown in recent days—soon they will be as large as those that dropped when I wrote the letters for your trip.—You know how I urged you at that time to accept the hand of a sympathetic man if you should meet one on your way. Have you not met anyone for whom you feel more than indifference? I always thought that you might be engaged when you return, and you know that this would give me genuine pleasure. So, just tell me that I can become indiscrete—but between us can there be any indiscretion? I would like so very much to see you happy—but you will, of course, in all happiness preserve your noble spirit.

Everything must be blossoming around my rock. Why can't I go there?

Your father gave a most extraordinary lecture yesterday! It was the most brilliant synthesis between scholarship and the arts that one could imagine. When I came home, I wrote cordially to congratulate him. Next winter, at the President's Ball, you will be the queen. I will look at you bashfully from the distance. According to your letter, you lead quite a fashionable life at Hamburg. I beg you, can you once give me a quiet evening with your thoughts? That would make me feel good—very good. If I think how hard it was for me to tell you my plans for the future—the thought that you know everything now gives me courage to hold on to my plan. I have undertaken the following. I would like to have two boys between six and eight who do not have anybody. As a first step, I have contacted Dr. Schwander, the director of welfare programs at Strasbourg. He promised he would notify me when he finds somebody.(I have not told him that I am the one who would like to take in the boys.) Next I wrote to Mühlhausen. They also made promises, and so did the people in Paris whom I asked about children from Alsace. I want to realize my plans at last.

If you discover anything in Hamburg, please let me know—that would be the most wonderful, if the solution came from you. This long waiting has been painful, but, on the other hand, it has given me time to think over everything. How often have I told myself: "If you want it, you can turn around; you will be happy, just as others are, and you can do much good."—But the inner voice told me every time: "You see the road you want to follow; do so. Only in this way are you true to yourself, honest and strong." There was not the slightest struggle. My feelings were so strong that if I were to act otherwise, I would be destroyed. I don't fight my destiny; I follow it as quietly and happily as rarely a person has done. This alone is my life. Soon I will be thirty years old.—I know very well that every word I say in a sermon would drop to the floor the moment it came out of my mouth if I do not follow my road. I must continue. It is moving to see your life so absolutely clearly before yourself and to know that spiritual happiness is enough to fill our lives—and to feel the communion of thought with a few noble souls who have the right to know. Sometimes it seems to me as if I had climbed beyond clouds and stars and could see the world in the most wonderful clarity and therefore have the right to be a heretic! To know only

Jesus of Nazareth, to continue his work as the only religion, not to bear what Christianity has absorbed over the years in vulgarity. Not to be afraid of Hell, not to strive for the joys of Heaven, not to live in false fear, not the fake devotion that has become an essential part of our religion—and yet to understand the one Great One and to know that one is His disciple. Last night before I went to sleep, I read the twenty-fifth chapter of the Gospel of St. Matthew because I especially love the verse: "Truly I tell you, just as you did it to one of the least of these who are my brothers, you did it to me." But when it came to the last judgment and the separation of the "sheep from the goats," I smiled: I do not want to belong to the sheep, and in Heaven I would certainly meet quite a lot whom I do not like: St. Loyola, St. Hieronymous, and a few Prussian church leaders—and to act friendly with them, to exchange a brotherly kiss? No, I decline. Rather to Hell. There the crowd will be more congenial. With Julian Apostate, Caesar, Socrates, Plato, and Heraclitus, one can have a decent conversation. Yet, I serve Him because of Him, only because of Him—because He is the only truth, the only happiness.

**47. A. S.**

> [Strasbourg]
> Sunday afternoon, May 1, 1904
> Coming from the church

I preached to my good women about gratitude—which is not difficult, if one's heart is so filled with gratitude toward "God" as mine is. I often ask myself whether I thank Him enough for all the gifts he has given me. Did you know that we performed a St. Matthew's Passion that was considered by the critics totally faithful to the classic tradition? We had rehearsed for it with great enthusiasm. My lectures last semester were most successful. It is truly marvelous to lecture in a full hall and to feel that you are carried by the sympathy of the young people. At the seminary, it also went very well last winter: no incidents, either with the students or the personnel. The chief cook is a cow, touchy as the devil: I disarm her with even-tempered and special politeness. You would have a good laugh if you could see me in that role. But those are insignificant things: I feel that I have brought to the seminary a certain spirit, that I can convey something that those who have lived with me here will carry with them. I was touched by the expressions of sympathy of several students when they left the seminary. That gives me courage. Yes, I will not have lived in vain. I have a certain vision of immortality: our thoughts are what is immortal and immaterial in us. We live when our thoughts are reborn in others. This is why Socrates and Christ live. That is living immortality! Why do we need another one?

Because I am somewhat rested, my head is filled with philosophical thoughts. It is painful. Basically I am a philosopher—but I let myself be caught by Him, the greatest, the most divine of all philosophers in whom the most sublime thought leads back to the most simple. Because of this obedience He will forgive my heresies: I am like one of those Satraps[1] who were sent to the border of the empire and enjoyed certain freedoms because they defended and protected the country.

## 48. A. S.

> [Strasbourg] Night before Sunday
> May 29, 1904, 10:30 P.M.
> Moonlight

The moon plays with its light on the wall and the furniture of my bedroom. I could not sleep because I was somewhat excited after I had accompanied Handel's *Messiah*, which was performed last night at the Wilhelm's Kirche. With open eyes, I followed the gentle light of the moon and thought of you, my hands folded, and all that I owe you. If in all one's spiritual struggles one can find refuge with a human being who is of such pureness of thought as you are—then it is easy to live and to carry one's head high.

No cloud in the sky, only the moon shines straight into my room. I write you in the light of the small lamp. I got up and put on my gown. I took your little photograph out of its case and put it against the paperweight (your paperweight) because nobody can bother me here. I don't like it too well, this photograph; there is still something too youthful in your looks— you look different now!

Shall I tell you about my life at Günsbach? Have you thought about the two days we spent there at Whitsuntide? In the evening, I walked with the dog and saw the two old women, the two neighbors on their little impro-

---

1. Governors of a province of the ancient Prussian Empire.

vised bench—like last year, so I sat down with them, we chatted, and I saw you sitting with us, just as last year.

I have worked constantly copying the *Bach* manuscript; almost two hundred pages are complete; they will go to Paris before the end of the week. How wonderful when I get rid of that job so I can devote myself completely to the third section of *The Last Supper*.

Today I preached to comfort myself: In Paris, they still search,[1] but nobody has been found yet. The same in Mühlhausen. I told myself that God is not a sentimental man who trusts in the first enthusiasm of humans, but He tests people to see whether they persevere, and only then does He accept them for His service. But I persevere, and I am sure that everything will come out all right. Gerold,[2] who is usually reserved, said as we left the church, "Your sermon was beautiful." How are you? I see you before me. May God lead you on the road to happiness.

Did you know that I have gotten involved in church politics? I did not intend it; I don't like intrigues, but now the time has come: Liberalism is in great danger in Alsace, and my friends have forced me to become involved in church politics. My first action: I did Nowack[3] a nasty trick. He was sure to be elected to the council of the state church, but now he most likely will be defeated because I declared that we, the younger clergy, did not want him. Now the assistant professor has plotted against the oldest faculty member. I have done my duty because it would be a catastrophe if Nowack could control everything; he already sticks his nose into issues that are none of his business, and, in addition, he has lost all idealism; he is a stickler, only interested in taking part in everything. This is the first battle in a long war that will start between him and me. I enter this war calmly because I have no personal antipathy. I will get involved in all of this and prevent him from further action because it must be so for the welfare of the church.

How beautiful the moon is tonight. I feel as if you could not sleep either, that you look at the moon and let your thoughts travel . . . Good night.

1. For orphaned boys.

2. Karl Theodor Gerold, pastor of the Nikolai Church, was Schweitzer's supervisor at the church.

3. See p. 17n.

How pleasant was this hour of conversation. Why don't you write? I ask myself whether you received my recent missive.

Yours,

A.

## 49. H. B.

Hamburg, June 5, 1904
26 Papenhuderstrasse

Just a brief word, you shall have it! I am so happy that the *Bach* is completed—please tell me what you do now. Have you returned to philosophy? Do you realize that you walk like a crab? You go exactly where I came from. Your ideas concerning immortality, these impassioned visions, that our thoughts are reborn in the people who follow us, these I had before I arrived at those that I told you on the road to Günsbach—do you remember?—In this respect and in all humility, I came closer to the great Kant,—and this gives me great joy. And now, when I reflect upon this, I find a union of both: When our thoughts live in others—after our own life has come to an end— and when they reappear, perhaps in a purer form—is that not the sign of highest perfection of which Kant speaks—even if he did not think of immortality in human form and on this earth? But has this philosophy not existed for a long time in the concept of transmigration of souls? If this is nonsense, please forgive me, but I have not studied philosophy! If this is what you call atheism, I have been an atheist for many years. I remember a discussion I had with Kuck and Rudolf Spindler[1] on our return trip from Weissenburg to Wingen, and that I told them: "All in all, I am a heretic," and they answered, "You must admit that you cannot dissociate yourself from Christ; to be a Christian does not imply anything but *to love Jesus Christ*." How often have I thought of this when I have spoken with people who have ideas similar to mine, but they did not dare to call themselves Christians? What else is that, but a question of name? A name is a sound and smoke.[2] I wish that a minister, instead of secretly calling himself an atheist, would tell those who think independently and who reject the formalities, the trimmings and all that goes with it, those

1. Two young ministers.
2. Helene is quoting here from Goethe's *Faust*.

who have lost the courage to call themselves Christians (because *unfortu-nately* they came to the conclusion that these formalities were the essence of Christianity), those who are not always strong enough to stand on their own, I wish that that minister would say freely and openly what true Christianity is: To love Jesus Christ, and those who do should follow Him. He will find out what I have frequently observed: that their atheism is nothing that is in conflict with Christianity—and he can tell them much better than I ever could and can.—

Yes, people are "fashionable" at Hamburg, but we find life only in this world, and I had to find it. This means that I, too, was flying high and above the clouds, but a little too high because I had little understanding and feeling for the value of life—now I have found it again. You probably would be surprised to see me quite often as happy and content as a child. The reason for this lies in the fact that we both—as I believe—have found in each other a trustworthy support and in this way have learned to walk alone, *totally alone*, not to depend on anybody—inwardly, of course.

I attended here two wonderful performances: *The Three Heron's Feathers*[1] and *Tristan and Isolde*, the latter conducted by Nikisch.[2]

I read a little (even Ernst Haeckel[3]), and I will recommend some books to you when I return. [ . . . ] My brief word grew into a long one—but I was really quite proud of you and hope to be even more so! Therefore, much strength and good work, but not at night, please do remember!—and tell me how you progress! Now I must close, Adieu!

## 50. A. S.

[Strasbourg, October–November 1904]

*I*

So you are at Strasbourg and will remain there throughout the winter!—I am so happy—but am also afraid. Will we find the right kind of companionship, or will we fall back into the old pattern, and will I hurt you, "Sister Helene"?—No, all must be happiness and light, as at that time

1. A play by Hermann Sudermann (1857–1928), 1889.
2. Arthur Nikisch (1855–1922) was a famous Hungarian conductor.
3. 1824–1919, zoologist.

when we saw the sun coming through the trees. You will follow your path; I will stand aside and be happy if I can see you now and then, hold your hand, and know that you are "courageous" and happy. Only in my thoughts I will say b.d.f.[1] to you.

If you could know how despondent I am at times. Waiting and waiting in order to realize my plans! The boy I hoped to take in, one of my candidates for confirmation, was adopted by his aunt—an upright woman.—I wait. In Antwerp, they promised to notify me if they find somebody.—

But I am proud of my tenacity: the greater the difficulties, the stronger my determination. I see clearly that this is my road. What comforts me is the feeling that I have a good influence on my students./

Let us go ahead.

I write you in the light of the small lamp that shone on my pages when I wrote the *Kant*.[2]

## II

What I felt when I saw you was a shock—. At last I saw your sincere eyes again—.

And how handsome you looked in your suit. Nobody dares to tell you this. You looked so charming, more attractive than ever. Forgive me my clumsiness. It will be difficult to court you—let us joke a little—

Things are a little better. The affairs of the seminary are improving. I had an awful fight with Nowack, who again pokes his nose into things that are none of his business. I am dead tired from my work. When will I be able to give you the completed *Bach?*

## III

During the vacation, I frequently thought of you and spoke with you in my thoughts. I would like to write a book about the problem of being, about what I think, what I suffer, where I triumph—a book only for you. I will call it: *Wir Epigonen*.[3]

1. The meaning of this abbreviation is not known.

2. His doctoral thesis: *The Religious Philosophy of Kant* (1899).

3. "One of a succeeding and less-distinguished generation"—the first mention of this book, which Schweitzer never finished.

Perhaps I can write a part of it during Easter vacation.—

It will be yours. I feel again this inner excitement, just as I felt it while I wrote my *Kant*, this excitement of happiness when I see the whole world before me.

## IV

I come from the Knapps,[1] where you were, too, to celebrate the birthday of Else Gütschow.[2] I don't like your blouse! It is not beautiful. Please, do not wear it again when you go anywhere where I am. What a tyrant I am. Please forgive me/. When my fingers went over the keys of the piano, we were at the Rhine—You wore the lace collar with your old blouse, and we did not speak—.

I was exhausted when I got up from the piano—not one note for the others, all, all for you./.

## V

After the return from the soirée for *His Magnificence*.[3] Was I formal enough? You have to tell me.

While I ate the delicacies that were served, I was only dreaming. What a happy idea at least to seat me where I could see you. While you conversed with your neighbors, I told myself: "It is thrilling to tell myself that I know her better than anybody else who is here, and she, too, knows me so well,— with my struggles, my goals, with the idea that keeps me alive—, and that I know that she is more than the daughter of the Magnificence; she is a noble, a great woman, a unique soul—who searches and fights"—I heard you talking with me on the road to the Fischbödle[4]—I saw you sitting on the rock.—Why do you have such a pensive friend! Yes, we will, some day, talk together, and I will tell you much. I am so proud to know you and to share in your thoughts—you help me, you push me ahead!/

1. Elly's parents.

2. Student friend, the first female student at Strasbourg University.

3. Helene's father was a chancellor at the University of Strasbourg. "His Magnificence" was Schweitzer's pet name for him.

4. A small lake in the Münsteral Valley.

But I want you to marry! An honest man—do you listen! It is your fate to be a wife and mother. You know that otherwise my happiness is not complete. Frequently, when I see a man whom I respect, I ask myself: If he would marry her!!—

Well, so long!—

## 51. A. S.

[Strasbourg]
Wednesday evening
Seven o'clock

I am wrapping the package. You will find everything in it. I already returned *Aquis Submersus*[1] to you.—

Please return the first pages of the *Bach* to me: I must prepare the table of contents. Would you like to help me with the index? But only if your parents have no objections—.

I feel deprived because I do not have the books—when you were away, I spent several evenings rereading our treasures.—

Do you know how rich we both are because we know what it means to "live"!? Is it not the greatest gift we can demand from life, to know what it is: to live!

You will receive many letters.

## 52. A. S.

Dec. 21, 1904
At the seminary
In the evening

I must talk with you. This is the evening I always spend by myself, the evening of December 21st. In 1898, during my first longer stay in Paris while I worked on my *Kant*, I felt tired and nervous, weary of my work, and a little homesick. I was lying on my bed—heard a knock—at 20 rue de Sorbonne—and it was my aunt. She sat down beside me, the big sad child, and comforted me. I still see her in front of the fireplace, in the armchair—the

---

1. A novella (published in 1877) by the German writer Theodor Storm (1817–1888).

only one I had—and I sitting at a chair next to her. Twilight filled the small room, and the fire in the fireplace projected fantastic patterns on the wall. We lit the small lamp and spoke together: about Kant, about a new concept of life that this great thinker had opened to me.—What happened to the big sad boy? We put some pine branches into the fire to create a Christmas mood . . . and in this small room we became friends for life, and I felt a new worth of my existence through this deep affection, the first in my life.

Every time, on December 21st, I stay at home by myself and burn some pine branches to bring back the visions and thoughts of that evening. I relive everything; I see the room, the fire in the fireplace, . . .I go down the six flights with her—I hear the noise of the boulevard St. Michel . . . the tinkling of the bells from the carriage as she drove away . . . I hear myself give her address to the coachman, I walk back to my room alone, yet happy.—and I conclude the evening reading the few letters I still have from her.—

I want you also to participate in this evening. God is not a God of the dead but of the living—You have now taken her place; there are so many resemblances between you, resemblances that I always discover anew, my great, dear friend, my courageous companion. Come and sit in the armchair and smell the fragrance of the burning pine branches! I write you in the light of the pretty little lamp that I had at 20 rue de Sorbonne and with which I wrote the *Kant*.

This is a festive evening for me; I think that it is the beginning of a new phase in my life. The manuscript on Bach is completed! The last proofs have been mailed. I can devote myself completely to theology and philosophy again—and I want to be there for my friends again and for those who need me; I don't want to be an overworked, egotistical workhorse. With my thirty years, I begin a new life! What will I have in store for me? Will I find children whom I would like to raise? Yes, I want this; it must be realized; if not, I will not stay here. How can I possibly find fulfillment in my life? I have the desire to give, to give what I have in me and to improve through great and selfless action—and sometimes I smile when I see that people imagine that I have only one great wish: to become a "full professor"! Oh how happy I could be if I were that modest. If I could be happy in a modest way, if I did not demand so much of life, and if I did not feel so rich that I could give away a whole life! For the time being, I educate ministers and look for boys, but where will that lead? I hardly dare to read the journals of the French Missionary Society, Sister Helene, noble soul! Because every time I open one of them, I read, "We need people! Are there none?" And then I tell myself that it is easy to substitute the head of a seminary, an assistant professor, also the vicar and the organist for the concerts at Wilhelm's Kirche—but there I will be needed—. Let us wait: how this spirit of life, this mysterious Being that we call God will lead and guide me, the heretic priest.—

I am so content again. I feel as if a new leaf of my life has opened! And you, too, you are happy to have found a task! A goal and a commitment! I am so happy to give you part of my first free evening after a very long time. So I am not that character whom you met by misfortune on your road and who may have prevented you from finding the natural happiness that I wish for you—

It is strange that I have so little desire to speak with you in reality. When I visited you on Sunday and tried to smile graciously for five minutes, to utter banalities, a thought raced through my head: I saw you at the Rhine, at the Kanzerain,[1] at the Fischbödle, and I heard you speak about what we exchanged in the great moments of our friendship . . . and then I continued mechanically to talk about banalities.

It is almost eleven o'clock. The fire has died down. There is no fragrance of pine branches in the room anymore. You spent a beautiful hour of my life with me, one of those hours that stirs your feelings because you see a wide horizon of happiness before you.

I wish you could have been with me in church last Sunday. You are so very closely tied to all my thoughts, especially with the thought "about life"—with what we usually call religious thoughts, so I every so often say something for you, something only you could understand.

It would be ideal if I knew that you who share my thoughts were in the sacred room.

Good night—.

1. Hill near Günsbach.

**53. A. S.**

[Strasbourg]
Christmas Eve, December 24, 1904
(Holy Eve)

I spent the evening by myself, organized my papers, and prepared my sermon. Before I go to bed, I want to converse with you for a moment. What happiness to have time again to continue our dialogues. If you only knew how I suffered in those last months when I was nothing but a "worker" who could not be there for those whom he loves, who could not talk, not think, not even dream with them, only work. What impoverishment of spirit and soul! That is over now. It now feels like a bad dream. Now I belong to life again.

This will be the last Christmas I celebrate this way. Next year I should not be alone if my plans have come true. I am so glad I don't have to count my pennies these days but, in order to do some good, can spend as much as I consider appropriate. That is wonderful—you can imagine that feeling.

You don't know that I am thinking of a present for you! From the royalties of the *Bach*, I want to buy you a Christ medal like the one that I have always in a little box at my table. You know it well. I want you to have the same. My aunt had the same. I look at it often, this medal. It is strange to look at a man and to know that one is His slave.—

But what would my life be without this greatest among all humans?— Midnight. Where are you, where are your thoughts?

Good night.

# *1905*

## 54. A. S.

The bells ring midnight. I conclude the last year with thoughts of you and begin this year thinking of you. You are the most precious thing I have in this world. There are people who are devoted to me and to whom I am devoted because they are my relatives or because I got to know them well and over a long period of time, longer than we have known each other. With these, I share some of my daily life, and we exchange some thoughts.—But you are the person I "revere" the most; you have the greatest power over me. Do you think that that is sentimental? You have something genuine, great, and pure that draws me to you. This is something that surpasses love and is not tied to any emotion. When I am facing struggles and temptations, when I am in danger of losing the foundation that is the basis of my noblest thoughts, you immediately stand before me in my mind, whether they are great or little things. With everything I do wrong, I have the feeling that I betray you, to belie the opinion that you have of me. That helps me to pursue my path.

I thank you in this last and first hour of the year for what you are for me. You are somewhat like a little guardian angel for me here on earth. I cannot say that often, but I have to tell you once; I have to.

I wish you nothing for the coming year because our wishes are futile, and if I could shape your life through my wishes, I would not know how to do it. Accept things as they come to you, but (that is my only wish) be strong, noble, and good in everything you encounter. "Strong and noble," as my aunt used to say. I, for my part, will try to do the same.

We ask too much from life, too much inner happiness, which we hide

Albert Schweitzer, 1905. *Courtesy of Rhena Schweitzer Miller.*

defiantly, so we have the right to ask fate to fulfill our wishes. The only prayer I directed to God, the great Spirit, at the first ring of the bell after midnight was the plea to keep me pure and of noble spirit for what I must achieve on this earth. Aside from that, whatever has to come may come. I kiss your hand for a long time.

55. A. S.

[Strasbourg]
Thursday evening,
February 2, 1905, midnight

I come from a party—I must speak with you. If I did not restrain myself with all my willpower, I would sit here all night with the sheet of paper before me and converse with you. How can I convey my joy? It was a gray, dark day, but in the evening when I changed my clothes, I had a premonition that something good would happen. When I saw the seating order in the check room, I knew before I read it that I would lead you to the table. And when I felt your arm in mine, I felt happy. How one learns to be satisfied with little. But it is good this way.

I could not speak with you—only very little—but I spoke with you in my thoughts and looked at you from a distance. Since we met on the street, I wish nothing but that you accept the position with Schwander.[1] Please do it, I beseech you; I can see that you will be very happy!! Forget your education, your friends; work. You are not serious when you speak about egoism because I know better than anybody in this world that egoism has departed from you, that you don't have it anymore. Oh, how well I know that, and I *admire* you for that. Imagine, I sometimes think that one day we will meet facing a great task, and our paths will unite; I am sure of that!

During the rehearsal of the Beethoven Mass (while I looked at you from a distance), these thoughts came back to me. Let us each follow our path; be great, noble woman.—I am so happy tonight. I even love your gray hair that gives your face a peculiar serenity. Did I play my role well with the gentleman with whom we are "vaguely" acquainted? Was I indifferent enough in the presence of those people? In spite of the great ideas I have for your future, I always try to look among the unmarried gentlemen for the one whom I would like to see as your husband.

Mrs. von Dobschütz![2] That would be the right thing. While my colleague tried to engage you in a conversation as only a gentleman of the

1. In April 1905, the mayor of Strasbourg offered Helene Bresslau a position at the city's Office of Social Services, where she worked with homeless children.
2. Ernst von Dobschütz (1870–1934) was professor of New Testament theology at the University of Strasbourg.

world approaches a lady, I kept saying to myself: "Mrs. von Dobschütz." I
forbid you to accept this one. He is another edition of your friend Kuck, and
he would never understand you. I tell you all this as children would tell
each other. I have a supply of happiness until Saturday or Sunday, and I will
work hard and talk with you on little sheets of paper. You will receive them
on Sunday.

I stole your place card, of course. Yours and mine are together in an
envelope.

Good night. I will smile while I go to sleep.

## 56. A. S.

Saturday evening,
February 26 [25], 1905
(At the seminary)

At last! I long to speak with you. I have so much to tell you, and sad
things. If you were with me, you would find it difficult to comfort me.
Everything is lost! I searched in vain. Either the children I try to find do not
exist, or people don't want to let me have them and take my plans as fantasies. I had to swallow a lot. Some people, however, were quite touching,
for example Pastor Belin from the Neuhof Institute. I now have approached the people at Metz. If that should not work out, I have to wait for
some new chance, while I have lost another illusion. Have I told you that I
changed my plan? I would like to take in young men who leave school, so
they may learn something solid, or to see that they can become teachers.
You see, I have so much love to give, I will be so happy. When I meet a
homeless person—and they come around every day—and when I hear that
he grew up as an orphan, I tell myself that he would not be in this condition
if I had met him.

I am in the grip of a terrible despondency. But I never tell myself that
my ideas are fantasies. I am too logical, too rational to indulge in fantasies.
What I *want* cannot be fantasy. I am too realistic. But I want to free myself
from this bourgeois life that would kill everything in me; I want to *live*, I
want to do something as a disciple of Jesus. That is the only thing in which
I believe—and in your friendship. Because I believe in it! But people don't
allow us to step outside the ordinary, to detach the conventional ties. Yes, I
would perish in those. I must free myself.

If you only knew how sad I am. I was sure I would find my way. Now I am at a loss, forced into the useless existence of a "young man" who desires a "good opportunity to marry." This is how people see my situation. Look, I do good deeds. I gave all my money to the poor. On New Year's, I had nothing in my pockets. But what I want to give, my love, my life, my time—that I am not permitted to give. And that is for me a true need, more than my life. See, Lene, I don't deceive myself. This thought not just to contribute through scholarship, but through my life, came to me in an unexpected way. Like a small cloud from the distance, on the horizon—so it seemed to me. While I wrote my book on Kant, I felt the cloud coming closer: its shadow enveloped me. In my *Kant,* I have said more than I realized at the time: I destroyed everything that is essential in religion; I left the *categorical imperative* as the only reality. And now the cloud has become larger. I see nothing of what I once saw. Scholarship has become pale—I feel only one thing: I must act. Everything else feels like a comedy. I feel like I am play-acting; as long as I have not accepted this reality, my whole life is a comedy. Yes, if I could realize my plan, and at the same time educate future ministers at the seminary . . . I am happy at the seminary because I can do good, and Nowack genuinely respects me, but the rest? For the others, I am a young man who lives a pleasant life in a very pleasant home and earns 3,000 Marks, and it is exactly that that makes me so defenseless in their eyes. Always waiting. I have had enough of it. Will I have the energy to write the third part of my book on the Last Supper? I will write it without enthusiasm! But I will write it because the book will have its value. I already have everything in my head. I will need one year or, at most, a year and a half. I will force myself to write it. You will be satisfied with me. But my heart is not in it, as it was in my sketch *The Life of Jesus.* I expect something different, something that concerns my own life! I have given up the ambition to become a great scholar, I want to be more—*simply a human.* That will become the theme of your book, *Wir Epigonen.* We are not true humans, but beings who live by a civilization inherited from the past that keeps us hostage, that confines us. No freedom of movement, nothing. Our humanness, indeed everything in us, is killed by our calculations for our future, by our social position and rank. You see, I am not happy—yet I am happy. I suffer, but that is part of life. *I live;* I don't care about my existence, and that is the beginning of wisdom, i.e., to search for a value for this existence that the others don't know at all and that they don't accept. Not a professorship, a comfortable life—but something different. I have found it; I believe that I possess this value: *to serve Jesus.* I am less at peace than if my only goal were to attain a professorship and a good wife, but *I live.* And that gives me the tremendous feeling of happiness, as if one could see a ray of light in a deep hole, as if one could hear music. One feels uprooted because one asks, "What lies ahead, what decisions should I make?"—but *more alive*, happier than those who are anchored in life. To drift with released anchor.

I know one thing: If I cannot realize my plan to educate, to take care of young boys, I cannot remain here: I would despair. I would envy all those who serve Jesus, even the lowliest woman at the Salvation Army. I would conclude that I have to search for another kind of realization and would offer my services to the French mission in the Congo or at the Zambezi River because people are needed there.[1] If I listened to myself, I would leave here tomorrow instead of wasting away as I play this comedy. But first I have to write the history of the Last Supper and then, as my last book, our book, your book, *Wir Epigonen.* That will take three years, in which I will be tied to the seminary. Three years of waiting, of testing, of maturing. After that, nothing can restrain me. All these thoughts had already taken shape and occupied my thinking when we listened to Gerold's mission sermon together. I try to push them away, yet they always reappear. When I become totally absorbed in my study of the Last Supper, they are suppressed temporarily. But look, all these thoughts that entered into my life, which gradually came closer and closer from some distance and at last finally conquered me. It is my horrible logic that attracts these thoughts, that delivers me to them. This logic does not allow me any escape and forces me to search for what may fulfill my life!

I am at this point. It is difficult to write you this instead of telling it as "in the beginning" on the bank of the Rhine surrounded by flowers and sun. But look, difficult issues begin with an idyll, then the idyllic parable perishes, and what remains is the burden. This burden, however, unites those who know each other so well. But the idyll was beautiful—wasn't it!—

---

1. Schweitzer's first introduction to the idea of working in the Congo was through a newsletter published by the Paris Missionary Society. An article published in the fall of 1904, "The Needs of the Congo Mission" by Albert Boegner, provided the spark for Schweitzer's life work. See Albert Schweitzer, *Out of My Life and Thought* (Baltimore and London: Johns Hopkins Univ. Press, 1998), 85–86. Also see p. 115.

I would never want to lose a second of it. All is well, whatever will come to us.

I am so happy that you found a great task![1] It is like that: The last will be the first, and the first will be the last. Earlier I was closer to the goal than you, and now you are active, while I am simply a privatdozent—a human who lectures, who does not act. I am so happy for you; now I no longer blame myself for having uprooted you. Now you will find your way. And you will be happy. And if home and family await you, you will be very happy, and if you have to go your way alone, your life nevertheless will be fulfilled.

Do you remember that I have a promise from you, from the bank of the Rhine?: "If you need somebody some day, promise that you will call me." I promised you—and I often think of that. If I ever need you, I will call you, you can be sure. I guard your promise as something precious, like a jewel to pawn.

## 57. H. B.

[Strasbourg]
March 1905

I am returning your letters; I have not had time to peruse the sermons, to separate the old from the new; i.e., those I can keep from those you only "lent" me! I will send or give them to you later. You know that my mother has been very ill. She is better now, but I hardly ever got out this week. I had to postpone my work with the hospital for infants, so now I will have to be there until the end of the month and cannot go to Interlaken,[2] when Schwander gives me the job. I have not heard from him since our last conversation. When he told me: "I promise that you can begin work on April 1"—that is all I know—now we have to wait.

I have much to tell you, very much, too much to write.

Do you think about how much has happened, how much has changed and evolved in the three years since that March 22, 1902—and you become impatient—because you do not see clearly where you will be at the end of the next three? But I am glad that everything within you moves and

1. Helene's nursing program, begun in 1904.
2. In Switzerland.

rebels; nothing is as deadly as rest and stagnation—what do you know today about all the possibilities that you still carry inside you?

And your plan, did you not change it once already? How about dropping it once more, to take it up again in a way you haven't yet thought of? You may find the original seed somewhere else, purer and more mature, perhaps? Oh, how well I know this impatience when unused forces long for action. But where, my friend, is your usual logic? "Everything that happens is good and is as it is intended to be." Does that apply to one cause only and not to another? Be patient and of good courage, my friend; the sun will rise again and let the world radiate in new splendor, so different from what you imagine or dream today.

Are you angry with me for making a little fun of your logic? I had to think of the story about the candle that has always seemed to me a symbol of our friendship. Do you remember?

But let me be serious again. If we had had a chance to speak last Sunday, I would have told you about a conversation at the end of which I was in Paradise. And you had a part in it! I was so happy. To imagine that we can live in Paradise while we are strolling down here, below. Sunday morning during my little stroll, I sang all the time; I don't remember what; the words came without my thinking, and I recall only the little refrain:

> Car j'ai bien appris par toi
> A vivre seule et tenir foi.[1]

And then I felt your glance; you were sad and suffered, and I wanted to be twice as cheerful to make you laugh. But I cannot do that at the Knapps'. In that circle, I suffocate from the attention that is given to the merest trifles and to the manner, the thought that is used to deal with trivia in order to cultivate the art of conversation. I could laugh about it if it did not make me so sad. Individually, I love all these people, but I feel they slip away from me, and it makes me suffer. I seem to "remove" myself in principle from people— I have exchanged them for man*kind*—yet I love my friends, and Elly Knapp was so close to me. I, too, have love to give—may we give it to what we have

---

1. "I learned from you so well, / to be alone and to trust."

exchanged, and let us beware of the mistake that we can assume a soul totally for ourselves and expect something in return for what we give!—

While I took care of my mother, I also thought of you all the time—although I had no time to write, I had more time to reflect. And something
saddened me! I have always been very proud that my friend, that he never
asked anything of me—although he knew that I would do anything gladly
and with joy. But this time—although he understood that I could not
write—he demands an answer from me!—You see, my friend, there is much
that I would like to tell you, exactly about what you suffer right now, but that
cannot be put into written words. Any moment my mother may call, the
household needs me; I could never finish such a letter. And to begin when
one realizes that one cannot express oneself completely makes no sense.

It got late; you should have the letters tomorrow morning, to wish you
a good trip and very fine weather. Tonight is St. Wilhelm's choir. I can do
only one thing: be an example and show that there are ways to rise from the
deepest abyss of desperation and emerge at the top again. Will that give you
some consolation and courage?

I enclose with my letters my answers to your letters for my departure a
year and a half ago. I could not send them to you at the time because I did not
want to let you know how much I suffered. Today this will not worry you because you saw me all winter, so cheerful and content, even happy, recovered
because of my serious work. I say "recovered" intentionally because there
may be sections that might hurt you if they had come from a thoughtful
writer, so don't forget to read them knowing that they were written by someone whose soul was, at that time, really ill. You will understand—and please
return them at the first opportunity. If they can help a little, they have not
been written in vain, and the experience has not been lost; it was good for
me to see how one can get into something but also come out of it again.

I close now. I wish you all the very best for your vacation and much,
much rest.

How I would like to come to church tomorrow!

Why did you not give me any criticism on the article in the
*Protestantenblatt*? [1]

---

1. A Protestant newsletter.

Helene Bresslau, ca. 1905. *Courtesy of Rhena Schweitzer Miller.*

## 58. H. B.

[Strasbourg]
May 5/6, 1905

My friend, my great, beloved friend, I must thank you—as three years ago. Thank you that you are so much for me and that I can be so much for you! This is all so wonderful, so much more beautiful than we could have hoped or even dared to believe. I thank you for your faith with which you guided me, all the good forces you released in me and sustained, how you as-sisted me in my struggles, even when I fought against you and against my-self. I am grateful that you trusted me, that you held on faithfully to our friendship, even when you felt it to be your duty to warn me, to doubt my-self, my strength, and the strength of our friendship. I thank you for all the warm and good feelings that you have for me and cherish, and that I always could feel although you never spoke about them. You made me feel calm, at peace and protected, and assured me of the continuation of this trust that fills me with affirmation of life and with confidence.

I had to tell you all of this to thank you from the depth of my heart as forcefully as I can! The blissful awareness of all that you are for me, the priv-ilege of being the same for you—my gratitude for this, too, my friend! I feel such abundance of strength and joy that I ask myself with amusement how one can acknowledge this without bringing about "the envy of the gods." Is it because we have paid our tribute in advance, through our struggles and suffering? Now we do not have to fear anybody, not the gods, not humans, not ourselves; you agree, my great friend? We have the right to everything we have, even the secrecy that weighed so heavily and frequently on my mind, because those close to me, those to whom I owed the truth and in whom I wanted to confide, did not comprehend the faith I put in them; per-haps they were not able to comprehend it—so they misused my confidence to pull me away from my own, strongest convictions. That I allowed them to do this, that I granted them that much influence over me, has brought both of us much sorrow, and this will always remain my great guilt toward you.

I tell you this today, so you know that I am aware of it. At the same time, I ask you to bury this guilt, together with me, so it will not cast any shadow on our future happiness. We want to take only the good memories from the past into our bright presence and future, from the serious and the sad only the knowledge that our friendship passed through fire, and that it has been refined to a purity and strength that goes beyond our comprehension and that enables us to put all our efforts into our work—wherever we are or will be. May God grant that this be so, the God in whom we believe and whom we ask for His blessing!—

**59. A. S.**

> [Strasbourg]
> Thursday evening
> May 11, 1905

Would you like a little word? It is three o'clock in the morning. I worked all night at the open window, with the view on my tree that is in full bloom. And now I force myself to go to bed. What a joy to stay awake during the night, as I have begun again! My thoughts follow their path, climb up to the heights, rest in the shade of the rocks, look up to the clouds passing in the blue sky, sing, cry, laugh, and rejoice! I pursue them breathless: as the hunter in pursuit of the chamois.—What nights.—

Do you remember what I told you about the blooming cherry trees on the road to Günsbach?—

Your letter is so great and so noble. Why have I kept our friendship alive against all resistance? I had your word that you wanted to be my friend. And I believed in it and knew that you would find your way. But I did not know what I asked of you—the struggles I caused you when I accepted your friendship. I did not realize that life is more difficult for a young woman who is not permitted to keep her thoughts to herself, but who is expected to share them with those close to her.—.—and everything that followed as a consequence, until you understood that these are things that the others cannot understand, will never understand. But I accepted everything because I had your word.—Please, never ask me to forgive you for the grief you caused me. We are so close that neither of us has to forgive the other anything. Everything happened as it had to; what is great and everlasting had to be given birth, born out of much pain and sorrow!

## 60. A. S.

[Strasbourg]
Saturday evening
May 20, 1905, 11:00 P.M.

You did not understand what was meant by "insatiable." Is there any-thing you do not understand? You understand everything. "Insatiable." I wrote that down with a smile because I am proud and happy to surrender all my thoughts to you. "Insatiable" means that I have to struggle with myself not to spend all night writing to you.

Tonight—one hour until it rings midnight. This afternoon I had a dis-cussion with Nowack. He told me that I place too much importance on the mentoring of students and that the faculty does not look upon this with favor. I should not tutor them for their exams but teach them Greek and Hebrew. I listened with a smile. The whole plan of studies I had prepared collapsed in a few seconds: again the jealously of faculty members who do not allow me to be a simple teacher. They force me to do my duty, nothing but my duty—.

I listened to him without bitterness, and I answered in the same man-ner. I will fight, but like one who does not wish to strain himself. It is to no avail: The faculty is afraid that I influence the students. And I saw myself in a dream as the educator of the Alsatian ministry! I am giving up this dream bit by bit. While N. talked, I felt like a ship on dry dock, shaking slightly when a bolt is pulled out of the keel and it knows that others will be pulled out—then I will not fall over, but sail freely on the ocean. And I smiled,—he said to himself: "How friendly he is, this rebel, who used to enrage me; now he yields."

I sometimes feel that events run helter-skelter. But I am inwardly calm. I cannot remember a time when I felt so calm.

It was touching: a few weeks ago Reverend Knittel[1] told me that I will stay for another year. "You will receive a unanimous vote to become my suc-cessor, and after a few years you will be the canon of St. Thomas and a member of the church commission."—I am suffocating.

---

1. Pastor Michel Knittel held the office of inspector of spiritual matters in Strasbourg.

When I walked home through Ruprechtsauer Allee, I asked myself again and again: "Is it true that we both know of a happiness that others cannot conceive and that lifts us above anything that might happen?" What if I deceived myself, if all this happiness that is greater than the happiness for which we search before we understand that life may fool us and may withhold true happiness—if this all-encompassing happiness should be only a self-delusion, surpassing our own power? If one day we would stand before broken pieces of hope, and you tell me, whether you are here or far away—: "So this is the path on which you have led me!" But we will not allow what we have to be destroyed; we will defend it to the last breath, and only together; as our souls leave this life, we leave it because our happiness is the soul, our soul.

The tree seems to listen; its branches move. My tree—when I returned to the seminary, I told it that I would never leave it, and now!—Now I don't understand how I could believe that I was made to spend my whole life as director of the seminary. Oh—if I had found some children! But the others would have thwarted this plan, too. It was the wisdom of destiny that first showed me the plan that would have kept me in my surroundings, and only after that, when I was strong enough to climb the steep path, it showed me the other road that loses itself in the distance. Thanks be to you, destiny. The others will call you God, providence, accident. I call you "destiny." That is the most beautiful name: You unveil what you had determined in advance. Our whole life is "predestined."

*Saturday night, May 20, 1905*

These days are like months of my life. Every day is one month. I thoroughly enjoy and take full advantage of them! That's how it is.

The other day, during a meal at the seminary, we discussed "happiness." "We must know how to catch the moments of happiness, recognize them when they are here, not when they are gone; one must draw them to ourselves . . . hold on to them . . . raise them above everything to fully enjoy them . . . wrest them from life." The students looked at me baffled; they all started to spoon their soup. That was not theology—yet, it was.

I want you to be a little proud of me—just a little. Others give their women jewelry, pearls, diamonds; I give you only my thoughts, my thoughts! Not secondhand thoughts, not borrowed from somebody else,—

my thoughts borne out of my own mind. My thoughts, which, laughing or crying, I have brought forth with an arrogant pride of having created thoughts, of being a thinker. No, fundamentally I am not modest because to create thoughts that live is given only to few people, and if they have some, they offer them to the world; let them be admired, and everybody refers to them. Mine belong to me and to those with whom I want to share them, and the most beautiful belong only to you and me. These are my precious stones. You cannot adorn yourself with them. But you have something that only few people in this world can give you.

Romain Rolland, the critic from Paris, is with me. We spoke together, and our thoughts met. We both love solitude, love to go our way without any noise, without the desire to be recognized. You should see us together: he a sick man;[1] I strong and robust. We knew each other without exchanging many words.—

*Midnight.*

I force myself to stop. Otherwise, I would spend the whole night in dialogue with you. (Tell me: which of the two of us is insatiable?)

But tomorrow I have to preach. While I wrote the sermon, I was floating in the blue sky.

Good night.

Last Sunday I attended a lecture about the French mission. I gave 10 Marks; 5 for you, 5 for me.

## 61. H. B.

[Strasbourg]
Monday, May 22, 1905

Thank you!

You are right, I understood, but one cannot really talk if one has only two minutes in the streetcar and one can already see the Schillerstrasse.[2] When I left, I told myself: now he must think: "There she still is, the little girl whom I once thought had been drowned in the Rhine." But I do know

1. 1866–1944; heart ailment.
2. A stop near Helene's home.

that you were only teasing,—there are, however, times when I don't like to be teased.

There is something else in that letter that frightened me, and on this point our thoughts also meet—or rather our feelings. It is the abundance of happiness to which you give yourself and that then causes bad dreams, like that at the Ruprechtsauer Allee, with ghosts and self-delusions, etc.

Don't you think that it is dangerous, this theory of possession, of pulling things toward you, of indulgence, to give this to young people of whom many will not be able to comprehend our concept of happiness, who certainly don't know it? Might they not misunderstand you?! If they believed that one can search for it and force it?! How should they know that we have found it as we gave up what is usually called by that name, to renounce, to pass it on our way, because we had to pursue it without any thought of a happy reward? Look, I think this is something so tender, so fine, that one may not put it into many words, or it might get hurt. Only because our happiness gives us such divine strength, we sometimes confuse it and think that it were the strength in itself. It is, however, a nothing; it cannot be grasped—like a ray of sun, and it awakens the fullness of life. When I ask you from time to time: Are you still happy? And when I then see this ray of sun shining in your eyes—that tells me everything.—If you were to fill many volumes with your writing, you could not tell me anything more beautiful than the two things you once told me: Your friendship is my life—and I feel that all my happiness comes from you. That was on that Good Friday of the St. John's Passion when a little sheet contained the sentence, "I don't think of you often"—I was so glad—because that is how it should be; what we are for each other and what we give to each other must transform itself into energy that expresses itself in action, and the person must retreat behind it.—But let us not speak about that anymore, you agree?

There is so much of importance we should discuss—tell me, did the young boy not come? I always hope for a word about it—and if he did not come, what next?

And Nowack, who wants to hold you in close reins, will he be able to harness you? One cannot really hold it against him: So much fine energy, which under thoughtful guidance could produce fine results.

And Knittel, when I met you, I thought that you had no other goal but to become a minister—how times have changed—and people, too. But you see how today one door seems to open, tomorrow another one may show up, and at some point the right one will be there. You have what you need (including the ability to wait!): Courage and Confidence. But I thought that you looked pale; I beg you: Allow yourself more sleep! At least seven hours. Can you do that? Will you do that? Do you travel today? Was Strauss with you yesterday?

## 62. A. S.

[Strasbourg]
Night before Ascension Day
June 1/2, 1905

It is five o'clock in the morning. The lamp was extinguished long ago. I concluded the summary of David Friedrich Strauss's *Life of Jesus* with the rising sun. The night of work was good. Do not scold me: I felt so happy when I sat down at my table that the thoughts flowed on their own. I did the work of at least two days.

Before I sat down to work, I let my fingers glide over the piano keys. I heard a mysterious melody, without rhythm, without anything, great and beautiful, rising above a deep sadness, radiating in the light of a great happiness: I did not know whether I heard it in a dream or whether I played it. It was the words "perfectly contented" that I heard again and again, in the happiness of which you spoke about this afternoon. Can it be true that we are "perfectly contented"? Yes, it is truly so. Very simply: Because I have had your promise since that first open discussion when you suffered, yet you did understand me: Your promise (or mine, because I suggested it to you)—, to call you where and when I need you. I think that one day I may have to fulfill a major task for which I will need you—and then I will just simply ask you to work with me—and that, perhaps, providence will lead us toward working for the same cause.—

But this is on the far horizon.—One should, under no circumstances, think about it before one has a close look at the work—

And I will try to visualize myself working there[1] by myself, only carried

---

1. As a missionary in the Congo.

by your thoughts, which penetrate into mine and give it life. Your thoughts, that I will feel coming from a great distance, alive and noble, and that make me so happy now.

Contented—without wishes—

Yours

A.

**63. H. B.**

[Strasbourg]
Sunday evening
June 25, 1905

My friend, how I would like to talk with you if you were here—but you are there!

Your sermon this morning, so from the heart; they are, of course, always that way, but I could *feel* how it came from your innermost heart. . . .

Strange how I felt, not like a devout worship, but deep, deep reverence—

I cannot judge how others are affected because I always hear more, because I feel differently from the way others hear and respond to you.

*Monday morning*

That was all for yesterday. I wanted you to know how strong and lasting the impact of your sermon was on me. I thought that you would enjoy hearing it and that it would encourage you, although you do not really need that assurance because you have the strength and courage to pursue your aim.

It made me so happy to feel your strength, that you do not feel sorry for me, that it does not affect you when I am weak and downcast! I thank you for a good week! You see, people torture me, and I cannot live alone as you do. I cannot shake them off without hurting their feelings, and I am not as robust as Marianne.[1] I cannot ignore some of the trivia of daily life—the struggle for what I consider important is enough; yet minor issues seem to absorb us. What strangers think, I can ignore; a wasted hour or at most a

---

1. Sister of her friend Elly Knapp.

lost afternoon is bearable,—but my mother's quiet grief is hard to bear; she feels that there is more, something secretive that she cannot grasp and about which I cannot tell her more. I would like to help her to understand, to sooth her worries, but she only shows disbelief, hostility, and lack of understanding.

Forgive me for writing all this—I would not have done so if I were still afraid that this would upset you. This was the fear I had the other day when I said, "Leave me lying by the roadside,"—because I was afraid to see the fear and worry in your face that my complaints had caused. Now I can speak freely, so some of your strength flows over to me and sustains me. This was indeed strength, your joyful: "I have no pity for you, none!"—strength, and not only self-discipline or concealment of real worries—that made me happy, that gave me courage to speak freely.—I could not continue to hide anything from you and to pretend. I need your strength, which returns to me when I can tell you everything, and I feel how you are not touched by it, that you can pass over it—you must go ahead.

A conversation with my mother last evening was painful, and because it did not lead to any solution, it caused this outpouring—but now it is over. It also kept me from continuing to write last night. I would have sent you two pages of my diary from Genoa and Rapallo of November '99,[1] which I wanted to copy for you. I used to refer to those six months in Italy as the happiest time in my life, one that would always remain a most precious memory. It was the only time when, as an adult, as a thinking human being, conscious of her good fortune, innocent and without any inhibitions, I lived in a fairyland: I was happy. I am grateful to my fate that it gave me this time to dream, to gain insights, just as I am grateful that it made me wake up again to show me the dauntingly serious and the sublimely beautiful, the only true life. When I compare the two, I am afraid that I may not have the strength to withstand the second after my knowledge has made the first impossible and undesirable for me. But I must be strong; please listen, *you* must not have any fears or pity for me. To be strong or not to live at all, there is nothing else for me. I thank you that you believe in my strength.

When I felt resigned, the medal lay in front of me—I am ungrateful that I complain at all—

1. Schweitzer was planning a trip to northern Italy, where Helene had been with her parents in 1899.

When I consider that there have been in my life six whole months and then many moments, even hours, in which I realized that I was perfectly contented—

And that there is one human who—that you exist for me—

## 64. A. S.

Saturday evening,
July 1, 1905, around 11:00 P.M.
Günsbach

No, I don't want you ever to be disappointed because of me, never, never! Now I feel comfortable to talk with you, not in my room, but in my brother's, that is more elegant than mine. The son of Eugen Münch[1] is in mine. I gave it to him for six weeks; he is with us to gain some strength.

Do you realize that I talk with you? My work goes well, but it must leave me enough free time to share my thoughts with those who have the right to know—and the one who does have all rights—is this not more than a "declaration of love," which I never stated formally? And I will never do it. Because I do not want the shadow of external customs on our friendship. We found each other, and nothing on this earth could be more beautiful than that. To do, each in his sphere or together if destiny wills it, to comprehend life and, together, walk the high peaks, to be indebted to each other, and to give to each other. We are rich through each other! I felt that on Monday morning when I woke up and read your letter. These I saw as streams of light that flow over my whole life. I have been able to give you something that lifted the burden from your thoughts that had hurt you, that had poisoned your life and your heart. I knew that you would suffer—how much I only realized on the day I read you my sermon for Maundy Thursday. You see, I sometimes have the feeling that the words I say in the name of Jesus Christ do cause some good because, tender as they are, they are filled with struggle and peace, as is my own life. I believe that every so often, one has to look through the blue sky. Yet nobody but you can tell me that because hearing it from others would make me vain; if you let me know it, I feel humble and happy. I can't express it in any other way.

1. Schweitzer's organ teacher.

Then again I tell myself that I am wrong when I regret that you cannot participate more strongly in my life and my feelings, that you cannot be with me, at my side to hear the fleeting melodies I hear, the melodies that rise from my soul when I sit down at the piano. You share my greatest feelings, and all the best that I have inside me I have shared with you.

I think of you as somebody, as the only person who has the right to judge me. The power of your thinking envelopes me, protects me, and sustains me; I feel it all—, sometimes I have acted differently than I would have in order not to hurt your thoughts, which are with me constantly.

I tell you this; you have the right to be proud, and you will be so in the right way. I feel good not to have to fight with you. I surrender completely.

You see, the freedom we have with each other, the respect in which nobody wants to dominate the other—that is most beautiful. Each is a part of the life of the other, and yet we are free; each becomes a personality through the contact with the other.

This is so strange. Who can understand it? We do not cause each other unhappiness anymore! No, for sure. This I sometimes sing to unusual melodies. For example, this morning, when I got up from my desk to see the sunrise through the leaves of the big tree. When I looked at the portrait of my aunt on my table, who has watched over my work for many years, I asked her, the first (jealous!) friend, whether she was jealous of you? Already at her grave in Paris, I told her of you. I know that she is not jealous.—

Us, and our relationship, I understand correctly only when I think of Him, our Lord. It is He who brought us together, not in any wrong or mystical way, but as two laborers whom He met in the morning on the street and whom He sent into his vineyards. We are on that road. When the day gets long and hot. . . ? But we must work; the sun rises. So we follow our road—and when evening comes, what will He tell us? We will not ask Him for anything, no future salvation, nothing but His spirit and some of His strength.

## 65. A. S.

My faithful comrade,

My hand shakes a little: I just put the letter in the mailbox in which I tell the director of the Paris mission that I am ready and willing to leave in spring 1907.[1] This is a peculiar day. I participated in an organ concert, and while I played, I asked myself: "Will you ever be able to give this up?" It seemed to me as if I had never before played as well—and yet I could give it up at any time. Afterward a charming five-year-old girl came to me and put a flower in my buttonhole, and I gave her a kiss. When I came home, I played a little for the sister of Mrs. Curtius (she herself is on a trip). I improvised, and suddenly my melody took hold of me—I had only one thought, always the same, to leave, to go home to my room, and to write the letter that has been on my mind for such a long time. I sat on the folding chair that my aunt had given me; the shadows of the tree moved on the floor and came to me. There was a lovely mood with the light only coming from the outside.—I asked those last questions—always, yes. I reached for the lamp on the stove and in the darkness knocked down a beautiful vase that my housekeeper had put there by mistake. It broke into a thousand pieces. I smiled. What is the meaning of this? We must be able to part with things we cherish. That was the beginning.

The letter has been written: clear, precise, without any sentiments, almost like a business letter. I carried it to the mailbox; when I returned, I stood still for a moment and looked at the two towers of the Thomas Church that stood above the courtyard enveloped in a soft light.

I am happy. It is done. But I am afraid, not that I might regret anything. No. How can I live while I feel the obligation to go there? I go! But what will be my fate? How will my death be? What about my suffering? I go there to be with Jesus; He may do with me what He will. I will find Him, that I know. And to pray: "Thy Kingdom come!" I want to find out what these words mean, that He said: "Who loses his life for me and for my word, he will keep it."

---

1. In this letter to the Paris mission, Schweitzer offers his services as a missionary.

If He only feels that I am worthy to serve Him.—

And now, at this moment, nobody in the world except you has the right to know my thoughts. The others, including my mother, have had their share of my thoughts; the last one is for you. Do not say anymore: "And what shall those who remain here do without you; don't you think about them?" And how I am thinking of them! My faithful, selfless friend—more than my friend—I will cause you pain, I cannot show you that I feel how much you will suffer because I go, how lonely you will be. Good night.—

Will we have to separate in order to come together again?

I will tell the tree now that the decision has been made—. Oh, Lene, why do you have to love me so deeply while it will bring you only sorrow—but I thank you that you love me so much, a thousand, thousand times—I do not wish it to be otherwise. I feel as if a clock had stopped, and I would wind it up again.

When do we see each other?

With all my heart,
Your[1]


**66. A. S.**

[Strasbourg]
Monday evening
July 10, 1905


My head aches. I had a restless night, and this morning I feel as if my soul does not live in my body. It follows my letter, wants to bring it back, wants to be free again to decide, to make the decision.

But this restlessness had to come. Just as objects gain their shape when we see and don't just imagine them, when they become reality, which our will cannot destroy anymore—and does not really want to.

Therefore, let us walk our road and follow our Master. In all this restlessness, I do feel that I walk on the highest peaks of life, that I do not want to descend into the valley and limit my efforts to become a professor of theology, a full professor and canon of St. Thomas! Oh no!

---

1. Not readable in the original.

But I tremble when I imagine that the director of the mission has read my letter and, in his thoughts, assigns me to a distant mission station.

I always knew that a new life would begin when I became thirty years old.—

In spite of all the restlessness, I draft notes for one of the most difficult lectures of my class. My mind functions independently, almost like the hands of the knitting woman who pursues her work while her thoughts are somewhere else.

My father had supper with me, but it was difficult to have a conversation with him. /

Good night

## 67. A. S.

[Strasbourg]
Thursday morning, July 20, 1905
During the confirmation class

I am desolate; it is almost an attack of despair. I wait in vain for an answer from Paris! The director sent me a most cordial card; he has received my letter and will answer as soon as he returns from a trip; every morning I wake up and wait for the mail—nothing; at eleven o'clock again—nothing. Today on my way to the confirmation class, I dragged myself along the Staden; the eleven o'clock mailman shook his head again. It is so painful to learn this: to wait. I felt like breaking my cane on the railing of the bridge and throwing it into the water—and now I rehearse Bible verses with the children; everything calms down. Divine peace seems to radiate around me. The children learn: "Are you not more than the others, ye of little faith?"

These words were soothing. They must learn the next verse, and I write it down for them, smiling. How beautiful these words are—yes, everything will be all right. I tell myself that there must be a reason when we are forced to wait; one has to ask oneself again whether one will be able and ready to undertake what one has set out to do. Is our heart truly prepared? Is it pure and spiritually ready to go ahead with the inner fortitude we need—Why are these words of Jesus so beautiful? Yesterday they learned in the confirmation class (Matthew 18:19): "Truly I tell you, if two of you become one on earth as they ask for something, it will be done for them by my Father in

Heaven."—After that I was at peace about our common fate because we are one exactly like that.—The children learned the next verse. I must leave you now—to *learn* the words of Christ! What a lesson—and that is life. I feel that I wander through the countryside with white clouds and blue sky above me—

Albert

So! Let's close the books and see who knows the verses by heart!—

## 68. A. S.

Grimmialp,
Monday morning
August 21, 1905

My dear friend,

I can give you only good news. Your new friend "per Prokura"[1] is better, indeed much better. When I arrived, she was still languishing; the previous day she had been up for the first time. Since then she feels better every day. I am still a bit of a nurse: every day we take short walks, and I have to hold on to her arm. But I am confident as far as her future is concerned.

For this reason, I am quietly content. No worries about my two friends. I have not felt that way for a long time.

We fixed a pleasant study, the same I have had for the last four years. I look at the entrance to the valley that is closed by a huge rock. On the other side is the world, and I tremble when I think that each passing day brings me closer to the time when I have to travel around this rock and return to the world. I enjoy every moment, every second. The distant sound of the brook rocks me, and my thoughts are like children who wake up smiling.

My free time, when I am not occupied as a nurse, I spend on my studies. If I did not restrain myself, I would work all day, my head feels so well. Indeed, you will be busy. The first two chapters[2] are completely revised. I mailed them to a young minister, a friend of mine, yesterday, so he can check the spelling and punctuation. They will come back soon, and then I

1. Adele Herrenschmidt, Schweitzer's friend from Paris, with whom he spent many summers (1901–9) in Switzerland.

2. Chapters of *The Quest of the Historical Jesus*.

will send them to you for higher criticism. But first I have to have a word from you and find out whether you have a permanent address because I don't want this manuscript to go astray.

This afternoon I will start to read my notes for the last chapter, which deals with the last twenty years. It must be completed by the end of this week. I do not allow myself to read anything for fun so I will not be distracted. But I do play the piano quite often, and when I play Bach, I always have attentive listeners. [ . . . ] My head is filled with melodies. If you only could have heard my improvisations yesterday! But aside from a genuine, deep community of thought, we do not share anything in our daily lives. It is good this way, although there are moments when one would like to share impressions of the moment.

I wrote to my two publishers, offered Siebeck and Mohr[1] my *Quest of the Historical Jesus* manuscript and Breitkopf[2] the translation of my *Bach*. When both contracts are settled, I can live for two years without worries. You will hear about that.

Your new friend will not be in London until September 20th. She will come with me to Günsbach to get a good rest instead of going to Paris and Scotland. In London, she will pick up her students. You are mentioned frequently, not without a trace of jealousy. And if you should still be jealous, you might indeed envy her because she spends every day with your friend and writes at the same table with him. And I, who in principle never bring the people I love together, enjoy the thought that you both will meet someday, that you will become acquainted with each other.

You have the ocean. I know how much you love it. And I know that your thoughts wander to the Grimmialp. I receive them and thank you. Be very happy. You will receive further news. I feel so strange to have to tell you in long letters what I do.

Yours
Albert S.

I did not send anything to you in Strasbourg.

1. Publisher at Tübingen.
2. Music publisher at Leipzig.

## 69. A. S.

Grimmialp
Sunday, August 28 [27], 1905
In the morning, before lunch

My dear friend,

I worked all night until 4:00 A.M. Yesterday in the evening the plan for a new chapter with which I had struggled for some time stood suddenly before me. Now I have won the battle, and in that joy I have forgotten all fatigue and the headaches that follow a birth. And you have been neglected because of this chapter.

What you told me about our walk was not new to me. I knew what you were thinking. You must know that there is nobody in this world with whom I feel so absolutely free as with you, and nobody whom I consider as free toward me. This freedom grows as we become closer. We achieve something that few souls achieve: To be something immeasurable for each other, and at the same time each remains himself, knows it, and wants it that way. We also remain free with respect to our decisions, how we will be together or not, only happy in the thought that we live one with the other and through the other. This is the impression our last walk left with me. There was no fear afterward; everything seemed almost like a dream, and yet it was so natural that I cannot find words for it.

Yes, we talk about you frequently, about you and my future, Miss H. and I [ . . . ] Your letter was good for her. "This young lady," she said, "is destined for you; she has waited for you, and she will share your life and work." Refrain, "marry her"—this amuses both of us now . . . [ . . . ]

Great news: Breitkopf wants my German manuscript and promises me also an English edition! The German will bring me 1,500 to 2,000 Marks! Good-bye worries! For the Jesus book, I expect 400 to 500 Marks! That will be enough for two years! I am so moved! You will not get the manuscript. It is in Tübingen: The publisher will look it over before he sends me the contract. Poor collaborator. In September, you will get something.

I leave here on the 2nd and plan to arrive at Günsbach on the 3rd. Please write there; I don't want you to feel inhibited. You have the right. Tonight a longer letter.

Yours,
A.

## 70. H. B.

[from England]
August 28, 1905

Thank you for your short note; it was nice that you sent me a greeting for Monday morning. What did you do yesterday? I was at a church that lies at some distance, and I walked along the cliffs to have an enjoyable walk; in this way, I did what a normal human being in England does on Sunday morning. After that, I was invited for lunch and then devoted all afternoon to the mother of my friends; they had to leave the old lady all alone. (Was I good enough for an English Sunday? If so, it has to make up for many godless German afternoons.) But when she rested for ten minutes, I went down to the piano and played "Tomorrow the Sun Must Shine Again," by Strauss and Schubert's "Ranschendes Bächlein."—Do you remember the texts of those two songs?

It rains this morning; a good day to write. But I will wait for a reply from London before I mail this letter to give you my next address. Tell Miss H., along with my cordial greetings, that she should not feel too sad if she has to give you up for one or two days because of your work. She should remember that she has you for the rest of the time. How long will you stay at the Grimmi?

But if I continue to chat with you like this, I will forget to tell you about the evening when I learned about the Congo. It took place at the chapel of the "primitive Methodists." Two speakers lectured, one about his work here, the other about work in the Congo. It was first emphasized that we should not point to a great difference between "home work" and "foreign work" (that was said especially for me, don't you think?). In both lands, we work for the same purpose; only the means and the people are different. Some of us are destined to serve at home, some to go abroad to serve God better and to do what he has to do (this is very English, to speak briefly and to the point when you have to decide about difficult issues, don't you think?). Afterward he spoke, not as much about the work of the missionaries (he was—if I understood him correctly, at the Baringa Station; his name is Dr. Gratton Guiness), as about the awful conditions under which the poor natives have to live in the Belgian Congo. He wanted to appeal to public opinion to shake people up so they would contribute to the development of this area into a genuine state with a government instead of being at

the mercy of one single person who, although a king, has almost only com-
mercial interests. I will send you the notes I took, although I am not sure
that everything he said is correct. But it was horrifying, even if only half of
the cruelties he reported are actually committed there. I told my parents
about this evening and, for the first time, mentioned the Congo to them. I
wrote that if the description of the atrocities is based on fact, no responsible
person could remain a calm observer.—At the conclusion of his lecture, Dr.
Guiness asked whether anyone had a question. I thought of you and of your
director in Paris.

**71. A. S.**

> Grand Hotel Grimmialp
> Wednesday morning,
> August [30?], 1905

My dearest friend,

I envy you for the long hours you have to collect your thoughts; I would
love just to have that many minutes. The three great chapters, however, in
my *History of the Life of Jesus*,[1] which are currently occupying my thinking,
don't let me rest. It is an awful stress that makes me nervous. Nobody bene-
fits from my presence, and my other friend suffers from the preoccupation
with my work. She was very sad to have to take the children for a walk this
morning by herself.

For moments, when I can enjoy some rest, I am happy. I am now em-
barking on a new path. I see more and more that this is the right one. I do
not worry anymore: What shall we eat, what shall we drink, what shall we
wear? Now my beloved Bach book, the child born with so much pain and
effort, will have its father. That art sustains me at a time in which I had inwardly taken leave from it, that art helps me to prepare myself for the future, is that not part of the wonderful harmony that makes my life so
beautiful? Breitkopf offers me 1,500 Marks for this edition. I will ask for
2,000. They also consider an English edition! In several respects, the German *Bach* will be a completely new book. The historical sections of the beginning, which bothered a certain professor's daughter, will be cut, and the
chapters on the conclusion, as well as the principles for the performance of

1. Published in 1906 as *The Quest of the Historical Jesus*. See p. 33n. 2.

Bach's work, will receive more extensive treatment, according to their importance. The second *Bach* edition will be more intellectual and spiritual. You will see it as it develops. At Christmas, I will begin.

The contract for the *Quest of the Historical Jesus* has not been signed. I hope that this will be possible soon. I promised to send the completed manuscript on the first of October. What a September that will be! Several chapters are very good: those I will not change. Others have to be completely new. The most difficult, the last three chapters, I write here. I work well. But I am so exhausted! Perhaps it is because of the altitude. Departure on Friday . . .

## 72. H. B.

Tuesday morning<br>[September 5, 1905]

I just received your letter—thank you! There was also a card from London confirming that I can have the room that I reserved. My address will be: c/o Mrs. Forbes, 78 Ladbroke, Notting Hill, London W. I will definitely stay there until September 9th, perhaps even to the 10th or 11th, if I don't stay in Holland on the return trip. On the 12th, I intend to be at Strasbourg and would like to ask you to communicate with me again with those small sheets of paper you gave to me after your return, if there is nothing of special importance (as, for example, an exchange with the director of the Paris mission). In that case, please write to the following address: Miss Helene Bresslau, City-orphan Supervisor, Office of the Mayor, Section III Community Orphanage Office, Schlossplatz 5. In the meantime, I look forward to receiving another letter here and then one in London with the good news that tells me when you are in Günsbach, or wherever, so I know where I can find you in my thoughts. I don't like very much to write to Günsbach; please do not be angry (I believe it is my pride). I don't like to write you to where one does not know me. But I do wish you a very happy time there, you and Miss Herrenschmidt. I have the strange notion that we will not meet in spite of our, or rather, my desire.

I congratulate you on the good news. You see, your friend did not give you bad advice in all these years when she said that there must be a German edition of the *Bach*. This nation has a right to have one! But your friend is resigned; she foresees that your promise will not be kept in this case, as in all other promises about cooperation. If it does not already exist, one will invent a very special orthography and punctuation that an uninitiated cannot comprehend, is it not true? And in the end, everything will be done under great pressure, and whole nights will be spent working? How well one knows this, and one gives up as to even being surprised or disappointed. Oh, how disobedient our friends are! Once in a while one has to scold a little, don't you agree? I am afraid he has been spoiled recently. And, in the end, he does not want to have to do anything with the one who speaks her opinion freely. And then?—well, you understand—perhaps one has to change one's tune in order to overcome a great disappointment.—Why hide things from one's self? And why hide something from you that I cannot hide from myself?—

And yet: yours
L.


**73. A. S.**

Thursday Morning
October 12, 1905

The time has arrived.[1] The sun was shining just as on August 13th. Yesterday it was Wednesday. I spoke with the director of the missions in the Parc Montsouris, and after five minutes we were friends!

On Sunday, we will continue our discussion. It was touching. I explained to him how I arrived at the idea. He was moved by the simplicity and the logic of my thought. He himself is quite liberal, but there are people on the committee who are afraid of an assistant professor from Strasbourg; but he is sure that I can win them over through the simplicity of my words.

I will, however, see to it that the question of dogma will not come up.

Well then: two years from now the Missionary Society will call me to the place where I am needed. If they have a vacancy before that time, I will go. I leave the seminary and will begin my medical studies already this winter. If the society considers it useful to let me complete my medical studies, they will let me do so. This is the solution I like best because then we both feel more at ease. My religious views will then be a private matter. But if

1. Schweitzer finally had received an answer from the Paris mission.

they need a missionary sooner, I will not finish my studies. Officially, the society knows that one week from today I will be available.

You see, that is almost like a contract with a publisher. But I am for clear agreements. After our discussion, they had the send-off party for several missionaries who return to the Congo. I sat, not knowing anyone, in a corner of the chapel. What an hour! I heard how these simple men took their leave; I was surrounded by women in black dresses, sad yet joyful, everywhere an animated atmosphere; the walls were decorated with pagan weapons . . . in the dim light of only a few gas lamps, my whole life passed in my thoughts, and I saw that everything had to come this way. And I was happy that I have been faithful to myself . . . and in the dusk of the chapel, I saw you at the day of my departure . . . you were smiling.

These men are simple and of great depth. No veneer. One of them asked with a sad voice whether there was anybody in this assembly who would come and help him in the Congo . . . If there is an invisible communication between souls, he must have heard my "Yes."

The director, who had been moved by our discussion, used many of my phrases in his speech . . .

At the opera that evening, I told Miss Herrenschmidt during the intermission what had happened in the afternoon. She was deeply moved. "This is good," she said. "I am sad, but also proud of you. You must go!——."

The ballet continued . . . It was *Armida* by Gluck . . . and strangely: I listened to the music.

My head is tired, but I feel like a free person . . . Ahead, I go now to the cemetery. Tuesday morning I will return.

The other friend's[1] tumors may become serious if it is not possible to arrest their growth. She is serene and in good spirits and sends you sincere greetings.

Au revoir.

A

1. Adele Herrenschmidt.

**74. H. B.**

[Strasbourg, November 1, 1905]

All Saints Day—the day when everybody consecrates their graves. I do not have one in the whole wide world—many must envy me. And yet today those seem to be homeless who cannot make a pilgrimage to a grave. I went out to our place, thinking of the one who has been dead for many years, who never knew anything about me, yet to whom I feel somewhat related—am I presumptuous to have such thoughts? Please forgive me! I love her because she loved you so much!

It was beautiful out there, total death and disappearance, but with the force and beauty that carried in it the promise of resurrection. The trees are shimmering in the brilliant colors of their leaves, which any hour can take them away. To die like this—not to fade away slowly, but to radiate in the last richness of life in bright flames that will devour you—

Our Rhine, so blue, so clear, gossamer veils in the distance, which still do not obstruct your view, a smile over everything, the knowing smile of those who, in leaving, know that they have not blossomed in vain—our summer!

If you had been here, we would have taken leave from this summer hand in hand with a radiant smile—but I did not languish over your absence. I think of you with some anxiety—don't you work too hard? I also have several questions—among these, whether you are angry about my recent notes? But I will be patient; I beg you, don't write unless you have some leisure—as much as I enjoy every word you can send me, I would regret it if you had to force yourself to write it.

Good night,
Yours,
L.

**75. A. S.**

[Strasbourg]
Monday evening, December 18, 1905

Here I come again to chat with you. I write in bed with my fountain pen. These moments I spend with you are my only moments of relaxation. The rest of the day rushes by like lightening. I feel a little better.

I changed my plan. I no longer have the right to spend Christmas Eve by myself because the Christmas days I can spend with my family are now numbered. After my sermon on Sunday, I will go to Colmar to spend time with my sister and the children. Come to the church, please. That will be our Christmas.

What has this child done to our lives—no, not the child, but the man!! I see so much clearer now what I did not realize before, when I was still a theologian. Today we had our faculty meeting. Everybody was very cordial to me, but when the program of courses was determined, I thought with a shudder that perhaps I might have spent my whole life preparing course schedules.

Oh, I would like to talk with you so much longer. Sit at the bank of the river, smell grass and hay—but quickly. Yes, we are happy, in spite of everything.

Good night, my most faithful companion.

**76. A. S.**

> At home, for the last time on
> New Year's at the seminary
> New Year's Eve 1905

My dear, most faithful companion,

Come to me, we want to say good night to the old year. It goes to its rest, as we will at some time go to our rest when our time has come. And we want to thank Him, not like those people who make so much noise outside . . . but thank Him as calm people.

What have you made of us both, you dying year, when you were young, enjoyed bringing forth leaves and blossoms, when you yourself had to fight with the old winter and when you were strong and full of joy?

My faithful companion, what has it done to us? Today on my return trip from Paris, I outlined in pencil the definite plan for my two lectures on several large sheets. One thought that gave me constant joy was the feeling that I am a free man who can say everything he thinks about religion, and now I can offer people something; even if it is small, it is something alive, a small candle on which the other can light his own. . . . I am so happy and calm. You and I, we must always keep our religion to ourselves, keep it a secret because what God and immortality are for us, others will see only as

atheism and negation of the soul. For us, it is enough to live and to die . . .
in our poor state we are rich, and there will be a time when the whole world
will be poor in order to become rich again, after the borrowed and mort-
gaged goods that are now part of the accouterment of religion have been
lost. In the past, I was afraid that I had taken something away from you;
now I have no fear of that . . . none.

This was the decisive year for our lives, for yours and for mine. A dark,
long road . . . but we must and we want to pursue it because the other kind
of happiness, a good position and the other things that mean happiness to
so many people, would turn us into liars and thieves . . . You have helped
me to see clearly and to walk straight. I want to hold your hands and look
into your faithful eyes, you who have become so strong in your struggles . . .

A happy year, my faithful companion! . . . Happy in our sense. I did not
think of my mother, nor of my brother and sisters or anyone else but only of
you, and I don't want anybody around me except you. It will be this way as
long as I celebrate this New Year . . .

Come, say good night to the tree . . . now we will think of those who
have a claim on us; each for himself . . . that we don't hurt them and that
they let us follow our road . . .

Good night . . . /.

# $1906$

## 77. H. B.

My friend, happy birthday from the depths of my heart!—And yet a wish for happiness? Only as we understand it, the happiness of those who do not strive for their own, at least not the happiness of those who pursue only their own. Two years ago I wrote you from Stettin in a stolen minute— today, also stolen, yet under such different circumstances! You must and will follow your road, although less than ever before I can envision where it will lead. I do not try to project the future, to know what it cannot reveal. But every good thought is accompanied by one prayer: However hard it will be, whatever you have to do, wherever you have to go—may it not be *in vain*. Then it will never go beyond your strength.

This is the birthday wish for the man in whom I trust because I know that he will never do anything because of ulterior motives. You will do only what you *must*, do it out of inner necessity, and I want to assist you as much as I possibly can, to my last drop of blood. To call you my best friend is the pride and joy of my life.——

I celebrate your day in the mountains, in the snow-covered solitude of the High Field,[1] where I can be closer to you in spirit than here among other people. You will accompany me in spirit; thus, it will be a good day. It is not our fate to celebrate personal anniversaries with public parties. My small gift, which is no real surprise, you can fetch on Monday noon, yes? I enclose the promised pages of the diary and a few not totally unsuccessful

---

1. Ski area in the Vosges Mountains.

photographs. Once upon a time, I had hoped to be buried surrounded by these mountains; today I know that such splendor is not for us; my grave will be more humble. But the day at Genoa shows you *how* we have "worked,"—Rappallo—*how* we enjoyed! You will see all of these places, also my favorite place at Portofino, and with more leisure. It cannot make a deeper impression on you that it did on me, and it is still incomprehensible to me that all of this took only two days, memories that will stay with me for years.

Good-bye for now.

And may God be with you in this and all the coming years.

From my heart
Lene

## 78. A. S.

[Strasbourg]
January 25, 1906

Your birthday! I feel a great urge to converse with you and to tell you what I think on this day about you and for you.

Yesterday my birthday was celebrated at the seminary in the evening because earlier it would have distracted me too much from my lecture. The students said, "Stosst an, Frauenlieb lebe. . . ,"[1] and everybody probably thought about one girl or several whom he courts. Their eyes were happy. Mine, too, but in a different way . . . because I know the true meaning of a "woman's love" . . . what struggles, what strength, what renunciation, what richness . . . and one shakes and trembles when one accepts another's existence so totally, the other's thoughts, the other's fate . . . and at last one does not resist anymore to accept the responsibility . . . because one feels that here is something stronger than anything else in this world.

What shall I wish you on this day? I don't want you to have the feeling that you get older! No! I beg you. That is what causes me pain because I tell myself that if fate had not led me to you, you would have a home and family and no feeling of aging.

But I think about all the strength you need and will need to live at

---

1. "Lift your glasses to the love of women."

home, within the circle of your family, who suffer in the realization that you do not choose the path of happiness, who will hurt you in major or minor ways because they want you to return to the right path, like those who cause suffering because they do not understand the person's destiny. . . .

This is a difficult task. I cannot wish you anything that others would want to have because that is not in accordance with your own plans; it lies beyond your life's horizon. But the strength and the inner peace to remain yourself without hurting others, to follow your road, the gentleness and firmness that you will need . . . that is what I wish you because you will have to renew this resource everyday.

And I must tell you this once, you are, for me, one of the purest and deepest souls that ever lived in a woman. [ . . . ]

I take both your hands and thank you with all my heart / /
A.

## 79. H. B.

[Strasbourg]
End of January 1906

You would like just a word—what can I tell you? That it was an excellent lecture—aesthetically perfect as a speech? These were comments I heard, and that is self-evident, of course. What I enjoyed more than this or that brilliant part, more than this or that striking image, was the power of your words that I felt and that you transmitted to the audience. My soul, so tightly strung, was vibrating with yours and tried to sense whether others in the room responded in the same way. Not just that your words might be of comfort to some or even might bring a feeling of redemption, but rather that they saw themselves face-to-face with a vaguely perceived enigma and now felt the reassuring call: Go ahead, be yourself, and be truthful! That is what remains for me today; for that I thank you in my own name and for the others.

And because some criticism should not be left out: a little too long, a little too unctuous in your delivery. You don't mind if I tell you? It is only my humble opinion. My faithful companion in arms, now sleep and rest,—I hurt knowing how tired you are.

## 80. A. S.

A farewell letter Monday evening
February 27 [26], 1906[1]
At the seminary in my study

This is the last letter I will write you from the seminary. My room is partly empty; the writing paper is already packed for the move; tomorrow the piano will be taken . . . The large tree moves in the wind on this warm February night.

I leave this room for the third time. The first time as candidate, after my exam, to go to Paris and Berlin. The second time after my two years as vicar, 1898–1900, and the six months as acting director of the seminary! How painful it was at that time! My aunt wrote me to comfort me . . . I just did not yet see the road.

And now I leave peacefully, pensively, and smiling . . . Out into life as fate ordained. I feel and know that here I would never become the one I meant to be, a human who plunges into life and gives everything he has in him, whatever his lot may be.

It hardly hurts to leave my tree. A sentimental trait (in the best sense of the word) gradually leaves me. I think completely clearly, in spite of my fatigue.

My rooms are quite messy! No curtains, no rugs—nothing. I have not invited anyone. Events like these should not be celebrated. One morning I just told my housekeeper: Please take the curtains down tomorrow. The previous evening Gillot[1] had supper with me, and we were in a happy mood. My new apartment will be very attractive, almost too beautiful for me.

There is hardly anyone left at the seminary. The students have gone out to have fun. You see, I am no longer suited to educate future ministers. I become unfair.

As I write you, I take a long break after each sentence. On my table, I have a few snowdrops. Smoke comes from the lamp, and I did not even notice it; the room becomes even more inhospitable, even the stove does not work anymore.

1. The day before Shrove Tuesday.
2. Hubert Gillot, lecturer in French at the University of Strasbourg, with whom Schweitzer consulted in preparing the French edition of *J. S. Bach*.

What has become of the person who had planned to end his days here, dreaming under the tree? This artist—monk . . . Dead and buried! I feel as if I had never known him, so far removed is he now. I feel and now understand what it means: "If someone is in Christ, he has become a new creature." . . . How our values do change.

What else can I tell you from this table? Shall I call you, so you can sit once more in the easy chair at my right side, where you stayed with me through long nights, where—interrupting my work from time to time, I have spoken with you in simple, but loving words . . . words you have never heard, words of admiration and of deep gratitude, words full of anxiety and worry about you . . .

The moment has come. Have you taken a look at everything? You see how the branches of the tree swing in the dark night . . . a large serpent that wants to hold me back . . . one could truly believe that there are snakes that move . . . —

Ahead. Let us get up. We have been here together for the last time . . . and we only look ahead, not back . . . Lord, send whatever You ordain. So You care for us . . .

## 81. H. B.

[Strasbourg]
Sunday, March 4, 1906

[ . . . ] Do you know that your letters accompany me everywhere? [ . . . ] and that it was hard for me, yesterday, to put them all together for storage. How shall I thank you my great friend? How rich I am, blessedly rich—I was moved when you came the other day—you felt that, didn't you—

That you yourself told me such words—can that be true, possible, that I can be that much for you, that my thoughts, that I myself am always with you?—

How proud I am, how happy—well, these are words that cannot really express *how* I feel—. It seems that I float high above the clouds but not dizzy, but firm and safe, so blissfully peaceful and secure—

Thank you—

When you read this, you will have woken up for the first time in your new home. Did you have pleasant dreams? You know that dreams we have in the first night at a new place will be fulfilled! What shall I wish that you might have dreamt? That the anxieties in the times of struggle that you experienced in the rooms you now leave, in view of the tree we both want to keep dear, may never return. This I cannot do because I know that they will return. Not in the same way, but for different reasons and in different shape, but they also will be fiery and severe—unless we would give up, and that we do not want, not even for that price. That we may keep our strength and confidence, that we face whatever comes with renewed fortitude, this is my wish.

That we may look back to every phase of our past humbly and with gratitude for the power that guides us, and that we become aware of our own strength with pride and joy. You are already able to do this—I have not yet forgotten how weak I have been during this long winter, that your patience and goodness had to support me. I will not forget it but also hope that it will be done with and remain in the past.

And now ahead into spring. I have such a good symbol of the new, sprouting life, which I intended to send you as first greeting to your new home. Do you remember when at your birthday I was at the High Field, it was such a beautiful day, still a little snow but already the beginning of spring. We walked down the hillside, you with me; we saw the setting sun and walked over the soft ground with bouncy steps, in spite of the weight of the skis that weighed heavily on our shoulders, as they could not make our feet glide. At the left side was the larch, bare and dormant, yet some of its decorative cones were still holding on gracefully to the branches. We took some of these branches home, put them into water, and some began to sprout. I planned to send these to you for your move. Now I am not able to do that, but something happened that is more wonderful than what I had thought. I put the branches into flowerpots, filled with earth, and yesterday when I tried to take them out, I noticed the beginnings of tiny white roots. So I left them there. I don't know yet how they will develop; I will wait and take good care of them—wouldn't it be a miracle if branches that were cut from a larch tree would root and grow? If so, I will transplant them into several pots, and you will get some of them. Not all branches showed signs of roots, and those I will take to your place today. If you find time, please send me a little good-bye greeting with the mail for Wednesday morning. Salutations to Paris and to Miss Herrenschmidt. And greetings to you.

**82. A. S.**

Tuesday, on the train to Paris
March 13, 1906

Tell me, is this me, this man who travels through this cheerful country-side in the March sun? At this moment, I just saw the woods in the distance, the woods of August. There is a great distance between the sun at that time and the sun today, a long, dreadful night of toil. Is it possible that life is so beautiful, tell me, is it possible? For us both, the sun always comes out when we need it, when we have reached the bottom.—My head is so sick, but a few days of rest will cure it. The sheet on which I write you lies on my anatomy book, the only one I took with me. It is in tune with the sunlight.

I can hardly tell you anything. I want to close my eyes and repeat only the one word: Sun. Later I will review the new page. I think of the 22nd.—The Vosges Mountains come closer. Miss Herrenschmidt will come on April 2nd. You must get acquainted. [ . . . ]

*Zabern*

[ . . . ] Now comes the Hoh-Barr.[1] Once on a foggy fall day, I climbed up there with my aunt. She leaned against me, shivering: "Do you lead me to the sun?" she asked me. "Yes, always." On top was the sun, and two years later I had the privilege of leading her from the agony of death toward the sun. I can never ride past here without thinking of that sun!

And you? Have I led you toward the sun? I must be sure of that, so I do not have to worry about you. Yet, it feels so good to worry about you. How strange: To worry about you does not hurt anymore. In the past, I asked my-self: What will happen to me when I see her friends marry, and she remains alone and grows older? Now I do not think of that with sadness. Now I think of you with pride.

Tunnel. No sun—but only a few minutes—then sun again. Is it not something wonderful, life, just wonderful?

When will we write our book, *Wir Epigonen??* Your book, which should satisfy you to the last line; how happy I am to be able to give you a present! You have given me so much—more than I can put into words.

My mother cannot yet accept my plans. She recently wrote to me that

1. The ruin of a castle above Zabern.

The Cycling Club, in Saarburg, 1906. Helene Bresslau is second from left, Albert Schweitzer second from right. *Courtesy of the Albert Schweitzer Archive, Günsbach.*

the reason why I looked for my ideals in distant lands is that my friends were almost only women! She does not think of Curtius, Ziegler, Widor.— But, you know women have more strength and are more naturally in tune with life than men. I am sure that no friendship with a man would have helped me, would have taught me as much as you have, not to forget my aunt and Miss H.[1] There is an elementary superiority and naturalness in a woman—or did I meet only those?

The sun is blinding me. Keep this sheet, the words of an unspeakably happy human being . . . Last night I sat down on the couch and asked myself how I have earned so much happiness. Saarburg . . . I think of the day we spent there and our way home.

Yours

A.

The little paper of this morning was left in my desk drawer. How much you have to forgive me. Will this be a good day for you? The branch of the larch is put away safely, and it will be on the grave as a greeting from you.

1. Adele Herrenschmidt.

**83. H. B.**

[Strasbourg]
Monday evening [end of March]

Now come, we both are alone and therefore together. (Why can't we keep company when we eat by ourselves, or is yours not solitary?) Now you can stretch out on the couch, poor, tired friend; you can relax totally while I finish the corrections—for once without disturbances and without interruptions—and then we will say good night.

Now I must tell you that I find the last pages not as clearly written. It must, of course, be awfully difficult to explain everything clearly, but I would like to see it more concise, so it becomes more lucid. Forgive me. I should finish first.

Finished and so tired, spring fever. Perhaps the cause lies in myself, that the last part does not seem so absorbing . . . I want to see your argument so cogent, so forceful that nobody would even think of contradicting you. Now I can see how they will begin to take it apart. It does not matter; you will rebut them, but it would have been nicer if they did not even start [ . . . ]

For now, good night; bon voyage.

Auf Wiedersehen

**84. A. S.**

Günsbach
April 29 [28], 1906

Letters from Italy are here.[1]

In Italy, I did not find time to write, tired and exhausted and torn inside. But you were with me frequently, in Florence and in Portofino.

My general impressions? I had not been wrong: Italy is not for me! I felt like a stranger from beginning to end! I was homesick for the North, for the sparse spring in our land . . . I had not realized that I am such a barbarian. I truly suffered.

On the other hand, your friend is too demanding! He cannot enjoy anything surrounded by all those curious people who walk around with

1. Schweitzer had been in Italy at Easter with his sister Luise and his friend Adele Herrenschmidt. Helene had given him her diary pages from her Italian trip in 1899.

their Baedeker,[1] those people to whom the essence of this country has been sold. Fiesole seemed like a beauty with makeup, to whom one pays homage. How could Böcklin[2] live there in this crowd of foreigners who behave in this environment as they do in their homes? . . .

I could have cried. Impossible to dream in the countryside, to love it. Everything was noisy, presented to be admired. No concentration! The most distant mountains are desecrated by these curious people. Because I could not stand it anymore, I dragged my friend and my sister behind the cemetery, far away from the people . . . and at last there was a moment of inner collection.

Everywhere it was like that. Pitti Palace, Uffizi! I was moved, but I did not enjoy it. Aside from Michelangelo, I do not understand Italian art; imagine that. When I came to the room with the painters from the Netherlands, I broke out into a happy laughter, as if I had come home. My dear Florentine, *mia bella*, what kind of a friend you have!

In Florence, I read your plan to my friend—the other friend. We followed it completely, and she wants me to tell you that she showed me everything you wanted me to see. When I saw the early Italian masters, the *Adoration of the Magi* at the academy, I was with you. It was Palm Sunday and sunset time. It is amazing how everything you have told me is engraved in my memory. I like the cloister gardens best—O, San Marco! This peace! But to be there by myself, to dream, to weep, to hope . . . and not always those curious people, with their books in hand, who come for five minutes and behave as if they were at home and who spoil the silence with their endless cackling. Why is all this sold to foreign visitors? I am so selfish, so selfish for the countryside and the art! I could commit a murder to get rid of them; they don't leave me alone when I need it . . .

Savonarola, great man! They trampled through your cell like cows in their stables. I stood at the window and folded my hands. People came, remained a minute, others came, and again others; they swallowed what they saw the way one swallows medicine . . . those intruders of Florence . . . I fled, and I wished I could have been with you for a second, you, the mournful monk, to speak with you . . . —Don't stop, go ahead, don't lose time!

1. A tourist guidebook.
2. Arnold Böcklin (1827–1901), Swiss painter.

One has to see this and that before supper. Should one walk? Should one take a carriage?

I don't like the Italian churches. How I did laugh when I saw the Duomo of Milan! It is a masterpiece fresh from the confectioner. Petty spirit in its grandeur, that is the spirit of the Renaissance. I, as you can see, do not like the Renaissance; we overrated it, as romanticism overrated the Middle Ages, we idealize it. And everywhere Catholicism is in evidence; everywhere, it triumphs over all efforts of a new spirit, a free spirit that did not have the moral strength to win and to prove its right to existence. Only Michelangelo . . . You must tell me about Michelangelo's lady friend.

And all those saints and martyrs on the turrets of the Duomo of Milan! That is grotesque. One would like to stop and talk with them because I am sure that they are bored. The interior is bearable. But as soon as you look up to the ornaments on the ceiling (like fret saw work) all enchantment withers away—

I must admit to you that I hate marble. I like only granite. How much I love the church La Trinita! That was a minute of deep joy. Santo Spirito not so much. Ten o'clock—

Ten o'clock I never forget! Once, when I went to bed earlier, I thought of it beforehand!

Santa Croce! I love that church. It is worthy to contain his[1] tomb.

San Miniato . . . The weather was fine, and I would have liked to dream in this church, instead of visiting it as a sightseer. La Certosa: A monk played the sophisticated guide, to entertain my friend. He was blessed with heavenly bliss, a fat paunch, and he smelled from his feet to his mouth! And he was stupid, too. Another one who will keep me from entering paradise. Would you be kind enough to share Hell with me?

I would like to see Florence without tourists because I comprehend only when I can dream. Yet, I would never, never love it. There is not enough that is natural. . . . The Boboli gardens enraged me. I don't find them at all beautiful. If there were not the view . . . When Goethe pondered about his Tasso,[2] there certainly were fewer visitors.

Uh—what a mood! But I knew this all beforehand. And the fights with my friend preoccupied me too much. She is so scatterbrained that I suffer

1. Michelangelo's.
2. Torquato Tasso (1544–1595), Italian poet of the late Renaissance.

from it. She can never be silent in nature; she does not like nature in a simple way. Our sensitivities are so very different . . . On the last evening in Florence when we were by ourselves, everything just burst out of me. There was a moment of great sadness between her and me—and then we found each other again . . . that was very good. I felt that her thinking was freed from some stress and that now she could follow me again on my paths . . . also the steep paths. Afterward it was very beautiful. In the evenings, we had long conversations, and since her return she has written me touching letters . . . I feel that I can be for her what I wanted to be for her, . . . and what I must be for her.

But I was afraid to think of you . . . —If I do that, I become unjust toward others, especially the other friend. There I give . . . from you I receive. You rose slowly in my life, like the moon who sends a clear light through the trees, which we recognize only when we ask ourselves: why is it so peaceful everywhere? Peace, nobody but you gives it to me! You remain completely yourself, more independent toward me than anybody else . . . And yet, I do not sense you as somebody else, but as myself. With the other friend, I feel a pain, until we get used to each other again; I suffer deeply, almost physically, when we say good-bye, and I ask how we will find each other again . . . None of this with you. No pain when I leave you . . . You will always be who you are . . . and in spirit you are always with me . . . You follow me everywhere, and you understand everything . . .

We should, however, be forbearing with the other friend. She needs me and is so happy because she would be alone . . . I was touched when she said: "You are so good to me! You always pull me up when I am sinking . . . and I feel no jealousy of the other one anymore, none whatsoever for the other friend." (Will it be beautiful in the fall in Paris?)

We spent three days at Santa Margherita. One morning when the weather was fine, I said: "We should eat at Portofino." "Oh, one wants to be with somebody else," my companion said. "No permission to speak with you today." I don't have to add that she did not keep her promise. Nevertheless, I had many moments with you on that day. It was the only day of peace. We went to the top and then walked around the promontory. I walked slowly behind the others. Tata[1] sat on a rock where we spent an hour, calmly and quietly. I picked flowers for her. On the way down, we

1. Schweitzer's nickname for Adele Herrenschmidt.

bought some lace in the narrow street. I got some for my loyal helper. I wanted to have lace from Portofino, for all your cooperation with my book. If you don't want to show this present from me, do not show it to others; just keep the little package until you don't have to account to anyone, what concerns only you and me . . . and then you will wear them. Until then they can rest in our cash box . . .

At Mühlhausen, I learned about the death of one of the women missionaries from the Congo. Her husband had died there three years ago. She remained to take care of the sick because she had had training at hospitals in Paris. She died suddenly . . . For some time, I could not shed the thought that some day she has to be replaced . . . perhaps through another Alsatian. She came from Mühlhausen.

Please forgive me that I tell you this.

Tonight I will return. The article from the *Kunstwart*[1] is very good. The other friend was very proud of it. She had read it first, in the morning before breakfast.

Are you not embarrassed to have such a barbarian friend, who returns from Italy and has no desire to go back? Only Portofino . . . and why? . . . I love the region! . . .

## 85. A. S.

[Strasbourg]
Sunday evening
May 6, 1906

We walk into the dawn. The eternal spirit that battles with the world, the spirit that searches for clarity and that can become conscious of itself only within the individual . . . this spirit needs us. Everything else is unimportant! What matters your solitude and mine? My lack of some comfort . . . What does it all matter? Waiting? What does it matter? To be tossed to and fro, to be humiliated . . . even that, what does it matter? To be tired? What does it matter? Nothing, nothing, nothing!! Oh, if you had to live again without your sadness, without your struggles . . . how poor you would be.

When you hear the evening bell ringing, do you tell yourself that we will carry these sounds far, far away? Until then we do not live the real life!

1. A review of Schweitzer's book on Bach.

Do we dream? Can't you dream? Oh, my great companion!: Must I carry you, lift you up? . . . Is it so long, so long that I still must learn? . . .

And with all of this, you are an immeasurably happy woman . . . for that reason I cannot feel any pity for you . . . never, never. Oh yes, I will comfort you . . . but do I have to comfort you? . . .

You noble being, you unpretentious, great woman!—I want to kneel before you and kiss your hands . . .

Do you want to humiliate me and believe that you are missing something while you own what is most genuine and beautiful in me . . . and as I am supported by your thinking?—

## 86. A. S.

[Günsbach]
Wednesday morning, at your place
June 6, 1906

Last night I worked a little. This morning, what a scandal. I had breakfast in bed and stayed there until 10:00 A.M. My father came, we talked together, and in-between I often thought of you! How strange, I cannot see you separated from your work. If you did not work at the orphanage, you would not be the same for me. I love this person who has searched for and found her calling. Do you remember the day when you told me, at the Staden, that you would most likely find something in the mayor's office? I was trembling with joy.

At the moment, I work on my next course, in which I intend to give a complete survey of the research on St. Paul. I know that I love this work because I do it aside from the other occupation. How beautiful, what the pious Baur[1] at Tübingen wrote in 1845: "The essence of Christianity can be understood only historically" . . . He was honest. There is great ardor in his work. But we have gone beyond this. We know that Christianity is a constantly creative spirit, a spirit that remains itself only through constant work.

Now that my thoughts have rested, I see everything much clearer than ever before. And I want to have the strength and the health to live my thoughts, so they become life.

1. Ferdinand Christian Baur (1792–1860), professor of theology at Tübingen.

Albert Schweitzer in his study, 1906. *Courtesy of the Albert Schweitzer Archive,* *Günsbach.*

I think that you get more than just the hour of every day that I promised you.

**87. A. S.**

[Günsbach]
Saturday, August 19, 1906,
on my rock

It seems to me that you must feel how happy I am. Indeed, I believe that I can still learn everything that I must learn. You know, sometimes the "universality" of my mind frightens me. I carry it as a burden and tell myself: how happy must be the people who have only one profession, who master one field. But then, when I have the strength again to carry my head firmly on my shoulders, I am proud to have more versatility than the others, and I have confidence in my strength to cope with all the different claims. What joy this is. In the evening, before I go to sleep, I bury my head in my hands and could weep with happiness. Then I tell myself that it must be so.

Siegfried Ochs[1] was touching. When we parted, he said: "You have told me the words I expected from Christianity and that I have never heard. I understand you, and I never would try to persuade you to give up the road you have chosen, not even for the sake of art." I probably will go to Berlin next winter, to his Bach concerts, if I find the money for it. The day after to-morrow I will begin with the preparations for the translation.[2] Be happy with me.

You know, you are the only person who can really be happy with me because you live entirely within my own thinking. I feel that so strongly, more than I can tell you. That is my happiness.

I have been writing to you already for one hour because I pause after every sentence to follow each thought to its end.

I have my organ fingers again. You will hear it when I accompany *Israel*.[3] I like this work more and more. But it does not touch my heart. While I practice, I can think of other things.

Grafe[4] and Wrede[5] have written to me. They admire my work greatly, but they cannot follow my thinking, my new historical interpretation of the life of Jesus, although it has made a great impression on both. I did not expect anything else. It is impossible for them to accept a new view immediately. Wrede will review my book in the *Göttinger Gelehrten Anzeigen*.[6]

## 88. H. B.

[Strasbourg]
2:30 A.M.
Monday, August 27, [1906]

My dear, great friend,

Don't worry that I write at night—it is the heat that always wakes me up in these midsummer nights. Because I had a good, restful day and went to bed early, I am happy to use this time for a conversation with you.—my

1. 1858–1929, conductor.
2. The work on Bach.
3. Handel's *Israel in Egypt*.
4. Eduard Grafe (1855–1922), theologian from Bonn.
5. William Wrede (1859–1906), theologian from Breslau, major New Testament scholar.
6. A prestigious scholarly journal from Germany.

great, faraway friend. I feel as if you do not sleep either, at this moment, and as if you could hear me. Is that right? But if so, you are working, and that worries me, to see you chained so tightly to your work—I implore you: think of your health and take a good rest! What does it help if one returns as tired and weak as one departed—and then the daily grind begins again, and moments of relaxation are rare—(even if they are ever so beautiful!!). Don't feel sorry for me because I am still here. I don't envy anybody (except just a little bit those who are right now at the Grimmi[1] (that includes the cow who grazes in the garden!). But you understand that it is not so serious that I suffer, so it is not worth mentioning. My vacations will come soon, and they will be enjoyable! In two, at most three weeks, I expect the dear visit of sister Ella.[2]

Yesterday we celebrated my mother's birthday—for the first time in several years, we celebrated it at home, and I did not miss the excursion to the White Lake, although it was a beautiful, bright day. In the morning, I had already received the expected answer from Miss Barrère[3] and the next part of her translation, a delightful letter from Emma Münch (the first), and then one from a beloved somebody far away—you must agree that this was a day to celebrate! How I wish that you could feel the deep peace that I feel and that you could share it—I am so afraid that you are too exhausted and tired. Your health and that of my father, Papa, are not very well. He really had a dilatation of the heart, which has somewhat receded but still causes him pain. The doctor ordered total rest, something that is very hard for him, and he cannot wait to leave. Because he is very nervous, this condition adds to his impatience; I hope that the doctor can give him permission tomorrow to travel in a few days. I don't have to repeat my request that you will not talk to anybody about this when you return.—

[ . . . ]

And the manuscript—what must you think of me? I chat along forever, without saying a word about it.—what do you want?—the best comes last, that's what I practiced as a child, and I kept the most delicious piece of cake for the end.

1. In Switzerland.

2. A friend who later became the director of the home for unwed mothers that Helene helped found at Strasbourg.

3. Helene Barrère translated a section of Romain Rolland's *Jean-Christophe*. See also p. 75.

My dear German *Bach,* I need a Sunday to read you, a double holiday. For this reason, I gave the whole day to read your Bach book, with the exception of a few hours in the morning, which belonged to the birthday child, and then I needed to make order in my room. One certainly cannot read *Bach* in a messy room!

Now, the critique: I find it very good, easy to read, clear; it does not show off the enormous knowledge on which it is based. I asked myself whether you don't go a little far with the simplicity and ease of style, but I believe that it is good. Those who know will recognize the depth of your foundation, and the others can enjoy the building without having to bother about that foundation. What I miss, unless you plan to replace the whole first chapter of the French *Bach,* is an introduction that explains the importance of the chorale for Bach and the need to get acquainted with the chorales first. That could be said in a few words at the beginning of the chapter about the origins of the texts and would relate directly to the content. The severe cuts are most helpful to the lay person, who can orient himself without any effort. That the book does not lack in scholarship is vouched for me by Mr. Schweitzer, the scholar and artist! Do you want to keep Widor's preface? If so, please let me do the translation—tell me.[1]

With the exception of the beginning, where one somewhat feels the difficulty of entering the subject, almost nothing has to be corrected. We can discuss the little details that should be changed when you find time after your return to Günsbach to devote an afternoon to the manuscript! I have the bold hope to gain permission to ask you to come to us again because I did not notice the slightest sign of displeasure after my confession, but now I can write this in only very small letters! I wait for your quick reply and wish you all the best. Enjoy yourself; enjoy the beautiful, beloved countryside.

Yours,

L

Monday morning. Last night, when I lay down again (at five o'clock), I thought of those nights when I got up, secretly, desperately, to write to you to help you out of your sadness and to save you from a dark day and to pull myself out of my own desperation, and I was filled with gratitude. How

---

1. Schweitzer did not retain the preface, but Charles Marie Widor, his organ teacher and friend, wrote a new one, dated "Paris, October 20, 1907."

everything has changed and turned out well! Don't you think that we can have faith and face the future with our heads held high?!—With all my heart, L.

## 89. A. S.

[Strasbourg]
Sunday Evening
10:00 P.M. October 28, 1906

The bells are ringing. In the fireplace, my dearly beloved fireplace, the fire is dying down and projects twitching fingers on the wall. It feels as if it were the last true Sabbath for me for a long time . . .

When I prayed last night, the prayer of the last days to gain strength for the coming winter, I asked myself again and again: What is God? Something infinite in which we rest! But it is not a personality; it becomes a personality only in us! The spirit of the world that in man comes to the consciousness of himself. Prayer: to feel the stirring of the highest being in us, to give ourselves to the divine within us and thus find peace. I wonder whether I can ever express this more clearly? But you understand me, don't you? I think that without my telling you so, your religious thoughts are becoming like mine. I am so happy to get out of all the theological noise and to find myself alone, to think the thoughts I want to think—not as I am going to teach them, but as I want to live them, quietly and simply . . . and that you share them with me, although here, too, you remain completely independent. You understand me and know that this happiness in the thought of not having to teach is not egoism on my part, but it is the growing of truth and strength within me. If I had to tell anybody what my religion consists of, I would not be able to do so . . . but you sense it, and you know it.

Now good night. The fire goes out; may God give us the strength to endure . . . we will ask for nothing else!

Good night, you faithful, great soul . . .

## 90. H. B.

[Strasbourg]
Monday evening
10:15, October 29, 1906

I pull myself out of my dreams—I am very, very sad. There were only ten people at my lecture—that was such a disappointment that I had difficulty concentrating, and I am afraid that I did poorly. But on the way home, I promised myself to be twice as good even if only half of the people who came will come again. It is so painful when you intend to do only good, people do not want it. But it is a good lesson for our vanity—I feel as if I became too proud of my lectures last summer, and now that is punishing me—and rightly so.—

On the way home, I thought of you all the time; you walked at my side; it was a good, quiet, sad way home,—but the kind of sadness that becomes a blessing. On my desk lies the page of the *Frankfurter Zeitung* with the review of your book.[1] Papa had put it aside for me, isn't that touching? In front of me in the vase are the flowers from the rock, the medal, and the picture of the choirboys of St. Sulpice—both are always on my desk, and nobody has yet asked any questions about them.

Tomorrow night Boegner[2] will speak here. I would like to go—may I? But I don't know in which lecture hall.

I reread your short letter—I was touched and moved. That great trust that you have in me—I don't feel worthy of it but try more and more to deserve it. So often I have such a deep longing to get away from here and to begin our work. I believe that at your side I will become a better person. You radiate such strength, and the weary are longing for strength,—but I must arrive at that by myself.

I am digressing—good night! It is past eleven, and I have dreamt rather than written, and all the time I think about what you said about God, but I cannot find a way to put my thoughts into words.

---

1. *Von Reimarus zu Wrede*, later published in English as *The Quest of the Historical Jesus*. See p. 33n. 2.

2. Alfred Boegner (1851–?), head of the Paris Missionary Society.

**91. A. S.**

[Strasbourg]
Tuesday evening,
November 27, 1906

My Great One,

I have not been very generous recently, yet there is so much I would like to tell you. You will read this letter tomorrow after I have been with you, and it will tell you good night from me.

How happy I am that you have regained your enthusiasm and your energy! . . . I suffered so when I saw you so depressed. And on Saturday I was worried when you said that it seems so long until we can begin our work together and that we would be old by then . . . I know that we will be old. Already now our early youth lies behind us, the April of our life, and what lies ahead of us, the years of further learning; for you the "waiting" will consume another portion of your youth. You must, however, believe that when the hour for our work arrives, we will have great strength in spite of everything. We will not be old: we will begin a new youth: we will celebrate our fortieth birthdays as we celebrated our twentieth . . . because we must believe in the words: "They will run and not tire!" This keeps me going!

Those who come after us will have it easier. They will plan their lives differently, and they will not take all the detours we had to take before we found the right direction. They will find their road sooner. Look: nothing has been lost in our lives: no detour, no effort, no struggle, no hesitations . . . believe me . . .

When spirit is a reality, when our lives realize themselves in the spirit, then it will carry us. I believe that if it were not for the spirit, I would have long ago succumbed to exhaustion. Spirit is stronger than anything: that is my faith.

You don't know how happy I am that I can be together with you some time tomorrow . . . you cannot know it . . .

Good night. Has it been a good Wednesday?

## 92. A. S.

[Strasbourg]
Sunday evening
December 23, 1906

M. G.

It is one o'clock in the morning. I preached today and have done many other things but am so happy and so filled with my *Bach* that I wrote the difficult section about the portraits, his head and the bust created after an earlier sculpture, with playful ease. Now, as I go to bed, I already know the sentences with which I will begin tomorrow morning. It feels so good to work in peace and not to be interrupted while you are involved in your subject . . . If I think that my whole life could be like that and that it may be in my power to belong to the happiest people who can devote themselves always to one task . . . well, that cannot be. And it is probably good. But when I enter heaven, I demand that I will be given one task only: to polish stars, to scrub the moon, to load the explosive for thunder, to play music to entertain the mother of God, or whatever, even to write the sermons of the Berlin court chaplains in shorthand—but only one job! I would insist on that, even if I had to be rude. In this hope, I will accept my fate on this earth.

Since this afternoon I have been thinking of you on the train. Where are you now? My poor child . . . I hardly dare to lie down in bed and to go to sleep when I think that you have to sit straight on your bench until tomorrow morning. What a stubborn child you are to travel in the night!

I am sad because I have no Christmas present for you, nothing but a little bouquet of violets. I was not able to think of anything, not a book, not anything. And you are so good; you want me to have my package! With great difficulty, I found three hours yesterday to buy a few presents for my relatives and for some poor families . . .

But I am thinking of you . . . often and with gratitude, and tomorrow evening you will be with me when I am alone.

When you read this, we will have seen each other. This little letter will welcome you tomorrow evening when you come home after the exchange of Christmas presents.

Yours
A.

**93. H. B.**

[Strasbourg]
December 25, 1906

Thank you, my friend, for your words. You are with yours and happy. It does not matter that we cannot spend one day together, I wish you many good hours—how beautiful they must be; your mountains and woods in their white, festive snow cover!

I accompany my parents to Baden-Baden and will return tomorrow night.

Can you come on Saturday for the Barrère issue? Around 4:30, when I return from the organ at Ruprechtsau. And you are invited for supper! Please write me whether this Saturday is convenient or whether you would prefer another day. I will not be free until then, but all of next week.

In any event, we will take our walk on January 1st, won't we? We still have to set the time for that.

I received a great surprise this morning from Tata, and I look forward to showing the present to you. I just wrote her a cordial letter. How nice of her to think of me in this way.

Good night, my Great One; I wonder whether you are asleep now? I began this letter when the clock struck ten—it took me one and one-half hours to get this far,—because I fell asleep for a while—

Good night, sleep well, my most beloved friend—

**94. A. S.**

[Strasbourg]
Friday, very late at night
December 28, 1906

I saw *Tristan*. I had been asked to accompany the cousin of Suzanne Harth, who is here right now.

There was no time in which the music did not move me deeply. I admire it very much still, but the music of my own life is so very different, and if I consider the way in which I am bound to the soul that is dearest to me, that is different, too.

I thought so intensely of us both that I was far away at times. Our magic potion is the ideal of duty, and this to me is as beautiful as the other way to belong together through magic . . .

Thank you so much for your good, good Christmas letter with the two tiny pages! I am so happy and so relieved now that I know that you are content. Now it seems to me that we enter a part of our travels that leads us through a quiet bay . . . we must accept it with gratitude.

I have asked you to give your New Year's Day to my mother. You know she is recovering, but her hair has become white, and she has aged. When I told her that I had to work and could not come to Günsbach for some time, she was very understanding. But when she begged: "You will be here for the Christmas tree that we always decorate for the Ehretsmann children[1] won't you, I beg you," I said without hesitation, "Yes" . . . in your name. You have the right to this day because of its significance in our lives, . . .it was the day on which you came over the bridge in the morning, tired, and then there was the light in the evening. . . . if you give this day to my mother, it will bring us happiness.

I have this premonition that you have been chosen to do much good for my mother and that she will find a great support in you, that you will in some ways be her favorite, and she will think of you with many good thoughts. My chapters are progressing. I even wrote after the theater.

Yours,

A.

## 95. A. S.

[Strasbourg]
New Year's Eve 1906
Forty-five minutes before midnight

Do you remember the little note on which I gave you for the first time the last minutes of the year?

Now everything is so natural—.

We have to thank this year for so much . . . We did not expect that the year would end like this when we stood at its beginning. I am so happy that the estrangement with your family now has been lifted . . . I am just reflect-

---

1. The children of Schweitzer's sister Luise.

ing about my sermons of this year; have I been faithful, have I been great
and pure enough to say what I had and wanted to say? . . .

I am lying in bed because the fire had gone out when I came home; for
a long time, I have been lying with my eyes closed.

Two years ago today, at this time! I felt that something in my life, my
life itself, came to a decision. Now it flows in its riverbed, one year of prepa-
ration and waiting after another. May the spirit whom we want to serve
support us.

I take your hand and kiss it. It is midnight. Thank you for everything
that you are, you noble, pure soul. May this be a good year for you . . . the
work that waits for you! I was so proud and moved when I came home on
Sunday! And I wanted to write you a long letter about that today. You are
happy! Why must you have such a tired friend who cannot even write to
you about such wonderful things! But he will regain his strength again and
again, you can be sure of that.

Goodnight.

Yours,<br>A.

# *1907*

## 96. H. B.

My Great One, my Very Great One,

I have been lying down, dreaming, my head on the pillow on which your hand has been lying, and I felt as if as I rested on your hand, that you carried me—in the twilight only a little light in the corner shone above the chest . . .

How you carry and hold me, you, my most beloved, my only friend—where would I be, what would I do without you! What a wonderful year is coming to its end now—.

How can I thank you enough for what it has given me? I don't have to be ashamed anymore; I don't have to hide it like a sin that I have the best, noblest, and the purest, greatest human being as my friend—I have won a sister who is sensitive and loving—I live in a sphere of peace and harmony, and those who are dear to me know and respect each other and are perhaps not far removed from loving each other—

It is almost too beautiful, Albert, I am not worthy of it—I am not enough for the others, am too egotistical, not faithful and humble enough—may God help me to grow into this, the God into whose hands I put my life because I can think religiously—the spirit is above everything and yet not too sublime to act even in the smallest detail. "God is love, and who lives in that love will remain in God, and God in him."

Albert, I thank you for what you wrote about your mother—you do not know how I admire and respect her. I believe that I could learn to under-

121

stand her if I could get a little better acquainted with her; she would lose the slight shyness she now feels in my presence. And your father, this fine and warm man,—I do love him, although I hardly know him. And I feel guilty toward him, a guilt I do not want to take into the New Year—I will write to him today—he will not take it amiss.

## 97. A. S.

Friday morning,
January 25, 1907

Your birthday! I woke up with that thought and was sure that the sun would shine today. Now the sun travels over this sheet of paper, and the small pen draws its outline with a certain coquetry, as if it knew that this is a birthday letter for a young lady.

I imagine that your family may have a few sad thoughts today. They think of your contemporaries who have their own home, who have children, and who are happy—what people used to call happy. And earlier, before I saw our path clearly, and yours, the same sadness was also in me; I worried about what would happen to you when your first youth had passed, whether you would not accuse yourself of having wasted it, whether you would be sad as you approached your thirties.

All this fear lies now in the distant past. I congratulate you on your birthday, smiling. May they come, the years . . . we will fill them working, waiting, preparing ourselves for the great task . . . and years cannot bother us! And every year we will live as if it could be the last, will love our lives for what we want to do, and will face death smiling as the destiny that may call us when it has been fulfilled . . . and just for that reason we will love life passionately like those who know what it means to live! To want to live: that is what I feel always through all strain . . . and you feel the same.

I like it that you are a little younger than I am, but not too much, so that this feeling that you are a "finished" personality, a feeling that underlies all my thoughts of you, is real. I like your seriousness . . . just as I prefer the first summer months to the beauty of spring . . . when you sense that the fruit that is forming inside the blossom. And for me you will always be young . . . always. Don't worry about the years that come, and don't worry about the hair that gets grayer . . . not about anything: What I love in you is the youth and the strength of your spirit, the youthfulness of the inner you that does not pass and never can pass, that is always reflected in your face and gives it freshness and beauty . . .

May our God protect you . . .

Yours<br>Albert

### 98. A. S.

[Günsbach]<br>Tuesday evening<br>[March 1907]

Dear Miss Bresslau,

Your pie arrived in excellent condition. My mother admired how perfectly I delivered it. Everybody thought that it was charming of you, and Mrs. Schweitzer proved to be the genuine mother of her son when she immediately began to eat the orange slices! That is called Atavism. My father was a little disappointed: He had hoped that it would be a yeast cake that you can dunk in your coffee. I promised him that at your next visit, Saturday night, you would bake such a cake. He cannot believe that you actually made yourself what I brought with me. [ . . . ]

### 99. A. S.

[Günsbach] in the woods<br>Thursday afternoon<br>May 24, 1907

M. G.

No, I don't write you a letter! This will be a large sheet. I feel how sad you were the last time you only got a letter.

First: Last night when I came home, my father asked about you. I told him that I had met you, that you looked so tired, and that I asked you to come on Saturday afternoon. Both Father and Mother were delighted. When we took a walk, my father said: "If the day were to come on which you tell me, 'Helene Bresslau will be my wife,' that would be one of the most wonderful of days for me!" You see how much he likes you. One takes it as a matter of course that I invited you. One does not consider whether you were here a long time ago or more recently. Marguerite[1] may not have returned. But I wish you would know how unimportant this is for my parents. They would like you to come visit them for their sake! My father is already looking forward to having somebody whom he can court a little. You also have to bake something for him while you are here.

This is the situation. You have to decide. I don't mention myself; however, I would like so much to discuss my chapters[2] with you . . . Yesterday, when I walked at twilight through the blooming fields, when I was breathing this peace, when I was enveloped in the fragrance of the wildflowers, I told myself: "How revived she will feel when she comes! . . . How happy will she be, how invigorated!"—If you do not come, you will hurt my parents! They would like you to feel at home at the Günsbach parsonage . . . The flowers around me call you! I asked Sülti[3] . . . he said "yes" and stuck out his tongue! He, too, looks forward to seeing you . . . Please come—It will be the last beautiful Sunday for a long time.

You are dressed up at the Knapps. When I passed the railroad station on my walk, I sent a telegram. Perhaps you will read it right away, and your spirit will leave the party and come to me. The weather is beautiful and will stay this way. Our oracle is speaking. One will put an easy chair in the garden and will let you rest. My mother will be offended if you do not come to admire her blooming wisteria . . . I notice that I push too hard, and I should not do that. But never before have I tried so hard to invite you to come here because I see how much you mean to my parents. And I don't want them to feel that you come only to see Marguerite. You must come for their sake—because it is your right to be in this house and because I like to have somebody who keeps me company for Sunday breakfast. In my own favor, I can report that I have worked already on seven cantatas today, and the chapter will be very good, so I need somebody who can enjoy this with me . . .

For months I have not worked with such ease! How happy I would be without the worry and concern about my friends, the Curtiuses? . . . Wear

---

1. Schweitzer's youngest sister, who lived with her parents.
2. Of the *Bach* manuscript.
3. Schweitzer's dog.

your gray suit and solid shoes! A hat, too, with which you can walk in the woods . . .

5:30 P.M.—I have to go home.

Yours,<br>Your G

In the evening!
I completed ten cantatas today!

## 100. A. S.

[Celerina]
Sept. 2, 1907
six o'clock in the evening

I sit all by myself in the woods on the road to Pontresina. Tata and the others left for a great excursion in a carriage, and I stayed home to finish the chapter. It is done! I could jump with joy: Motets, Christmas Oratorio, B Minor Mass, the small Mass,[1] all of this, twenty-eight very difficult pages since Thursday morning! And I believe that it is good! Now only the last chapter. No fear of not completing this work; only one chapter left to work on in peace, eight or ten or fourteen days for just one chapter. How have I earned this good fortune? Be happy with me, very happy.

I knew that you needed a letter when you returned to your work. But tell me, why are you so tired again? Your letter is so good, but concerning this, so sad. See, as I put this letter in the mail, I add the invigorating air of the Engadin, my best thoughts, and the fragrance of the pines. I think of you so many times. Often, in the evening, in the middle of a difficult sentence, I put down the pen to spend some minutes with you . . . and at the same moment the church bells of Celerina and of Samaden begin to ring. That was so beautiful. As if your thoughts came with the sounds of the bells.

My room looks out toward the mountains, and I work all day at the open window with a view over fields and rocks. Where did I get the energy to accomplish all this so quickly? But you will also notice how my hand shakes!

Yesterday morning I took a walk alone with Mrs. Schumm[2] and told

---

1. All included in the English edition of Schweitzer's book on Bach.
2. Charlotte Schumm, a widowed friend.

her about you! She was completely "understanding." Tata often speaks with me about you. Yesterday afternoon she interrupted me in my work—it was Sunday, but it had to be half an hour to tell me that nothing could separate you from me. I did not answer a word. She was moved to learn that I owe it to you that I could come spend some days with her.

The printers wrote again that they need more pages of the manuscript this week. I lived in such anguish before I finished that chapter!

I can think very clearly, but I am exhausted and have spells of nausea. This afternoon I was very pale, but now I can breathe normally again.

The hotel is very elegant; I don't fit here with my worn suits. If it were not for Tata, I would not stay here! And these genteel people. They don't even greet each other on the stairs! It is so sad to see this. The Engadin would be beautiful; these elegant hotel guests make me feel like a stranger.

Good-bye. I want to take a little walk to get my blood going, to look for a piece of bark to carve a little boat! Yes, a real boy [ . . . ] Oh, the letter of the two Helenes. Pine fragrance. And Günsbach was good. I am spending every second with you until 10:45 in the evening.

Yours

A.

## 101. A. S.

[Celerina]
Wednesday night, one o'clock in the morning
September 4, 1907

M. G.

I just finished rereading the three chapters I wrote last week. Now I will wrap them, and tomorrow morning they will begin their travel to Strasbourg. You can read them in peace—this is not a request to correct too much—toward the end of next week, you can then mail them to me at Günsbach. We will stay at Celerina until Wednesday, then our ways will part—to Günsbach and to Paris. It would have been too tiring for me to come to another place. Tomorrow I must begin with the last chapter.

To relax, I carved today two little boats from bark, one for Tata and one for Lottie.[1] Tomorrow I will begin to work on a very special piece of bark, for whom? You must guess. My hand hurts from so much writing.

I have to tell you a story about Tata. Yesterday we were invited for brunch by friends of hers at the Grand Hotel at St. Moritz. Luxurious hotel, elegant dresses, music, champagne, beautiful ladies: in short, me in my shabby gray suit, I felt like a flea under the shirt of a beautiful woman. I tried to make conversation with a pleasant young girl and at the same time tried to keep my thoughts with the plans for my chapter. Suddenly, Tata, who had been reading the music program, called laughing from the other table: "Albert, they are playing the waltz from the beautiful Hélène."[2] General amazement. I blush. Lottie bursts with laughter. Tata is very amused, and people ask: "Who is the beautiful Hélène?" At that moment, Tata, who had just gotten her champagne, lifts her glass: "I ask all of you to drink to the beautiful Helene," and the glasses clinked with a beautiful ring. Where were your ears yesterday at 1:25?

In general, my life here is quite monstrous. The printer urges and urges! Just a while ago, I got a rather unfriendly card. I let the others go for a walk and remained here by myself. With Tata hardly any conversation: I read her three of my sermons! That is all. I am too tired. But she is happy. She becomes more understanding . . .

Today we had snow. I went out in the snowstorm and took the road in the direction of Pontresina. Tonight I played a little music.

Will I get a little word from you tomorrow? Do you know how much I think of you? The doors clatter in the storm. I must go to sleep. My eyes begin to hurt. Good night.

Yours,

A.

How did the photograph turn out—the picture the other Hélène took?

1. Charlotte Schumm's daughter; Schweitzer was her guardian.
2. *La Belle Hélène* by Jacques Offenbach (1819–1880).

**102. H. B.**

[Strasbourg]
September 6, 1907

M. G.

Thank you, thank you for the two letters! After that of two days ago, I expected the manuscript, which arrived today with the second letter. To send it on as quickly as possible, I worked assiduously on the index. Do you realize that that takes much more time than I had anticipated? I planned to do four pages an afternoon (this week is completely scheduled for that), but I don't always get as far as I hope because it takes five to six hours. Can you send me the files of Emma Münch? That would be very helpful. I'll stop now; the streetcar is too bumpy, and I will continue later at the office, with what is left concerning our work.

2:45

I continue to write on this small sheet, so you at least see my good intentions to write immediately. That was, however, impossible. I would have written today, anyway, because I don't want you to pass a Sunday without a good-morning greeting from your friend, yet I was a little sad that you expected a letter today and were disappointed. And what you say about your eyes worries me. If the hand gets tired, it can recover, but pay attention to your eyes, I beg you! I know too well what it means to damage good eyes— how it happens, almost without one's noticing it, and how disagreeable and painful the consequences are! Aside from that, you need them for both of us! So, you must promise: avoid working too long with artificial light— what would you do if one day you could not do it at all?! And because there is only that last chapter to be done: arrange it so that it gives you joy, so you will keep good memories of it—the work on this book that meant so much to us and still means much—from the moment when you signed the contract in the Neuhöfler Forest—it is almost two years ago—remember?—to the moment when you held the first bound copy in your hands. It is this book that helped us to justify our liaison to our families, and it will contribute to the building of our future, yours and—

[ . . . ]

Tell me, M. G., from your letters I have the impression that you feel refreshed but far from rested. What is the cause? Nothing but the work? Or the elegant hotel? But that cannot have such a strong effect—just think of the wonderful suits you will have when the *Bach* is completed! Are Tata's and Mrs. Schumm's company not good for you? What about Lottie? This is the first time you mention her, but you don't tell much about her.

I laughed heartily about the brunch story (I hope my friend did not get upset—he does not mention it); this is further evidence that we experience everything together, even such mundane events! Do you know what we did on Wednesday? We, that is the Hoff family (including the oldest daughter of the grass widow, Marie Landsberg) and family Bresslau,[1] and my mother, also a grass widow. We went to the opera and heard *The Merry Widow* in a jubilee performance. And now I understand why I felt such a desire (which I politely expressed) to send you a picture postcard from that place: It was the long-distance effect of the champagne of St. Moritz. Is it possible to prove more convincingly the demoralizing effect of exuberant champagne brunches of distant friends on the friend who has been left behind?—Tell me whether you, too, laugh.

## 103. A. S.

[Günsbach]
Saturday evening
September 14, 1907

M. G.

A word for Sunday morning. I hope to finish in time to bring it to the eight o'clock train; it is almost eight right now. Thank you for the manu-script and the proofs! I cannot answer your question about the Bach family: that must be done when we see each other and can look at the family tree. At the moment, I cannot think of anything but the last chapter. The progress is slow. Without all my energy, I cannot stay at my desk . . . fever . . . To help my father out who is a little nervous, I will substitute for him at church tomorrow with one of my old sermons . . .

Listen: You must come next Saturday because of the index and then stay for Sunday. By then, I will have concluded the last chapter . . . if all goes well. I am too tired to come to Strasbourg, and everything must be

---

1. Hoff, Landsberg, and Bresslau—all relatives.

completed. Do me that favor. [ . . . ] The tired head sends a thousand good wishes for tomorrow morning . . . another eight days of slave labor! Do come on Saturday! We will celebrate the liberation together . . . Do not worry about me . . .

> Yours with all my heart
> Albert

## 104. H. B.

> September 26, 1907

Good morning, M. G.—free man! How do you feel? Has one had a little rest?—

This demanding friend thinks immediately: Now the twenty-four hours of sleep, or at least absolute rest, are over—will I get a little word from my friend tomorrow morning? A note in which he tells me how he enjoys his regained freedom and sends the letter of recommendation for the French Hélène, a request I did not dare to repeat during your days of strain and labor? Can I even risk bothering him to assist me concerning the "Home"?[1]

I dare ask you, my friend, because I need you, your assistance as writer. I have to draft an article that should be published with the most recent list of contributors early next week, in order to present it to the committee at its first session. Content: Thanks for the gifts and for the sympathy plea to continue the support by joining the society—perhaps also the suggestion to donate practical gifts as contributions to dowries?—But don't rush; if I get it by Sunday, it will be soon enough! A good, good night, M. G. I have to write now to Naples. How good to know that you can sleep more than the four hours I get,—I think of that at night.

---

1. A home for unwed mothers that Helene founded in Strasbourg.

## 105. A. S.

[Günsbach]
Friday, September 27, 1907

M. G.

No, you could not have any news from me this morning; I was too drowsy and sleepy yesterday! I wanted this letter to be a joy for myself . . . for the first time in many months, I can write you with a carefree heart, without worry and not in haste! Tell me, "Is it possible that I should live like other people, with hours to breathe freely?" I almost cannot believe it.

And the telegram, what a surprise! What did they say? Yours arrived just at the moment at which we drank to Bach and to my recuperation; then my father lifted his glass and asked us to drink to the health of "intelligent women in general and to that of Miss Bresslau in particular." And that we did. What do you say to that?

## 106. H. B.

[Strasbourg]
Monday evening
September 30, 1907

M. G.

I have to thank you so very much. Since the telegram, I have not had a chance to really speak with you. It is so difficult if one thinks of so many things, yet cannot express them—tonight I felt especially how hard it is not to be able to send you a good word—when one feels that the other may need it.

I am thinking all the time of your mother, the energetic woman, now tied to her sickbed—this figure so imposing that one gets the impression that illness cannot touch her—I feel how deeply I revere her.—And your father, worried, nervous; and you, weak and tired, having to think of everything, watch for all—you poor thing; how I wish I could be with you, to help a little! I am anxiously waiting for your news of tomorrow.

What am I doing? I pity you instead of writing an encouraging letter—

Your telegram! What wonderful news![1] I knew immediately that it was

1. Message: "The *Bach* is done!"

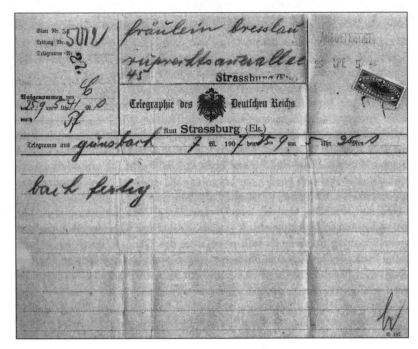

Telegram, 1907: "The *Bach* is done!" *Courtesy of Rhena Schweitzer Miller.*

from you, but when I opened it—I found it when I came home five minutes
after it had arrived—when I saw "Günsbach" my heart seemed to stop for a
moment—I had to push myself to open it all the way. I did not take any
time to reflect; I ran to the post office to send mine and only afterward the
thought came to me: what will they think there? Might it embarrass you because of the people at the post office? Thank you; with your good letter of
Friday, you reassured me and freed me from my worries—thank you with all
my heart for this letter and for that of today.

My eyelids are drooping. I intended to write you about the Dutch review, but I will do that tomorrow. Good night, M. G., a good night for the
Günsbach parsonage and all those who live there!—

## 107. A. S.

Günsbach
Friday evening
October 26 [25], 1907

M. G.

I have just packed my things; my table is empty— . . . the room looks already uninhabited. In spite of the cold and fog, I open the window to hear the fountain . . . and I say good-bye to you in this room . . . I recall our vacations here, from the first time in August when you came from Drei Ähren to us at Günsbach, to the day when you came "to us" at Drei Ähren this time. My heart is filled with deep gratitude. You were so self-sacrificing and kind to the exhausted man, you helped him, encouraged him, and the shared work on Bach has brought us even closer. I relive every moment of our vacation again . . . I see myself at the street near Walbach, when friend Sülti and I waited for you . . . I see you coming up the hill . . . I greet you . . . I push your bicycle . . . everything is like a living dream for me, and I am deeply moved . . . Dream and real life have fused in our lives and become one single thought, one single feeling, and that is the secret of our happiness. I read the letter again that you sent to me at Celerina, in which you speak about our vacation and my room. I see myself at the station at the last visit. You were so tired when you arrived at Günsbach; I explained to you why I had dared to ask you . . . I sit at the bridge at Türkheim with my chemistry book and see your coach approaching . . . and then the good dream . . . then I am in the train that goes up the mountain in the morning fog to Drei Ähren, and in the great curve I see the steam from the engine of the train that goes to Strasbourg and takes somebody with it . . . now Sülti is sniffing . . .

Good evening . . . you see, what we have experienced together in those weeks makes up for all toil and sorrows of life, and it is the deepest happiness humans can experience, . . .I feel and know this, and, filled with gratitude, I kiss your hands . . . Adieu, vacations . . . Adieu, M. G.

Yours

A.

Sunday 10:00 A.M. I just left Günsbach . . . our good Sülti ran after the train and was very sad.

**108. A. S.**

> [Strasbourg]
> Thursday evening
> December 10, 1907

M. G.

Why do I imagine that I will see you tonight? . . . That you will come by here to bring me the basket! . . . I had such a longing to see you . . . I feel tired, very tired . . . Will I see you? I should now begin with my sermon.

. . . It is seven o'clock now. To this moment, I had the hope of seeing you. If you had come, we would have discussed the sermon. Your easy chair expects you.

7:30. I just finished the draft for my sermon: About the Son of Man . . . What is human in religion . . . that true religion makes us true humans . . . and that this is the aim of religion.

. . . But now I am coughing, so much that I can almost not think and write . . . In any case, I will not be at the Dehios[1] after the rehearsal on Wednesday: the rehearsals are so long and tiring. I must go right to bed when I come home. . . . When do we meet here? I am searching in my poor head: Thursday is not free, Friday is not free, Saturday is not free . . . Sunday is not free . . . We poor children!

I expect *Bach* early next week . . . We will celebrate that together . . . A little note. The first since when?

> Yours
> A.

**109. A. S.**

> December 31, 1907
> Toward midnight at home in Strasbourg

M. G.

The last moments of this year are yours. What a conclusion of a year for us—a dream. You at Günsbach at my table, in the quiet and the peace of our house. And you have before you the medal[2] with which I have spent the

---

1. Georg Dehio (1850–1932), professor of art history at the University of Strasbourg.
2. A Christ medal Schweitzer had given to her.

Letter from Albert Schweitzer, 1907.
*Courtesy of Nancy Stewart.*

last hours of the day. It looks at you. Thank you, 1907, for everything you have given us. You are a blessed year. It feels as if we had found our direction and as if we sailed toward the estuary of a large river toward the ocean. No doubts, no fights, no difficult decisions, only learn to wait, to look ahead, not this constant impatient searching. I have learned it, the waiting, but for you it is more difficult.

*Midnight*

Your hand. Let us look at each other. Onward, onward: I believe that we have looked at things at the deepest level. We want to be simple people and serve, serve him, the great and the simple,—the true man, our Lord.

My friend, it is difficult, this life that I require from you. I often ask myself whether it will wear you out, will consume you. You have offered it to me, and I accept it and know that we are deeply happy, and no other happiness would make you happier. So I say: whatever may come, whatever Destiny has in store for us, may we remain who we are, and may the eyes of the Lord always rest on us.

# *1908*

**110. A. S.**

[Strasbourg]
January 4, 1908

M. G.

A surprise. I see my letter waiting for you beside your cup . . . I must tell you that we are spending this evening together . . .

I was so unhappy on the way to the station. It was chaos: twenty-five sermons at once, and how to make a single one out of them? . . . And the fear of saying things that I have not explored deeply enough . . . to give a sermon that is "not lived"! I have been suffering from this since Tuesday, and for the last two days I have really been in despair . . . these are terrible crises.

Then there was also the fact that without showing it, I was very affected by the death of my aunt.[1] I owe her everything . . . we were not very close inwardly, but we had deep respect for each other, and I was very grateful . . . without her, I would never have become the man I am. And now this bond is broken, and I would have liked to demonstrate my affection for her and was looking forward to visiting her in Heiligenstein. I wanted to speak to you about her and about the sermon last night . . .

This morning on the way to the station I had the premonition that it would be a terrible day . . . I saw myself sitting at my desk until two in the morning, at the end of my strength . . . That is why I spoke to you about my sermon almost with loathing. It is terrible—a terrible birth, when you bring

---

1. Sophie Schweitzer.

your innermost thoughts into the world . . . when you must be a prophet and at the same time must say things as a curate . . .

On the train—which hadn't started to move yet—I took out my pencil and began the draft . . . and suddenly there was light. In Colmar, I had established the plan for the second part. . . , when I got to Strasbourg, I wrote a third of the remaining part before dinner, and now at 6:30, my sermon is lying before me finished! I have to share this happiness with you. Just think: to be able to memorize in peace, to rest, and to be able to preach tomorrow without suffering from weariness . . .

And you will know all this before you go to church tomorrow morning. If anyone asks you why I am writing you, here is the reason: I am asking you not to forget to heat the oven in my room.

And tomorrow, our afternoon! It will turn out to be ideal . . . very quiet and peaceful, without restlessness! The afternoon that I wheedled out of you without a word . . . and that I had already given up . . . With this page, I am beginning the big pad. You see that it has turned out to be true: I am making sure that you get letters in Günsbach.

Good evening, m. G. . . . And your pains? And who is lighting your candle for you? . . .

yours

your G.

Good-bye. . . .

## 111. A. S.

[Strasbourg]

Wednesday evening

March 3rd [4th], 1908

I am sending you greetings using your paper and your pen holder—which I got from you. Come and sit by the table. I have lit the oven twice: now it is warm. My supper was sad; it was still cold in the room, and I cooked it for myself; i.e., I baked an egg and boiled milk—because I wanted my housekeeper to get some rest and not come over to my place specially.

I am looking at you in your armchair. I sit down facing you and take both your hands. What is it then, my G.! You unsettled me so much today . . . Why is there such a spirit in you? Was I not good enough to you? Are your heart and your thoughts not filled by the friendship that I am giving you? Have I not kept my promise about "all days that are feast days"?

You are suffering, I know . . . But even in the pain over death our friendship must be to us as the thing that is untouched in life, that stands above all pain and restlessness. I am writing to you as I would speak to you if your were here: disconnectedly, imploringly, beseechingly . . . m. G. . . . m. G. . . .

Apart from my duty, our friendship is the only true happiness in my life: the thing for which life with all that must be borne is worth living, living smilingly and cheerfully as serious human beings can be cheerful. Have you been disappointed in me? . . . I do not want to make you sad . . . Take this note as a loving message from the man who is proud of your friendship . . . and proud of you, but who has the right to demand of you that you be g. at every moment, even when you are exhausted, and who fervently begs you not to question our friendship, not even fleetingly in thought!

I kiss your hand. It is just turning ten.

yours,

A.

## 112. H. B.

Strasbourg i.E.

Ruprechtsauer Allee 45

March 9, 1908

[ . . . ]

I don't want to talk about myself; that is so boring. And now I have had so much light shown through me that there is nothing secret left. Bery,[1] if it were possible one day to photograph thoughts as we do bones—that would be horrible! And who knows what coincidence may lead the insatiable researchers to it one day. But my doctor is nice—what the English call "very decent"; he told me a lot about his wife (so he is already married), and yesterday on the streetcar he even introduced her to me.

I couldn't go to the Cahns'[2] this afternoon because I needed to have a third X-ray; the first two showed there is something there, but not in enough detail; in any case, it is nothing serious; perhaps a harmless bone splinter. So there is not the slightest cause for alarm; I will go to my profes-

1. A nickname the family had given him.
2. Dr. Arnold Cahn (1858–1927), a Strasbourg internist whom Helene was seeing for her back injury.

sor on Wednesday, and on Friday I will tell you what he said—when will I see you again, m. G.?

Good-bye—that is all that I am thinking—and happy days for you until then.[ . . . ]

## 113. A. S.

[Santa Margherita]
Saturday morning
April 25, 1908

[ . . . ]

I am a little bit sad because you give me no better news of Mr. Back and Mr. Sleep. How well I understand you when you say that you do things like someone who feels that he is already absent! But bear up, m. G.!

As for me, I am amazed at the enthusiasm with which I am tackling my studies. The nine hours of work a day are no burden to me. And yet it is not at all amusing to read lecture notes. But I have a certain taste for simple cramming! Your friend is a strange person.

The change of air did me an extraordinary amount of good. I am very peaceful and fresh. And so far I have progressed as rapidly as I had intended. So let us be glad. I am so contented that I can work. The fear of not finishing is no longer paralyzing me. I am enjoying the learning: in brief, I am seventeen years old! [ . . . ]

Good-bye, m. G.

yours,

A.

I am leaving you again and returning to Ewald's lecture notes. Mornings 9:30 to 12:15 physiology; 2:00 to 4:30 anatomy; 8:00 to 10:00 physics and botany. "That's how we live, that's how we live, that's how we live every day." [1]

---

1. From a student song.

Helene Bresslau, 1908. *Courtesy of Rhena Schweitzer Miller.*

## 114. A. S.

[On the train]
Sunday evening
June 21, 1908

St. John's Day . . . St. John's Day[1] . . . The train will be in Vendenheim soon: I have seated myself so that I can see the blue line of a certain wood . . . and the memories come rushing in on me. Do you remember the great expedition to Brumath when we danced in a ring in the evenings, when we "camped"? That was on St. John's Day, and we talked a lot on the way. I am trying in vain to calculate how many years ago that was . . . How beautiful

1. Schweitzer is quoting a passage from Wagner's *Die Meistersinger von Nürnberg.*

it is! The hay smells wonderful! What life, what power is revealed in nature! It might make you forget the sad underlying note of your being! If I had been able to take you along, we could have talked about the little sad note in your letter! It is true . . . we have had nothing of one another for a long time now. You did your duty to a friend and relative. That is the comfort we have: we are truly not egoistic.

Beside me, two little lieutenants are making enthusiastic travel plans: They will leave a week from tomorrow at 3:42: Constance, Lindau, Innsbruck, Kufstein, Munich . . . they are even discussing the hotels where they will break the journey . . . their anticipation is giving them such pleasure as only anticipation can. The Hofbräuhaus[1] plays a large role . . . We will never be that young again . . . I am almost jealous . . .

But I think as you do: We must have something of one another again! In five weeks, we will part, and who knows when we will meet again . . . While I am writing to you, I am dreaming. I gaze longingly into Nature . . . a white fog is covering everything . . .

[ . . . ]

Yours,
A. Your great one

## 115. A. S.

August 1, 1908
Saturday, 6:30

M. G.

M. G. is unpacking her suitcases at an unknown seaside resort, and her friend is sitting on the rock and dreaming. He has been dreaming since Thursday—if dreaming means living in a different place in your thoughts than in the flesh—but this evening he is dreaming with pen in hand, for he must have pages of letters ready to send off as soon as his friend's address reaches him.

On Thursday, he was in the situation of a herring being pulled apart by a student with a hangover: one friend was traveling from Basel to the Grimmi, the other from Strasbourg to Rotterdam, and he was sitting in the train from Basel to Strasbourg and thinking first of the one and then of

---

1. In Munich.

the other. And when I was back in Strasbourg, it seemed so strange to me that I could not visit you . . . My thoughts have been with you since then. In the evenings, I imagine that you are sleeping—or not sleeping—, rocked by the waves of the Rhine . . . I saw you lying all afternoon in a deck chair and dreaming. . . . At 3:00 today, I saw you throwing your arms around the neck of your cousin Ange,[1] and now I know where you are with all your beautiful dresses . . .

And your letter. I got it this morning when I woke up in bed and read it while I drank my milk. I thank you with all my heart.

I have not done much work over the last few days. I felt a need to re-cover, although I wasn't really tired. The meetings for planning the concert hall organ have kept me very busy.[2] And now a Saturday that belongs to me! But not entirely. I saw that my father would be happy to have a substi-tute tomorrow. I made him the offer. He accepted enthusiastically. But I will preach a good old-fashioned Strasbourg sermon.

I had just closed my eyes for a long quarter of an hour. It is very fine weather, a real August day . . . Then I saw myself at the commencement exercises at the Mühlhausen Gymnasium; coming home as a graduate . . . so many remarkable memories. 7:00—we must go home,—Sülti is remind-ing me . . . Workers are needed to cut beans in September. I advised my mother that instead of hiring Polish workers to deal with the shorthanded-ness, to take people we know, e.g., Frl. B. She will be informed; people were very pleased; i.e., my mother! (So was I.)

I kiss Cousin Ange's hand—

And am your G

[ . . . ]


## 116. A. S.

Thursday,
August 6, 1908[3]


Without your letter, I would have forgotten the 6th of August for I have no awareness of dates these days. It is as if I had lost the yardstick for time. And now your letter, which I received this morning, is plunging me

1. Johanna Engel. See p. 32n. 1.
2. The Strasbourger Sängerhaus.
3. The tenth anniversary of Schweitzer and Helene's first meeting.

deep in reveries that almost distract me. I am trying to imagine how everything was, and if the weather were not so vile, I would go to the Schiltigheimer Ring to see the house again. I see the table very clearly before me, and how we and "they" sat there. But I can no longer remember what your face looked like in those days. The face that impressed itself so deeply on my spirit later erased that first impression. Only I believe . . . that you are much more beautiful now than you were then . . . or was I not yet so receptive in those days?

In the evening, we took you home. What would have turned out differently in our lives without that meeting? When I say "ten years," a shudder passes over me . . . Ten years that I took from your life; you could be married and the mother of growing children if I had not stood in the way . . . and thus they were years of loneliness, of struggles . . . but also with moments of great and deep feelings of happiness. If I were with you, I would take both your hands and kiss them, even in front of Cousin Ange, for on such an anniversary some allowances ought to be made. But I am spared this temptation . . . I do it in thought from afar . . . [ . . . ]

In the evenings, I am so tired that I fall into bed. But last night, tired as I was . . . I wrote another consoling letter to poor Zeppelin,[1] a little bit of a sermon that may do him good. I don't know what led me to do it. But it did me good to let myself go. The letter seemed reasonable to me when I read it over—. At this moment, m. G. is reading her friend's little note. In spite of my weariness, I generally work at the organ after dinner.

You ask what the great one does at the hospital? First he does rounds with the doctor in Ward 124 (men's ward); then he assists with analyses, blood pressure measurements, injections, patient histories, and watches how X-rays are made. At 10:00, he goes to Ward 121 (men's ward); the game is repeated, except that he now performs auscultations and percussions on his own and has his results checked later. I have already learned an enormous amount.

My title of Ph.D. is very useful to me because everybody calls me Dr. Schweitzer, so that I get much greater respect than the other assistants . . . although some of them know more than I do. But it's the title that does it.

I am leaving you: I must rest, or else I will not be fresh for duty. And I

---

1. Schweitzer enjoyed seeing the Zeppelin prior to its accidental destruction on August 15, 1908.

still have to compose a wedding sermon for tomorrow . . . and my foolish
holiday brain just doesn't want to.

Will I have time to add a few words of greeting? I want to mail the letter as I leave so that it will go by the evening train. In any case, give my regards to Cousin Ange.

[ . . . ]

## 117. H. B.

[Katwijk aan Zee]
Friday, August 7, 1908

My Great One,

I am lying on the beach, and a very strong wind is blowing. Someone
doesn't have any idea how difficult it is to write him from here! And one
doesn't want to be in one's room, either, does one? I have already been in
there too long reading the paper. Poor Zeppelin! Now I am triply sorry not
to have been in Strasbourg on the 4th. Some are destined to experience
great historic moments, others to miss them. Cousin Ange finds that it is
enough if one member of the family experiences them. She is kneeling a
few paces in front of me in the sand and is painting a Dutchwoman against
the sea, a fine head with a very characteristic profile. The sea is magnificent
today, but it's my day to not swim. Yesterday the waves were excellent while
we were swimming.

Holland is not the country I thought it was.

This is the third letter, and I wrote two cards, and I have had just one
word from my friend.

Of course, I know that he has a lot to do, and that one letter was so
nice, with Günsbach air and Günsbach peace. But why so serious, m. G.?
You feel cheerful; is it only because we, too, are becoming older and more
mature, and because with all our happiness a serious life lies before us?—

M. G. is reading *Wilhelm Meister*. Do you know, I, too, had intended to
take Goethe along on vacation? But in the end I didn't do it, and it was
probably a good thing because I am without energy. But I would really like
to read something together with you. Do you know the *Elective Affinities?*
Or shall we plan to try it at Günsbach—that would be very nice; think of
the rock or the woods—at the campsites on the way to Hohrod!

How are things at the hospital? My great one will not seriously despair if he doesn't succeed just as he wants in everything immediately on the second day, will he?

Think of poor Zeppelin: the man can become a model and a source of courage.

Has m. G. already visited Ella? She will enjoy the story.

Yesterday I kept thinking of ten years ago and all the time that has passed since then, but I can't see it as a unified whole. I relive particulars, including all the little details, but it is impossible for me to think myself back into that former way of thinking and feeling. It is as if I were standing in another world today, separated from the earlier one by Sleeping Beauty's slumber and without the smallest wish to sink back into it. I often wonder that with all the rich and beautiful things that life has already brought me, I have never wished a single hour back again. It may be because I project my life too much into the future.—

Did you read the beautiful words of Liebermann and Hofmann at Leistikow's funeral?[1]

Now when I think of death, I catch myself thinking that I would not for any price exchange what I ought to and want to experience in life for what I have already lived. Another thought I had in these days: Bery, you have dedicated so many books to women, or intend to dedicate them, but none to your mother—or am I mistaken? I cannot remember to whom the *Kant* is dedicated.

Strange, all the things one has time to think about here—and day and night my eternally beloved ocean sounds in my thoughts and dreams. But it's not really dreaming. It's more a lethargy of thought in which one is not conscious of the where and why. I am perpetually astonished when I consider how little rest my great one allows his brain—and needs to allow it, if I compare it to my need to recuperate.—That is not human nature—it is something almost superhuman in your nature, my great one, which has such great reserves of strength!

[ . . . ]

Good-bye, m. G.! I will stop, I am all stiff!

> With all my heart,
> L.

---

1. Max Liebermann (1847–1935) and Hans Hofmann (1880–1966) were German painters, and Walter Leistikow (1865–1908) was a Russian landscape artist and printmaker.

## 118. A. S.

On the journey,
August 15, 1908
[On the train after Basel]

[ . . . ]

This sleeping car is somewhat better than the others, and your friend is happy to have a chance to have some conversations with a certain someone. The weather in Basel is fresh and clear. I met Moeckel from the orchestra with his bag and baggage and find it amusing to travel with him. He plays the viola. It is very remarkable to think that I am returning to the Grimmi again. I have a feeling that it is not even possible and keep asking myself how I deserve to have such happiness. You would not believe how much I am looking forward to it. I am like a child. Yesterday at four o'clock I kept telling myself that I would get into the omnibus the next day at the same time, and then I would once more travel the road that leads up into the little valley, with the hunchback as my coachman. It is as if I were being given a present. And then to see the stars tonight, to listen to the brook and call everything to mind that I have already thought and worked out. I rediscover a part of my life there. And I feel that it is something healthy and strong in me that keeps drawing me into this landscape that I understand: I am growing younger.

I already have the outlines of sermons in my head and will write them down on the Grimmi. I will even write whole sermons. Did I tell you that I am planning to preach sermons about the parables this winter?

I must tell you that your style in French is clear and really "French." One can tell that you write without any difficulty. If someone had told the professor's little girl who asked the poor little privatdozent while they were cycling at the polygon, "What is your language, then, Doctor?" and that so bluntly and saucily . . . that the professor's little girl would write to the privatdozent in French one day . . . but everything comes as it has been predetermined by fate. [ . . . ]

With deep and good thoughts for my friend.
Your G.

**119. H. B.**

[Strasbourg]
Saturday,
August 22, 1908

[ … ]

After I had written to you from Bonn, I got a card from your mother saying that she was going to Seelisberg and would probably not be back until the 3rd or 4th of September. She says that Marguerite will represent her and that I can come earlier and live in the upstairs room. From this, I conclude that the house is still quite full. Here I sit like Buridan's ass and am quite undecided. You will be angry with me again—I know that look when something does not suit you—and I am so afraid of it—but I can't change it—I am afraid of crowds of people, and on the other side the prospect of traveling with you is so tempting; the journey from Bonn to Strasbourg was so terrible again!

You see, Bery—I don't know if you can understand this—I have such an unquenchable need for rest—when I came to Strasbourg this time, I thought: "I will give up Günsbach entirely." You must not think of what I would take from you by doing that—I would be taking just as much from myself, if not more, for I suffer more when we are parted, and I do not have a second friend. You also must not think that this is the outpouring of a momentary dark mood—of course, people have more of the spirit of adventure when they are fresher and are deluded about their strength—but that is just it: the very sober judgment that I am constantly either deceiving myself or wanting to deceive myself. The fact that my beloved sea was too strong for me showed me how much I need to recover. But I *want* to go into the high country—even if I had to leave tomorrow. Now try to put yourself in my position; please try, dear, as much as you can. I look like the picture of health (it's true that Ella says I don't, but I have eyes of my own), and still all I want to do is lie on the sofa all day. I have not the slightest wish to see or do anything—quite the contrary. I shrink from it. I am going to Günsbach, to a house where people are as good and kind to me as if I belonged there—and where all their goodness and kindness cannot give me the feeling of belonging—quite the contrary. From time to time, they make me conscious of the fact that I have no right to it. You may call it oversensitive, but that doesn't mean that I can prevent it from happening again, nor can you deny that it has a spark of justification. And now look: I have written to cancel my visit to my relatives in Frankfurt who have known me forever and who let me do whatever I like because of the double journey. It is painful to me to take as much rest as I would wish and as I could easily have in the presence of people who do not understand my condition and who can't consider me so old and in so much need of recuperation. You must understand that it is the same in Günsbach—the painful part remains, even if perhaps it would be possible to obtain some rest because m. G. is there and tries to make things easier for me. And it is intensified by the fact that your mother's letter happened to come in the one good week, and I answered her so confidently that I hoped not to come back to Günsbach as the eternal invalid. If I am to keep this promise, I ought not to go there now.

I have not answered your last card: for one thing, I didn't know how, and for another, I didn't know where. I beg you to do it for me, and I entrust the decision to you. You know everything now. I am not ill, but I am at the same point, perhaps even a little further back, than when I went to the seaside. This journey, which was begun with so much hope, was a failed experiment that no one can do anything about because no one—least of all myself—knows what is the problem with my foolish nerves. That can't be changed now; the main thing is to make good use of the rest of my vacation (I will at least try to get an extension). I don't dare to decide what is right.

[ . . . ]

I *can* journey whenever I want or ought to, starting from Wednesday; write your opinion and commands. If I am to go to Günsbach, it would be nicest if you were to journey with me on the 4th. Adieu, m. G., and don't be angry with me, will you? Best wishes to Tata and Lottie, too.

Your foolish friend!

## 120. A. S.

[Grimmialp, Grand Hotel Kurhaus]
Monday morning,
August 24, 1908

I have just come back from my last walk with Tata; the weather was so beautiful. When I found your letter waiting for me on the table, I thought, "It must have better news." And again, it's sad . . . sad. But just think, I am not at all discouraged. I have a kind of deep premonition that you are moving toward recovery. I understand all your considerations, absolutely. Even the part about "justification." Now I want to tell you what my mother thinks. She tells herself that you are the woman who means infinitely much in my life, something deep and holy, and that you shared the work with her son when he could not have gone on without you! And that makes her proud, thankful that someone is dedicating herself in such a way to her son . . . and proud to have this woman with her. Here is no such thing anymore as the world's law, but only the deep, moral law. I implore you: do not come for your sake or for my sake, but for my mother's sake . . . and partly for us, too. When will we have such holidays again? The happiness of your friend who is resting will heal you.

Tata says that the sea was certainly too strong, but that you won't begin to feel how much good it has done you for ten days! She is determined to comfort me.

With regard to rest at our house, you probably don't know that Marguerite and the boys are there only while my mother is away and that she will return to Colmar with them as soon as my mother is back. So have no fear of people. . . . And then the "population shortage" in the country! Surely your strength will suffice for culling beans.

So because you place the decision in my hands, I am writing to Günsbach that we will come home together sometime during the day on Wednesday.

[ . . . ]

## 121. A. S.

[Günsbach]
Wednesday, three o'clock
September 23, 1908

I got up early to get your letter. As I was reading it, my mother came in to ask me about your news (I had told her yesterday that you would write to me about your visit to the doctor), and she seemed very concerned. . . .

So there it is, the news. It is what I had expected, and now it is a question of gathering up one's patience and doing one's duty. But I am already relieved at the thought that you are doing something for yourself . . .

Marcelle[1] came around ten o'clock this morning. We went to the vineyard to gather peaches and grapes. Then I packed up three packages: two with peaches only for the Münch families in Mühlhausen and Strasbourg,

1. Adele Herrenschmidt's niece.

and one with peaches and grapes for my friend. At noon, I took them to the station with Marcelle. My friend is to have the same breakfast as in Güns-bach because she is still on holiday! So, I'll see to it that this fruit is not fea-tured at the lunch table! The other members of my family can be granted some only as an act of grace. [ . . . ]

My family sends greetings with the recommendation that you should take good care of yourself, and I kiss your hand . . .

Always go to bed early.

Yours,

your G.

## 122. A. S.

[Günsbach]

Thursday morning

September 24, 1908

M. G.

I am sitting on the little wall of the vineyard with the peaches. We are expecting Cousin Elise for dinner, and I have been sent to gather peaches. Sülti at my feet, the basket beside me . . . sun, clouds, and a little bit of wind, a very beautiful mild autumn. It is just turning eleven. This morning I did a lot of work on medicine.

Yes, your letter was a surprise! And a good one. Just think, I was already planning to write to you today that you should change the hour to five o'clock! So that you can get a good rest and do your work! And now you an-ticipate my letter.

You cannot imagine how intensively I think of you at that hour . . . the hour of growing healthy for work . . .

My mother thinks that it would be wise for you to wear a very well-fitting corset for a time. I pass the advice on to you without insisting on it; in questions of the wardrobes of my lady friends, I get involved only if it is a matter of outer garments.

[ . . . ]

Yesterday I met Christian, the bailiff, and he told me that last week in the late afternoon he had seen "e Wibsmansch" [1] gathering peaches in our orchard. I said that perhaps it was you. No, he replied, "s'isch nit das wisse

---

1. Alsatian dialect: "a woman."

Mansch g'she, wo als mit der geht." [1] Since then, you have been called nothing but "s'wisse Mansch." [2]

I am going home. Adieu, sun, good-bye, friend.

[ . . . ]

## 123. A. S.

On the train to Barcelona
Tuesday, five o'clock
October 20, 1908

[ . . . ]

We have crossed the border, and you see that the Spanish trains do not prevent a friend from writing to his friend, as was the case on the French train. For the last two hours in France, I stood in the corridor, watched the landscape, and recited my lecture. I think that I have it in my head and can give it this evening if necessary. Tomorrow I will be busy all day getting acquainted with the organ, so that I won't experience what my friend does when she goes from the Ruprechtsauer organ to the St. Nicholas organ to play her little piece.

Georg Walter[3] is sitting across from me and asking me what I might be writing to make me smirk like that. Let him tend to his knitting.

It is just beginning to rain. Up until now, the weather has been very fine. A wonderful sunset over the ocean.

Spain is beautiful; magnificent colors. It is much more beautiful than southern France, and the land seems to be better cultivated here, too. I will go to the organ this evening so that my fingers can get used to the instrument. The Spanish women are really beautiful, but I find them so strange in everything that corresponds to my concept of women that they do not interest me. . . .

Now it's beginning to get dark. The Pyrenees are vanishing in the clouds. And I am thinking of the darkness breaking in on Sunday evening, of that hour of deep recollection together with you . . . The joy of sensing

---

1. "It's not the woman in white who sometimes goes about with you." Helene usually wore white when visiting Günsbach.

2. "The woman in white."

3. A singer who performed in the same concert as Schweitzer.

that you are gradually feeling better and of hearing your thoughts. It was as if we had tried out the two instruments to see if they were in tune, and they were. Everything that you said was so true, and I went home as if in a dream; everything was so beautiful . . . and I did not begrudge Felix the little bit of my friend that he got.

It has stopped raining . . . but I must stop writing you. The light has been lit in the sleeping car, and I am afraid of harming my eyes if I write to you by artificial illumination.

I am already trembling at the thought that I might forget the cards for your father. When will a word from my friend arrive? In case you have lost my address, here it is again: A.S. c/o M. Millet, 13 Alt de Sant Pere, Barcelona. Being yours, I kiss your hand! How far away we are from each other.

## 124. A. S.

> Sunday evening,
> November 22, 1908
> On the train to Paris

M. G.

All alone in my compartment. And next to me is a nice first-class compartment, completely empty; I will get into it in Avricourt because it will fill up after Nancy.

I feel so peculiar. Previously it was so exciting when the train began to move because everything that made my life bright was waiting for me over there. And now that is no longer true; nothing in my being would draw me to Paris except the thought of doing Tata good and comforting her . . . But I still think of those earlier times when my heart almost stopped beating as the train to Paris left the station as the most beautiful sensations of my life . . .

A terrible storm is raging; you can feel the wind throwing itself against the car, and the train struggling to move forward. The rain is lashing against the windows; everything is trembling and quaking . . . and my friend is nestling in her bed, closing her eyes, and turning in dreams to her G., whom the train is carrying out into the dark night, and telling herself that she is very happy to be lying like that, but that it would also be very nice to make this journey with her G . . . this journey that is a little longer than the one from Colmar to Strasbourg . . . Are you thinking of that day a week ago?

Zabern. You see how slowly your friend is writing to you. And he began right away in Strasbourg and interrupted himself only to eat three pieces of rum chocolate and to find them enjoyable, even if the papers are worried about the state of humanity . . . and that one must preserve tradition.

But all this is only the introduction. On the way home, I went to see Curtius, who was sitting alone in his office, smoking his cigar. "This Fräulein Bresslau is such a sweet girl! There is something enchanting about her . . . you have to like her . . . I wonder what will become of her?" . . . Silence . . . then Bery confirmed what the president had said. Please confess when the president kisses your hand for the first time.—But do you know (I dare to tell you this from a distance) that you had a very special charm that evening and that your soul was mirrored in your face as I've rarely seen it? . . . I may tell you that . . . and also that I am very happy about it.

Saarburg. In the mountains, the wind is growing calmer . . . I will think about my sermon. Good night . . . such a long letter! And your stupid friend has forgotten to ask for the air pillow! Another time his friend must think of it.

I kiss your beautiful hand.
Your G.

## 125. H. B.

[Strasbourg]
Tuesday morning
November 24, 1908

M. G. A letter from the streetcar—how long since B. got the last one? Thank you for yours, my friend. Did I think of the day a week before on Sunday evening? No, dear, not one tiny thought, not even of the possibility of making a rather long journey with m. G. What did you think about? Well, I will tell you about my evening: when the Great one had gone, I sat down at my desk to make corrections and remained there with a single interruption, namely, dinner, until ten o'clock . . . It was very good that I had not promised to come to the organ, for a little student came and stayed for dinner, and if I had not had to work, I would have had to help my mother entertain him. By ten o'clock, he had gone, and my work was done—as much as I could do that evening—, and I went to bed, and at ten o'clock I did indeed think of the Great one. I fell asleep immediately, and woke up a short time later, very disturbed, because I thought that I had missed the great one's departure time. But when I looked at the clock, it was 11:30. I accompanied him to the station, and when I had settled him—in thought—in a nice, completely empty compartment, I remembered the air pillow! I was completely in despair, and my first thought was to get up and take it to him. But I had to admit: too late!—And then I woke up almost every hour and thought of how my poor Great one was spending the night on the train.

*In the office*

I will finish up quickly in order to mail my greetings before I go home. Why didn't I send any yesterday? Your poor G. had scarcely gotten home for dinner last night before she had to prepare to accompany her father to the theater. He was in a bit of a bad mood and did not want to go alone; my mother didn't feel like it but didn't want him to stay home so it fell to me. A premiere, three one-acts, very interesting, even somewhat amusing. What did my G. do last night? The concert is tomorrow, isn't it? I can only guess because this time I know nothing at all about it.

The weather seems to be getting a little better—how is it in Paris?

Big committee meeting today, a string of urgent visits tomorrow; in-between I have to see how I can fit in practice for Gerold and my severe organ master. Was Felix there on Sunday eve.?

And how was it?

> Good-bye, my dear G., do not forget
> Your G.

**126. A. S.**

> December 31, 1908 . . . 11:30
> At home

I have been visiting my sister in Hausbergen; she is not well; and I just got back. It is no longer very warm in my room; I will get into bed afterward to await the ringing at midnight . . .

And I am thinking of you, my great one, with great and joyful peace. In your friendship, you give me something so simple and deep . . .

Our eyes are fixed more than usual on what is to come . . . We feel that it is coming closer . . . Do you know, we will have to do without many things, and we cannot yet imagine what it will be like to be thrown into a completely different kind of life . . . but we will triumph over it and help one another . . .

It is moving: you are the only person who has a share in my "future." When I think of the others, my parents, my brothers and sisters, Tata, my friends, I tell myself: you will think of them two or three more times when a year comes to an end and I am sitting in my little room on the Thomasstaden . . . and then you will be far away from them when new years begin . . . and you are a contrast to all these people . . . and you will share the anxieties of these new years with me . . . and there will come a time when I will no longer write to you on New Year's Eve, but only say to you with a look at such time: . . . forward . . . to meet the new year . . . one more step toward the end . . . the end . . . enigma of being, impenetrable . . . the end . . .

yours

A

# *1909*

Sunday evening
January 30 [31], 1909
[On the train to Paris]

M. G.

[ . . . ]

Since getting back from Günsbach, I think of our journey that evening every Sunday . . . and the feeling that I had from the beginning is growing stronger and stronger in me: that this was a beautiful hour in our lives, one of the most beautiful, and its blessings will accompany us . . . And when I then began to speak with you, I was so self-conscious and wondered if you would divine everything that I wanted to put into that hour . . . and you did feel it! Thanks from the bottom of my heart . . . Not until later did we become conscious of all that we said to each other and all that we agreed in silence for the time that we will be permitted to spend together . . . Can there be any other human beings for whom it is Sunday in the same way that it is for us? . . .

I will see Tata . . . how many times now? . . . then she will be lonely and will have nothing more to hope for from life . . . I was the only human being who kept pace with her and who could comfort her . . .

Now comes the forest between Zabern and Saarburg . . . I walked here with my aunt in the fine autumn weather.

Good evening. I kiss your hand. This is the letter of a dreamer.

Yours,
G.

**128. A. S.**

> [Strasbourg]
> Sunday evening
> February 28, 1909, 11:30

M. G.

We must celebrate this moment together . . . the beginning of my holidays. Do you have a sense of what this hour means for me. . . ? A terribly difficult winter lies behind me, and I survived it without injury . . . It held!

I look at the picture of my friend who died, and it seems to me as if she wanted to ask me if I really endured all that. And now I am going toward the spring. Eight weeks in which I can work in complete peace and recuperate at the same time! Isn't that splendid?

Celebrate this hour with me; I feel so wonderful . . . the feeling of still being able to do something and of feeling vital powers within.

Tomorrow Günsbach, the rock, the quiet manse.—Is it a dream?

Did you notice how moved I was this evening? The whole time I couldn't stop thinking that I would not give many more concerts at St. Thomas's. And while I was explaining the organ, you were there . . . and I will be separated from all these people one day, except for someone who stood at a distance today . . . And if it seems that I am completely taken up by other people, you must tell yourself that this thought is supporting me . . .

Was it beautiful? . . . I felt so solemn that I cannot judge for myself, and I only asked myself if it was worthwhile for all these dear people who came.

I am so happy that I am becoming stupid as a result . . . holidays, holidays!

And you will be free next month . . . and in medicine it's not all piecework any more.

Are you thinking at this moment that your friend is happy? . . . I had to pass by you so that you could feel it . . .

Good night. I was together with my dead friend and my living friend . . .

> Your G.

Helene Bresslau and Albert Schweitzer, 1909. *Courtesy of
Rhena Schweitzer Miller.*

## 129. A. S.

[Günsbach]
Thursday evening
June 3, 1909

M. G. Hyelyena!

It has just struck 8:30 from the Günsbach church. Sülti and I have settled down on the rock and are celebrating the first Thursday evening with
you. You can imagine the picture. I told him what is going on, and he has a
suitable expression on his face. It is lovely, very lovely weather. In the
course of the day, Nature was refreshed by a quarter hour of rain, and now
the fresh grass smells so good that you could fall asleep . . . Dog roses are

blossoming on the rock, and the scent of elder comes from the distance . . . there are caterpillars there, too, but I pretended I didn't see them because tonight is a feast day. A great feast: m. G. has arrived! She will rest tonight in a good bed. Is it really true that you have arrived?[1] I can't believe it, for since Tuesday evening I keep seeing you in the compartment; this morning, when the sound of the wheels on the tracks had ceased for me, I still kept hearing it for you, and it seems to me that it is only just now stopping.

Have you really arrived? How is your room?

It is incredible to think that you are so far away. This is the first Thursday evening, which I dedicate to you. It's nice that it is taking place on the rock. It is an evening in which nature lies in a dream, intoxicated by its richness and its scents; everything is drenched in saturated green . . .

M. G., what are you doing? The waiting is so long! But I am not worried (although I know that your back is hurting you now). But now rest, m. G. The time will come when you must work . . . how the river roars!

Now it is striking nine. By your time, it is already later, and perhaps you have already lain down and are waiting for "ten o'clock" . . .

Last night I celebrated ten o'clock at the moment when the train left the station in Munich, and it was like a relief to me to tell myself that for this second night I would share your lot of sleeping over the rolling wheels . . . or staying awake.

I want to tell you about the rest of the journey with the other Hyelyena.[2] I had finally found a nice place for my traveling companion in the corridor, the female attendant's seat, and an hour later the other seat in the corridor was vacant. That was very pleasant. We sat comfortably and had air, and we wrote and talked, and she really opened up. In Salzburg, we sat at a table, had lunch, and wrote cards. The other Hélène had my pencil holder and left it on the table. We were just on the point of getting into the cable car when some sense of unease made me feel for the pencil. I just had time to run back and get it.

From Salzburg to Munich, we took our places in the corridor and watched the scenery. She tied her handkerchief around her head, knotted

1. Helene is on her way to Russia.
2. Hélène Barrère.

in the Roman style, which gave her a very distinctive appearance. The scenery was very beautiful, with the evening sun falling on the Alps. We spoke little, but we experienced nature . . . For a moment, we seriously considered interrupting the journey and spending a day in the Alps. That was when we saw the Chiemsee. Both of us said, "If the other one were here, we would do it" . . . the other one who was traveling through the Puszta. I told her a little about you, and we got to know one know one another. We arrived in Munich at eight o'clock in the evening. I took her to her boarding house and invited her to have dinner with me because my train did not leave until ten o'clock! And that is what we did. You got the card . . . Farewell in the streets of Munich, and Bery had the remarkable experience of standing there without a Helene and having the feeling of a leafless tree . . . Strolled very calmly along the line of railway cars while others were hurrying because now he didn't have to look for a good place for any Helenes. The feeling of this carefree traveling was splendid and sad—

And then ten o'clock . . .

Good night. Almost nothing can be seen now. The first Thursday letter.

Good night, m. G. I kiss your hand.

**130. A. S.**

[Strasbourg]
Thursday evening
June 10th, 1909

[Mademoiselle H. Bresslau
c/o Dr. Amtschislawsky
Runowitschina, Southern Russia, nr. Poltawa]

M. G.

As it was striking ten, I was sitting in the corner of my sofa wrapped in thoughts and feelings. That was very beautiful. This evening belongs to you; it is so remarkable to tell myself that you, hundreds of miles away, know that this evening is dedicated to you and that you are thinking together with me. And it is so soothing.

You are sharing the evening with a draft of the sermon. I hope that is not grounds for jealousy. It is so good for me to have this peaceful evening for my sermon, too.

But I want to tell you. Received the letter from m. G.! And what a good letter. What is your back doing? Is it really going so well, or was the lumbago so bad that you didn't notice your back anymore? . . . On Sunday evening, I dined with the Bresslau parents . . . just the three of us! It was very nice. During the meal, I told the story of the journey to Vienna; I said that I had accompanied you to the station; then your father bewailed the fact that you certainly had not had enough money and asked me if I hadn't given you any. To this I replied . . . because I could not bring a "No" to my lips . . . —that I gave you fifteen crowns in Austrian currency, but you would pay it back to me on your return. It was also enjoyable to show the Bresslau parents that one is looking out for Mademoiselle Helene and that it is even permitted to become involved in her financial affairs.

Later we went over to the sofa, and I began to pay discreet court to Mother Bresslau . . . just as one runs one's hands over the keys of the instrument . . . it produced a good tone.

But I left at 9:30; I had to spend ten o'clock on Sunday alone in order to be in Vienna in my thoughts! How wonderfully all of this is suited to Sunday evening! I was in my room. And waking up on Monday . . . I didn't even forget the stroke of seven in the morning . . . and then the ship . . .

I know that it will be just the same again next Sunday.

The other Hyelyena will come at 3:10 on Sunday; we will pay a visit to your parents, go for a walk in Strasbourg, and in the evening—after dinner at my house—we will go to the organ at St. Thomas's. She will be leaving at 11:25 at night.

[ . . . ]

## 131. A. S.

[Strasbourg]
Monday, June 28th, 1909

M. G.

I am really losing the courage to write to you, and I could weep when I think that all the beautiful letters that I sent to your address are traveling around somewhere in an unknown region.

This is only a little word, for I really haven't been alive for the past week; my worries about you were scarcely over when my worries about Sunday began . . . and then there's rainy weather that makes one sad . . . It will pass, but at the moment I am merely vegetating.

Again it is midnight, and I have not done half of what I ought to have done . . .

The writing and the galley proofs[1] from Vienna are taking up so much time, and not a single free Sunday . . . All this only to tell you why I let Thursday pass without writing you; I thought of you all evening, but my pen would not obey me.

Thank you for your letters. Write me more often, spoil me a little . . . and tell me what your back is doing . . .

On Thursday evening, I will write you a long letter, for just now my head cannot go on . . .

This should not make you sad; it will pass . . . and I cannot disguise my-self . . . and otherwise you will not understand my silence . . . oh, the lost letters . . .

And this one may get lost, too . . .

I kiss your hand . . . ten o'clock is always there . . .

yours,<br>your G.

Please send me one or two addressed envelopes in every letter. Copying the filthy Russian letters makes me wild!

## 132. H. B.

Runowitschina,<br>July 5, 1909

M. G., my poor friend,

Your letter of the 28th has just arrived—the first apart from the two things from the 3rd, the card with Hélène Barrère and the letter from Emmy.[2] It is a little bit your fault; because you are not capable of doing what everyone else can do is a serious sign of the nervous condition in which my poor G. finds himself. And his friend is so far away and cannot even help him in correcting and mailing off the proofs—that is really sad—

I had written to you yesterday, as I do every Sunday, but my letter turned out a little melancholy—you can probably imagine it!—, so I am sending only the part that I am too lazy to write over again. At the same

---

1. For a book about organ building.
2. A friend from the Frankfurt hospital.

time, I am enclosing an addressed envelope, but because this letter probably will not arrive before the 12th, please answer immediately and just this
once send the letter by registered mail so that it is sure to arrive before I
leave. I would prefer to send you my next address, but I don't know it yet
myself. My plan is to go to Moscow for two or three days. Then I will travel
to Stockholm either via St. Petersburg-Helsingfors or via Libau to meet
Cousin Ange and perhaps also my brother Hermann. I am still waiting for
information about the sailing situation and possible difficulties caused by
cholera.

I do intend to be reasonable—no matter how horrible it would be to
have to give up St. Petersburg and no matter how much it would compli-
cate my journey. What does m. G. think?—You want to know how my back
is doing. It has had a good rest—like all of me—and almost always remem-
bers its duty to my G. to keep nice and straight, and what is more important, it is strong enough for it and capable of doing it. It arouses only a faint
memory of former pains when I have been forced to keep it bent for a very
long time, but because I am not doing much work, there is seldom occasion
for that. But a question in return: sometimes I wonder if my G. is not going
completely wild in the long absence of his friend? You do not write when
you are going to Bayreuth. Did I write to you that Ella is there now, superintendent of the Mainschloss sanatorium, diagonally opposite the Fest-
spielhaus, and that you must visit her if it is possible?

All I can see now is a golden sky through the trees. It is magnificent—
Every day we have very heavy storms, very unfavorable for the grain harvest, but very pleasant for us.

Good night, m. G., until tomorrow.

*Early Tuesday*

It is overcast. Yesterday there was hail and flooding in the neighboring
village—how sad it is to be in the country and have to experience the destruction of the whole crop. And the grain was growing so beautifully!
Where we are everything is still untouched, fortunately, but they want to
begin harvesting, and the weather is not good for it. I haven't gone out
much in the last few days, and sometimes I have a desire for movement—a
sign of fresh strength.

Because Russian literature remains inaccessible to me here, I am preparing for the north and reading Ibsen, Lie, Strindberg, which Lena[1] owns in German. But my antipathy against the neurasthenic Ibsen characters does not go away, in spite of all my admiration for his mastery of dramatic technique and knowledge of people.

I would so much like to know what m. G. is preaching about at the moment. Morning sermon again next week—I am keeping careful count, and if there is a shift, he must tell me.—How happy I am that the lectures will be over soon! I hope that he has signed up for only one hour next winter—what is this?—I was horrified when I saw the two hours on the schedule. But sending the plan was a fine idea—and today it is Tuesday, so Bery didn't have to get up so early. But now he must promise one thing very solemnly: to get to bed earlier. If you have to lecture at seven or eight, you must not be working until midnight. I will expect the promise in your response.

Adieu, m. G.

Yours always,
your G.

## 133. A. S.

[Strasbourg]
Thursday evening,
July 8th, 1909

My dear G. had to sacrifice part of her evening to Calvin. Today is his 400th birthday, and I have to preach a sermon on him on Sunday. Because I am afraid to start writing it too late, in spite of my weariness, I have forced myself to write down at least the first page this evening. That has been done, and now I am somewhat calmer. But it is late, too: almost midnight . . . for days I have not gone to bed before midnight . . . Oh, to have just one more peaceful Sunday. I haven't had any since we parted . . .

I am only beginning this letter . . . in order to get to bed, thus obeying the thoughts of Someone who is far away from here . . . and yet not far from me.

Is this Someone at least recuperating? That is what I want to know every day. Today we took the excursion to the Donon,[2] on which you met

1. Probably her hostess.
2. Vosges Mountains.

Greda Curtius four years ago. She reminded me of it today and asked me to convey her greetings. While working on my sermon, I lived through that day again . . . the forest . . . the beautiful sky . . . the descent . . . and for a moment I forgot the horrible weather here.

Good night. For you, it is already "tomorrow" . . .

Do not allow yourself to be eaten by the large dogs in the old princess's park, and do not carry a torch for the handsome Ivan Ivanovich, the Jupiter among station masters . . . You see that Mother Bresslau has informed me well about her daughter. I spent the evening with her day before yesterday, while your father was in the Graeca.[1] Paul was along, too. We entertained the two cousins.

One more good night. The hardest part of the week is over! Only three more after this one! . . .

Does my friend not have any time to spoil her friend a little with letters to make him forget his weariness?

Yours<br>A

[ . . . ]

## 134. H. B.

Monday, July 19, [1909]<br>On the train to Moscow

M. G. Your friend had to neglect you—she is ashamed and penitent—at the very moment when you ask her to spoil you a little in your exhaustion, and when she has to thank you for such a long, good, sad letter.

Listen to how it happened: By now you must have received the letter, which I mailed on Saturday in Poltava, where we watched the festival. It was nothing special—the city was very beautifully decorated, a crowd of important personages, at whose head we twice saw the czar, really everything just as we do it, but rather exhausting. On Sunday, we had visitors; on Monday, we went out to pay visits; Tuesday and Wednesday we were very busy getting our things ready for the laundry and for our departure; Thursday, I took care of errands in the city with my nice student, along with a lit-

---

1. Greek club.

tle expedition to the Swedish fortifications with the monuments and the church.

Bery, I had an experience in that church. It is quite modern, painted all over in oil paints, and over every altar there is a larger painting; the biggest one over the high altar is famous because the Christ in it is said to have the features of Peter the Great! But it wasn't that; it was a different image of Christ over a side altar. Evening mood. Not a "landscape," but a great, spacious, quiet plain. In the foreground, a couple of loose, boulderlike stones, and right at the front He is sitting—nothing soft, nothing ecstatic, nothing, nothing "forced," not even deviating very much from the traditional type, but with what depth! Spacious, great, and still like nature, but deep in thought—knowing this figure gives one peace and courage. I do not know who the artist is, but he is a friend to us. No picture has given me so much in a long time—perhaps this, too, is a sign of restored health . . . And now I am looking forward to seeing the Treyakovska Gallery in Moscow, the most important collection of modern Russian painters.

Yes, Bery, now I am sitting on the train and going to Moscow—alone—and the parting that lies behind me was as painful as any in my life. Here I must go back to the account of my week. On Friday, I wanted to write home and to my G. Then Zenia, my friend's little boy, fell ill. On Saturday, it got worse, and yesterday I left Lena in despair. I would not have done it; I wanted to telegraph a cancellation to Moscow and stay, but I had the feeling that it would be better to leave her entirely to herself and her care for her child. Bery, I think that with these late children, all the worries, all the troubles are ten times harder than when you are younger— [ . . . ]

Lena is quite devastated. So I left yesterday. Her sister could not go with me either, although she already had prepared everything for the journey, because her six-year-old boy had a sudden malaria attack with high fever. But there's no need to worry abut me; I am expected in Moscow by two people—by the brother of Lena's husband and by one of the Runowitschina assistants, who is spending her vacation in Moscow; both know some German. And I can make myself understood in Russian quite well if necessary.

Here we are in Tula already—and I wanted to put this letter in the box here! Perhaps the stop will be long enough!

I will stay in Moscow for only two days and then go to Reval, avoiding Petersburg, and from there take the ship for Helsingfors. The cholera is giving me a hefty extra railway journey, but what must be, must be! And fortunately it's not bad at all. Now at 12:30 in the afternoon it's definitely not hot. I hope it will stay that way; it was hotter yesterday, but still quite endurable. In all this time, I've had no more rain than was necessary and desirable for the cooling off, not a single completely rainy day. Do you see how right I was to go east? How sorry I am for the poor central Europeans—my Frankfurt relatives also have rain in Switzerland. I hope that August will be nicer and that the Günsbachers can then carry out their plan. As soon as I can, I will write to you in more detail; I already have sent you postcards a couple of times.

[ … ]

Bery does not have to worry about me. I can stand the train extremely well now—what progress compared to last year!—and anyway everything will be done with by the time we get to Reval. Then it is mostly by water, and then soon the journey home, which will be made in stages: Berlin—Dresden—Bayreuth—Nuremberg, Rothenberg, Strasbourg. Home by September 1st. Where will my G. be then?—

[ … ]

What's happening with the *Rules of Organ Construction?* Was it so essential to expand it again?

Good-bye, m. G.—perhaps a couple of postcards will come now before there is time for another letter! One gets so lazy in Russia—so lazy!

Yours always,

L.

## 135. A. S.

Sunday, August 1, [1909]

Bayreuth

Now I am in Bayreuth again. *Parsifal* last night . . . I was touched when I entered the hotel. They had given me the same rooms that I had with my aunt, and I took the one in which she had stayed . . . Thus, there was a Père Lachaise mood from the very first moment, and it still persists. I found myself sitting on the edge of her bed as I did in those days after *Parsifal,* and I cried during the first act, which hadn't happened to me since time immemorial.

*Parsifal* still does not quite satisfy me. But I think of the "knowing through compassion" and the Good Friday magic in my own way, in accordance with what it means in my life, and then it's moving. I trembled at the fact that in this crowd I was the one who knows what it means to say, "knowing through compassion," and whose life is being devoted to it.

But all the Kundrie stories leave me cold. I can't fit it in with the rest because I have come to know only what is great and beautiful in woman, not what is glittering and seductive.

But I was deeply moved.

Ella finds that I look tired, but I feel so fresh in my work.

Let us speak of Ella. I saw her three times in one day. In the morning alone, where she was staying. In the afternoon with my sister before the performance, and in the evening I took her home in the dark (she lives twenty-five minutes from Bayreuth and had come to meet us at 9:30 after the performance). From there, we went to dinner. When we went down from the theater it was ten o'clock.

I think that things are going well with Ella. She lives magnificently. My sister and I are eating with her today. But first I will chat for an hour with Houston Chamberlain, Eva Wagner's husband.[1] I had a good quarter of an hour with her at Wahnfried, and before the performance I talked with the family. Aunt Cosima[2] has taken to her bed. Eva Wagner[3] has become much prettier since her marriage.

I must break off to go to see Chamberlain. I will write to you before the hotel. My sister is going for a walk. She is in seventh heaven.

## 136. A. S.

[Grimmialp, end of August 1909]

So you are in Günsbach! I followed you on your journey on Thursday and saw you arrive. And since then I see you in the little dining room where you drink coffee, or with the pastor's wife, or in intimate conversation with friend Sülti, or in the pastor's study, or in the evening on the sofa with your lower back . . . so that I am sometimes very distracted. And then I ask myself if you are sleeping well in the little room upstairs . . . I hardly think

1. Houston Steward Chamberlain (1855–1927), historian and philosopher.
2. Richard Wagner's widow.
3. Richard and Cosima Wagner's daughter.

of the lieutenants at all . . . I cradle myself in—what should I call it? "security."

The work is progressing.[1] Ten long pages already! [ . . . ]

How nice to think of you in Günsbach . . . My G. "at home" . . . when will I have a word from you?

In haste: the post is going out, and I would like you to find this on your cup tomorrow in the little room.

Yours,

your G.

## 137. A. S.

[Grand Hotel Resort, Grimmialp]

Sunday, August 29, 1909

M. G.

The sun is setting. I am sitting on the little hill in front of the hotel where the cross stands and am writing evening greetings to my G. It is lovely weather, and all afternoon I said to myself: "Is it possible that I am breathing this air and that my G. is in the Ruprechtsauer Allee?" I had hoped that you would spend Sunday in Günsbach, too, but from the good letter that you wrote at my table on Friday and that I received today, I learned that you left yesterday.—To find my letter waiting for you this morning. So both of us had a nice surprise from each other at the same time this morning.

I did not go out this morning because I wanted to work on a chapter that I had finished in my head. Around ten o'clock, I saw from where I was sitting at the table that the postman was driving up the street. I interrupted my work and sang to myself: "The postman, the postman will not have any letters for me"[2] . . . but I was almost certain that there was one there.—

And what news! You know Aunt Constance and her children Louise and Paul Harth.—Oh Fate! Can I no longer hide my lady friends from each other? But it is good that it is so. And I foresee that one day as I walk arm in arm with Constance in Saar-Union, I will tell her what a woman m. G. is . . .

Blue shining fog lies over the mountains! And today is Sunday . . . at

1. *The Mysticism of Paul the Apostle*.
2. Reference to a song by Schubert.

this hour, m. G. was lying stretched out on the journey to Vienna, and I was looking into the wonders of nature . . .

And this evening is Sunday evening.—

How nice that you were in Günsbach. I, too, feel suggestions of autumn every day . . . something wonderfully beautiful and sad . . .

The work is progressing well, except that I don't yet know what it will turn into.

[ . . . ]

## 138. A. S.

[Günsbach]
Thursday evening
September 30, 1909

M. G.

When you get to the hospital[1] tomorrow, I want to be the one who is waiting for you and says "good morning" and "good night" to you.

I have been thinking about it all day . . . about everything you are giving up for this year, and it almost hurts me that you no longer have your home. So I will come often with my little notes, and you will have the feeling of being at home.

The first Thursday evening . . .

Today it was raining. I worked wonderfully. If I had not put on the brakes at the end, the whole Holy Ghost would have been finished, or almost all of it.[2]

The room seems empty to me now that there is no longer anyone sitting at the table next to mine. But you can imagine that I will be sure not to clear it away. At least the table will be a companion to me, and sometimes I lift my head and say hello to m. G. And later Sülti and I will make our way to the station, to the 8:00 train . . . and the "world" that I always think of when the engine with the mail car behind it starts moving and the steam rushes out gets a new meaning . . . something is added for a hospital in Frankfurt . . . for someone dear about whose health I worry.—And every time it is ten o'clock, I will think, "and that m. G. keeps her strength and health."

1. In Frankfurt.
2. A chapter of *The Mysticism of Paul the Apostle*.

Good night . . .

Are your hands warm, or do they need someone to warm them? . . .

Sülti is reminding me. It is time . . .

> Yours,
>
> your G.

## 139. A. S.

> [Barcelona]
> Monday evening
> October 19th [18th], 1909

M. G.

This is a little word that should reach Someone on October 20th . . . to remind that person of the day in Drei Ähren. I feel as if I were sitting on the bridge in Türkheim waiting for my helper . . . and then other pictures come, and finally an autumn morning, and down below in the valley a line of smoke . . . a train going to Strasbourg, and myself traveling up again in the tram, my heart full of deep, pure thankfulness for knowing the happiness of having encountered you on my way . . . I need to think of that these days, and so does Sister Lene . . .

Soon it will be nine o'clock . . . (ten o'clock for you) . . . and now I am thinking of the future, of all the October 20ths that are still to come . . .

People in Barcelona know of my plans, which arrived here via Paris, through someone who met Romain Rolland.

In a quarter of an hour, I will go to the rehearsal (orchestra and choir) . . . it will last till midnight . . . There has already been one this afternoon for the Rheinberger.[1] The orchestra was so enthusiastic that they began to applaud. (This only because it suits my friend very well when she is a little vain about her friend.)

[ . . . ]

Tonight the floodlights from the forts played over the mountains above the city.

It was wonderful . . . the evening papers are being hawked. That always makes me a bit frightened: what news do they bring? . . .

But inwardly I despise newspapers, which more and more serve up world events as entertaining news for the bourgeois.

---

1. Josef Rheinberger (1839–1901), a nineteenth-century composer.

O, the disgust: And yet we two smile because we are past that, are waiting to work for mankind. Do we know how fortunate we are? . . .

Good night. I want to read a bit of ophthalmology (ten mins.) before the rehearsal so as to finish a chapter that I did not master this morning.

The bathroom here is a pleasure: marble basin with running water and floor of stone tiles; there you can splash about to your heart's content, and then the sun shines warmly through the open windows, which I don't have to close because I am staying very high up (third floor).

> Yours with all my heart, I kiss your hand.
> Your AG.

## 140. A. S.

> [Strasbourg]
> Tuesday evening,
> November 9, 1909

M. G.

These are very restless days . . . I have to get back into medicine and get so much done! I have finally set up my schedule of studies. You will get it as soon as it is final. Almost every day until eight in the evening. But in the mornings I don't begin until 9:30. That gives me an hour for reading.

Tomorrow it is my turn for the practicum in the eye clinic. I have to read a lot more this evening to orient myself again.

The organ in the Sängerhaus is progressing. But I am still having a lot of trouble with it. Rupp[1] gave a wrong measurement for the relationship between the pedal and the keyboard . . . I must correct the error as far as possible. He is a featherbrain. What music was I supposed to send you? I've completely forgotten! I only know that it was something by Schubert.

[ . . . ]

I want to think about my sermon, too . . . I almost boxed Pastor Kuck's ears today: He stops me in the street and starts telling me that the pastoral sessions that "Lene" is obliged to attend are beneath criticism! Yes, childhood friends are a terrible thing.

> I kiss your hand, yours,
> your G.

1. Emil Rupp (1872–1948), organist in Strasbourg.

## 141. A. S.

[Strasbourg]
Wednesday 4:00
December 8, 1909

M. G.

The word "homesickness" in my friend's little letter cut me to the heart, and here I am. I'm coming with this little note as a surprise so as to kiss your hand, for you can probably imagine that I cannot leave you alone if you are homesick. So imagine that I am coming to you, am sitting down beside you and taking your good hands . . . So, and now let us not speak . . . for a long time . . . May we speak again now?

Frau Wölpert[1] was delighted to have seen you, and on Monday, in the morning when I was drinking my coffee in bed—quite ashamed that I had it so good and my friend already had to go to work—she began to tell me about you, that she had seen you and that you looked tired. And Greda said the same thing in the evening . . . And I had not noticed that you looked tired! Did your eyes, so beautiful and so deep, prevent my seeing the rest of your face? And I, who will always have to notice in the future when you are tired, to relieve and support you, to demand nothing of you . . . what will happen if I do not notice when you are tired! Dear great friend . . . But then you will tell me! Won't you?

[ . . . ]

I was in the theater with Widor, who wanted to see the *Walküre*, and at midnight I accompanied him to the station. And then . . . slept, slept . . . not without having thought a great deal of my friend, who must have reached home by that time.

And . . . this was my last great concert![2]

Did you feel that as you listened? It was the introduction to a final chapter! And it is well that it be so . . . The train passes from the mountains into the plain . . . how beautiful. But that m. G. was there, that was wonderful . . . Thank you for coming.[3]

[ . . . ]

1. Schweitzer's housekeeper.
2. Inauguration of the organ in the Sängerhaus.
3. From Frankfurt.

## 142. A. S.

[Strasbourg]
Thursday evening
December 16, 1909

M. G.

My first quiet evening in a long time. Yesterday we performed the Christmas oratorio. Everything went well, and my dear organ was wonderful . . . But it isn't what it used to be in the Wilhelmer Choir . . . Brilliant, but not simple and deep . . .

And this evening I really wanted to go to the theater to hear young Waltershausen's opera so that I can say that I've heard it. But then I found that the sacrifice would be too great and that my Thursday belongs to the two of us . . . and to my sermon.

It has just struck ten, and Sister Helene is probably already resting. Let me confess something to her: The little photograph of you is there on your chair beside me and is keeping me company! If people knew what an adolescent their vicar, privatdozent, and organist is! But it is all right for you to know it.

I'll put this letter in the box so that you will get it sometime tomorrow.

Dear homesick child . . . I, too, am homesick for my friend, but I have this wonderful ability to feel her so vividly in my life that I keep thinking she is there . . . although I am doing a lot of calculations in my head as to when the organ dedication in Bielefeld is so as to find an excuse to go to Frankfurt.

Christmas . . . and no friend coming to Günsbach! Yesterday my sister wrote to me to set a date for the Christmas tree in Colmar, and I could scarcely answer her, for I kept repeating to myself the whole time: "My friend will not be in Colmar this year . . . she will not be coming to Günsbach!" How will I explain that to our dear Sülti? . . .

I wonder what you might like for Christmas. I've already got a tiny little trifle. It will be packed up tomorrow so as to arrive on time. But it is not to be opened until Christmas Eve at 6:30 . . . when I open my little package and imagine that m. G. is coming to me. But I would like to give you a real present, too . . . tell me what. My weary head is not coming up with anything. The trifle is something that will find a place over your bed. So . . .

and you can't guess it, but you will be touched because it will tell you about the two of us, but in a way that only you and I can understand.

[ . . . ]

## 143. A. S.

[Strasbourg]
Tuesday, December 21, 1909

Dear *Sehnusuchtskind!* [1]

I know what your longing is . . . Everything that you can still give to your friend and be for your friend in life is stirring within you, as the ocean surges . . . and floods over me. That is how I understand your longing . . . in the depth of my heart I understand it . . . I will never think that you are sentimental . . .

Thanks for the little word you sent . . . the great word—I am writing to you, can you guess where? At Dr. A-a-a-a-l-l-t-m-m-m-a-a-n's house;[2] I have to speak to him for a few minutes because he judges Erb's symphony so harshly everywhere in the specialist journals. He is making me wait. So I am summoning my friend Lene to keep me company.

Last night I announced by telephone to your parents that I would come to dinner . . . and played the good little privatdozent. It is very amusing how my thoughts are interwoven when we three are together. And how calmly one speaks of the absent young lady!

Did everything arrive: the letter, the little package, the "pussy willows"?

Should one spoil the homesick child a little bit over the holidays?

This is the shortest day . . . isn't that good? Tomorrow the days will begin to get longer again . . . and then October will be here soon . . .[3]

I kiss your hand.

Yours.
Your G.

1. "Child of longing."
2. Dr. Altmann (first name not known) was music critic for the *Strasbourg Post*.
3. In October 1910, Helene would conclude her training, and Albert would take his final exams.

## 144. H. B.

Strasbourg,
December 22, 1909

M. G. I got your letter from Günsbach and the "pussy willows" and was touched by them— thank you with all my heart. Now the pussy willows are in a glass under the picture of the manse and the Russian Christ. They tell me of a friend who is so good and tender and kind to me that I can't even tell him, much less thank him!———

But I must tell you something amusing. The flowers arrived on the evening before the little letter, and so I thought at first—the postmark was illegible—that it was the promised Christmas package and didn't open it and admired the subtle strategy of adding a note to get it delivered immediately. I thought that Mama might possibly have told you that our packages are kept back until Christmas Eve and piled up for us, except when their contents might get spoiled. And we are told only that something has arrived. That is what happened to me today with the real package. In order not to draw attention to it, I let them have it, for they keep terribly sharp watch, and the matron[1] said that it had been addressed by the same hand in which I had already frequently gotten letters and in which the fresh flowers had come, too, and as she said it, she looked very closely at me—but I did not show any emotion and said very little. And she made compliments about the lovely small script "as if it were engraved" and the fact that the flowers were so nicely packed! And I would just like to know who is the sender named on the address that accompanied the package. Do write and tell me.

The enclosed is to be opened on Christmas Eve at 6:30. Farewell, m. G.

With all my heart,
your friend.

1. The mother superior.

## 145. A. S.

Strasbourg, Thursday evening
December 23, 1909

M. G. F.

The sermon for the afternoon of Christmas Day is completed, also that for the Sunday after Christmas! Tomorrow I will write one for the first Sunday after New Year's, and then your friend can enjoy the holidays.

These lines come to tell you good night. Tomorrow I will open my package at 5:00 P.M. because I am going to the Wyotts'[1] for the opening of the Christmas presents afterward; but on my way there, I will be with you in thought when you open yours at 6:00 P.M. . . . And in the evening, when I have returned home, you will be with me . . . because then I'll write you.

I am so afraid that you expect too much from the contents of my package . . .

Tonight I will begin to work on *Paul.* I have read him again these last few days, and I am moved by the beauty of several chapters.

Tomorrow my friend will receive another little surprise; some printed matter . . . I am so frequently in the rue de la Sorbonne . . . In these days before Christmas, my aunt came one evening after I had already lit my lamp, to rest quietly at my place . . . I still see her sitting in the chair, next to the fireplace, the snowflakes melting in white drops from her fur jacket . . . I sat on the floor. That was a wonderful evening . . .

Oh, Mother Superior! The friend of Sister Helene is a rascal. He put the name "Frau Wälpert" as the sender of the package. Poor Mother Superior . . . Have you ever in your life known what a friend is? I won't laugh anymore.

I kiss your hand.

Address all letters to Strasbourg.

Yours,
Your G.

What a beautiful letter you wrote me!

1. His sister's family.

## 146. H. B.

6:30 on December 24, 1909

M. G.

You are getting comfortable in your chair at your table, and a beautiful, peaceful quarter of an hour belongs to us. You take the photos—pathetic as they are, but the photographer sent the dozen to me without giving me the test prints and without asking me if I want them—and you imagine that Sister Helene is coming in to you and bringing you the little package that you are already holding in your hands. There aren't any of the usual cookies in it—Sisters like me are not permitted to think of such things—but a fresh supply for the dear pad of paper, so that you can keep on writing nice letters as you have been doing.

And now she is taking both your dear hands and looking into your eyes and thanking you for helping her so much through this year, directly and indirectly—for you don't even know *how* you helped her . . .

And so we both celebrate a lovely quiet Christmas—and think of a Christmas Eve when there will be no cold winter around us, but also no other people who are dear to us, and where we will have to be everything to one another—

## 147. A. S.

[On the train to Günsbach]
Friday morning
December 31, 1909

M. G.

[ . . . ]

This little letter is to tell you where you should look for me for the last hour of the year, which we will pass together in spirit. And that is in our room in Günsbach. I am going there to preach for my father tomorrow morning, on January 1st . . . if it had been up to me, I would have spent the evening quite, quite alone in Strasbourg . . . But I want to be there for my parents . . . After all, it will not be my lot to spend New Year's Eve with them many more times. And they go to bed at ten o'clock, so that afterward I will be alone with you . . . Sister Helene . . .

I must tell you how happy I am: I have seldom in my life worked as I worked in Freiburg! In three days, I wrote the next-to-last chapter of *Paul*, almost thirty pages! That's incredible! And everything is nice and clear! I will not reveal the average time I got to bed; that belongs with the old year's list of sins! I went for a walk twice a day! For which I want to be praised.

Tata was coming to terms with her fate. It was a regimen of quiet and bed rest for her. She lay on the chaise lounge in my room and read, fought bravely against the temptation to disturb me, but often succumbed. She was charming and straightforward. I have rarely seen her so truly straightforward and childlike.

She told me that she was suffering from having me as a friend, yet having so little of me, because I found no time to talk to her about my work, to educate her, to broaden her horizons. This morning in the streetcar I had to summarize for her what I thought of Paul! "Do you know," she said to me, "I would be ashamed to go back to Paris and say that I was together with you for three days and you were writing about Paul the whole time without my knowing what you were saying!" Isn't that touching . . . and almost sad. Yesterday she said, "I have lived with you enough to know that the woman who will share your life will suffer often and deeply by being bound to a human being who is so engrossed in his work and his thoughts . . . She will have to give up a great deal, your H. B. . ." That made me sad because it is so true. And it was said simply and touchingly.

Good-bye. You know that I will write to you tonight . . . and this is one of the last New Year's Eves when I will have to write to you . . . for in the coming years I will take your hand and look into your eyes. There will be a great thanksgiving that will lift you up above everything that the woman who shares my life finds lacking in me . . .

I kiss your hand
Albert

Until Wednesday in Günsbach
Your flowers provided great pleasure in Günsbach!

# *1 9 1 0*

## 148. H. B.

[Frankfurt am Main Bürgerhospital, Niebelungen Allee]
January 12, 1910

M. G.

It is visiting hours, and I am using the little bit of peace to come to you today—who knows what tomorrow will be! M. G., this will not turn out to be a happy birthday letter because I have been so homesick and often so sad in these last few days that I must make a great effort to pull myself together in order to endure. I can tell you this, can't I? You're not angry with me? I know you aren't. I also know that it will pass and that it is better not even to speak of such things in the first place—but you also know that I can never hide anything from you. Well, that's enough of that—there is no reason for it anyway. And I'm often sorry for Emmy because I'm not at all the right kind of cheerful company for her, and then I often make an effort—but that is not quite the same thing. Oh well, our time together will soon be over; if I don't get long night hours (seven to eight a week) next week—and I don't expect to—I will definitely get them in about seven weeks. And when that's over, half my time here will be over, too—isn't that splendid? Seven weeks—how quickly they pass. And then there will probably be a leave, too. And when is my d. G. coming here?

My friend, now you are going to be thirty-five years old—I always, always have to think of how serious you were on your thirtieth birthday. Now you are halfway to forty—it is wonderful how much you have achieved in this time—may God preserve your creative powers and energy, that is my warmest wish for you! Happiness? That is what it is for you—I can imagine no other happiness for you than being able to give something to the world

181

and to humanity—you, my wonderful, deep, great friend! I thank you for being that to me—I thank you for being as you are—

Last night was wild and stormy. This morning everything was covered in sleeting rain—now the view is open, and the outdoors are covered in sunshine. Sunshine, m. G., plenty of sunshine for your new year!

### 149. H. B.

[Frankfurt]
January 13, 1910

Your birthday is getting very close now, and I am with you in thought all the time—even more than usual, if that is possible!

You already have a little parcel from me—it has been set aside for you for a long time because I have one just like it (only a bit smaller, "ladies' style"!) hanging on my watch chain and always use it to sharpen my—your!—pencil! Do you like it a little?—I hope you behaved yourself and didn't open it early? I had to send it off that early because I couldn't get to the city or the post office after Monday, my free afternoon. At the same time, I picked up a parcel from the other Hélène at the customs office—an excellent portrait of her in a charming, elegant frame; I've never seen one like it before.

[ . . . ]

Good-bye, m. G.—I did so hope for a word from you today. It seems such a long time since the last one came.—

But tomorrow we will be together—completely—

yours, m. G., with all my heart,
your G.

### 150. A. S.

[Strasbourg]
January 24, 1910

M. G.

I wonder whether the mother who cuddled her sweet little daughter thirty years ago had a presentiment of what path the child would choose. That is the question I have constantly been turning over in my mind for several years. If anyone could have predicted it to her then, she would have been horrified. . . . When I saw your parents playing with your little niece recently, I thought to myself that they used to play the same games with you once upon a time, and I began to dream. What must they be thinking today! . . . And while you were lying in your cradle, I was playing in the courtyard of the old manse in Günsbach. Every Sunday I would throw a penny for the poor little black children into a poor box. It was a very solemn moment. When I think it over, I believe that it is one of my earliest childhood memories. . . . And now the thought, which I dimly sensed at that time, unites the child from Berlin with the one from Günsbach!

My darling, do you know how much you are giving me? Sometimes it chokes me, and I ask myself if it is right for me to accept it. What a modest and impoverished life I am offering you . . . what a struggle for health! . . . I shudder at the thought of living on charity one day and hardly dare to think that you will share this life. And a life in which illness and death lie in wait for us. . . . Please tell me, m. G., is it true that you want to work with me? . . .

I know it is, and yet sometimes I still cannot believe it . . . when you said at the great waters, "If you need me, it is my right that you should call me," did you have any idea of what significance it would take on in the future? . . .

And all these years of waiting you have sacrificed for me—almost ten! The most beautiful years of your life in which you could have had all the happiness that life has to offer for a woman—house, hearth, happiness, children—you have led a life of hard work, shaken by struggles with your-self and your family, full of sadness . . . with much heavy loneliness. . . . And all that for me! . . .

Imagine that tomorrow when you wake up, it will be W[1] . . . and that I will come to your bedside, take your hand to kiss it, and look into your eyes to tell you wordlessly everything I think and all I thank you for.

This morning I left the clinic at eleven o'clock and skipped Chiari's class (from eleven to one) to pack up your little parcel and to write to you in peace and quiet. It was not easy to pack up the parcel. But I think that it has turned out very nicely. In the book, look at the lower corner on pages 1, 50, 100, and 150! I am giving you my own copy. It has blank pages bound in

1. The meaning of "W" is not known.

on which you can make notes on the treatment of the diseases and on your experiences.

The *Orgelbau-Regulativ*[1] arrived yesterday! The little apples are from Günsbach! Your G. and Sülti gathered them during the holidays between two pages of St. Paul. They come from the meadow below the rock . . . the meadow in which the pastor's wife picked nuts.

All the very best!

Yesterday I was in Karsruhe at the premiere of the new opera by Siegfried Wagner. I left after the afternoon sermon. Afterward I dined with the family (Siegfried, Chamberlain, and his wife, Thode) and Thomas. It is beautiful music, really admirable. But the text ruins everything! Ficker, who was also there, said, "Thode and Chamberlain ought to keep an eye on him in these matters. . . ," and I thought, "You are missing one thing, Siegfried! You don't have a Helene, a cruel, severe, self-willed Helene, as I do! (only displaying these characteristics in matters of authorship, of course!) . . . Then you could create magnificent operas."

You see how much I value my great friend.

Oh, how comfortable it is to write in peace.

I kiss your hand.

Greetings to Emmy.

Yours,
your G.

## 151. A. S.

[Strasbourg]
Thursday evening
February 17, 1910

M. G.

[ . . . ]

Not long ago, last Monday, Prof. Gunkel from Giessen gave a lecture about the Psalms. I spoke with him afterward because he is also doing a lot of work with the New Testament . . . and it was so remarkable for me to feel the difference. . . . He, the professor of theology, deeply involved in all these matters, . . .and I, who felt the other part of me, the human being, so very strongly as I spoke with the pure theologian. It was such a joy that I

1. The manual on organ building.

can't even describe it to you! What does all my weariness matter when I feel this simplicity and richness within! . . . It was as if I were in a dream.

My first sermon on the Passion finally "grew" in a quiet hour as I lay awake before falling asleep. . . . So I am a happy Bery.

And my visit! Just think: I have two concerts in Bielefeld; the second on February 28th. So I will be in Freiburg on the afternoon of March 1. I told Frau Goehrs that I would see her daughter, too. But, of course, it goes without saying that my visit is intended primarily for you and that we want to meet alone! If it is possible, let's go out together. Are you a little happy now?

I kiss your hand.

Yours,
your G.

**152. A. S.**

Strasbourg,
March 22, 1910

M. G.

Now this sunny day[1] is over like all the others. But how beautiful it was! I will tell you about it. Outwardly it was not at all what I had dreamed of. Just think, I had the evening Passiontide service at 6:00 P.M.! So I couldn't drive to our place, tempting though it was; I would have been too nervous about getting a flat tire and having to push J26![2] Besides, I had myself looked at this morning: a pair of swollen glands proves that I really did have an angina—the fever in Bonn—tonsils still somewhat inflamed. Therefore no risking a cold.

Having to stay home on the 22nd, when the sun is shining so brightly!

So I transported myself to the land of dreams. I said to myself: "Do your duty," and in the afternoon I worked on my sermon for the sixteen people who were there, so that I should accomplish something good in spite of my weariness. And while I was doing that, I dreamed—of those days now and . . . then.

It is so characteristic of both of us that we weren't able to celebrate the 22nd at our place . . . It is simply that we have become externally unfree

1. The anniversary of the beginning of their friendship.
2. His bicycle.

. . . for what we wish to accomplish together. Is it possible that there was a time when I had my afternoons at my disposal and my friend had hers! . . . And without this freedom, our friendship could not have developed as it did. Everything is good just as it comes. How I thank fate that we were free in those days!

And then our "festive days" passed before me in spirit. I could no longer tell them apart . . . It was a forest in spring and you . . . and pieces of our life. And I was touched when I thought of all that. And it seemed to me that a prophetic spirit had spoken through me when I dismounted from my bicycle and offered you friendship . . . asked the question, "Do you believe in friendship between . . . ?" from which our life grew.

I thank you with all my heart for all that you have given me. How can you thank me for making a detour via Frankfurt to see you! For whom did you take this life upon yourself? . . . Tell me, for whom! My great friend. For whom does the bird let itself be locked in the cage . . . the migratory bird . . . even a migratory bird that is greedy for traveling. Do you think that it would be possible for me not to think about that?

That is how I dreamed while my head, still weary from the warm sun, did its duty and produced its sermon. Our fate was sealed for me in the phrase "being unfree" . . . but so was our greatest happiness.

And you were thinking all these things along with me. Imagination raised us above reality. We were both in the forest in spring . . . I saw the yellow branch from which you broke off a blossoming twig on the second 22nd . . . the avenue down below, where the path leads to the wooden bridge . . . and we were the two prisoners in our place. It has occurred to me so often recently that imagination is freedom. . . . Then it gradually became darker and colder. I went to church. And when I went back home, happy to have done my duty well, . . . read and be amazed . . . I telephoned Mama B. and invited myself to the birthday dinner to replace her daughter. That is something new that was not always on the program for the 22nd! And I thought of how you always took care to get home on time. . . . Your parents did not know what thoughts I had as I sat with them at table.

And Mother Bresslau serves me a tart and says that it is her dear daughter's favorite tart, and I must do it justice . . .

I told them boldly that you came to the station to welcome me, etc. . . .
[ . . . ]

> My most faithful comrade. Give me your hand . . .
> Your G.

**153. A. S.**

> [Günsbach]
> On the rock, Monday morning
> April 11, 1910

M. G.

Blue sky, sun, blossoming bushes, blue flies that buzz around me, birdsong, in the distance snow-capped mountains . . . in the middle Sülti and I. From the valley, you can hear the River Fecht, noisier and more powerful than in summer and autumn . . .

I am thinking of you. If only you could be here just for one hour . . . But as it is you are shut in because of me.

I am stirred up and moved by the parting from Tata. This was our last vacation. A chapter has ended for us. We will see each other and speak with each other again, but it is the end of the days when we lived together peacefully with hours of delightful conversations that showed me the soul behind this character, full of contradictions. The first great sacrifice. We parted smiling because we knew that the spiritual link between us can never be broken and that our friendship will always be sacred and does not need the beautiful, beautiful days of life together that gave it birth. So the illness and the solemnity of the days suited what was going on within us. . . .

I am writing this to you so that you will know what is moving me.

And Nature comforts me . . . On Saturday evening, I found your good letter waiting for me. I am so proud of the fact that you are a little bit satisfied with the style! I will go straight home and go over a couple of pages, which I do not like.

And now the "waning days" are approaching for you . . .

I kiss your hand with profound gratitude

> Yours

P.S. Yesterday I received a lovely set of medical utensils (scissors, etc.) as a gift from the mother of one of my candidates for confirmation . . . the first gift for the Congo.

> Again, yours,
> Your G.

This evening I will return to Strasbourg to see Cahn tomorrow.

**154. H. B.**

Frankfurt, April 26, 1910

M. .

It's been an eternity—at least that's how it seems to me—since I wrote to you—since the last time I had night duty, and that was long, long ago!—and almost equally long since I had heard from you until the good tired little letter arrived. It is getting so hard for me to think that while I am writing this, my weary friend is sitting on the train again and traveling to exhausting Paris—when will the weariness ever end?—I think not until we do!

—So I am a creature of the day again, and I have been put into the narrowest three-bed room. So instead of one roommate, I have two of them, but at least instead of one incompatible one, two very nice and cheerful ones. But it's impossible to do anything alone—so far I have not been able to touch the *Paul*. I'm very sorry, but for the next two weeks I do not believe that there will be great progress. After that, I will get a room to myself as station nurse and at least can get to it in the evenings—hoping that I won't be too tired! And then comes my leave. . . .

Today I did my first anesthesia, an easy case, and it went quite well. I am a little happier again—the last few days I was severely depressed by all the petty details that came down so heavily on me again. And again and again and more and more seductively comes the thought of going home, of continuing to work at home and taking the exam as an external candidate and that I was stupid to have come here at all—so that it is often really hard for me to endure.[ . . . ]

In my bundle of news, I forgot to tell you about the new pastor. He came here one evening to get to know us; I was ordered from night duty for the occasion (supposedly to play the harmonium). He had been in England for six and a half years, and there was a very lively conversation about the country, its people, and conditions.

Yesterday was the first lesson. The topic of his discussion with us is— the life of Jesus and research on the life of Jesus! He seems to be a distinguished and intelligent man, is extremely lively, and has brilliant teaching skills. Thank God, some stimulation after all!

Two more items of news: Cousin Ange was in Paris until last Saturday. She had a show at the Salon and obtained a commission immediately from a Baroness Dufour.[1] I don't know anymore details, but it's nice anyway.

Then my parents were in Berlin with a very musical gentleman (the brother of an aunt who lives here); he spoke very enthusiastically about the *Bach* and asked if they knew this Dr. S.—yes, the famous Bery!—

Yesterday my parents passed through here on their journey; they will go home today. And what about me?—I hope no later than the end of June— but no sooner either!

Is this a surprise?

Farewell, my friend—

From my heart
your G.

[ . . . ]

**155. A. S.**

Saturday evening
April 30th, 1910
Nancy

M. G.

The sermon is finished . . . and a great worry has been lifted from my heart. I am to preach tomorrow morning. I worked on the second part of the sermon from Paris to here . . . in magnificent sunshine.

No, my dear, the letter was not a surprise . . . I was expecting it.

The concert was moving. As the hall was emptying, I stood in front of my organ console for a long time and looked at it as if I were seeing it for the last time . . . and when I came down, people begged me to promise to come for the St. Matthew Passion in the spring.

My Paris stay was pleasant. Tata has made a good recovery and was de-lightful . . . if I satisfied her claims on your friend's time. [ . . . ]

On Thursday, I dined at the Marquise de Loys' with very elegant people who were invited in my honor . . . on such occasions, I always get so home-sick for you, the wrap, your Günsbach dress, Sülti . . .

1. No details known about this person.

That is when I feel that I really know what I have in you, in your simple, elegant style and the "talents" that dwell in you.

I slept a lot in Paris, so I will be getting a relatively fresh start to the semester. Tomorrow afternoon I will bring some order into my affairs . . .

Now to your letter. First of all, I forbid you to call my friend Helene "stupid." She is too smart and . . . too beautiful for that! I have the impression that you are experiencing a crisis of discouragement . . . sadly we are never spared that. As for me, I am always telling myself that 89 percent of it consists of exhaustion . . . I don't know if it is true, but I believe it. It is the first time that you have expressed the thought that you might not finish your year. You must know that you are completely free and that your friend does not have the slightest doubt of your energy and the strength of your will if you think it right to bring your torments of exhaustion . . . and of the shared bedroom . . . to an end! Poor friend! How well I understand all that . . . But in a couple of days of leave, the sky will grow brighter; that is my belief.

Oho, and this pastor fellow! I hope he's married! I wonder what kind of look he will give you when he finds out that you are the godmother of *Reimarus to Wrede*. Then he will have to make some strenuous efforts in his lectures!

[ . . . ]

Good-bye, in a few weeks.

I kiss your hand

Yours

Your G

## 156. A. S.

[Strasbourg]
Sunday evening
May 1st, 1910

M. G.

Your little letter was so alarming . . . It is just striking ten o'clock . . . This afternoon as I was planning to pay a visit to the Hoffs, I met the entire Bresslau family. They told me about your letter, and while your affairs were discussed, Bery sat in on the family council, on the sofa next to your mother. How times have changed. Well: I am of the opinion that you should give notice immediately if your health is suffering—oh, why did I have to hear again about our back! But if it is exhaustion and depression, then you should take that into account and not reach a decision until after your vacation. If I know you, you will be depressed if you have wasted these eight months for nothing; the business with the external exam will not work out.

In your place, I would drop surgery; I would try to get into the Internal Division and get leave soon; what comes next will follow in due course. But above all you must do what you think is right . . . your health is everything.

I find that you are too concerned about the general conditions in the hospital. Let it go and go your way; there is nothing that can be changed . . . the rule of women.

This was the "business" part. And I know best what my friend is suffering from: loneliness. See, my thoughts are coming to you; can you receive them? . . . Can our friendship and our future work still give you the strength to live with this loneliness? . . . If only I could speak with you for one single hour. Do you want me to have some business in organ matters down there and to visit my dear aunt in Frankfurt for a few hours if you cannot get leave? I can arrange it! And what are a few hours in the train compared to the homesickness and loneliness that you cast off after a peaceful hour with your Bery . . . and how much hope and sunshine I would like to give you. Say the word, and it will be done . . . in spite of the semester.

Look, I wish you could spend one hour in the room in which I am writing to you, so very still and peaceful, upheld by the thankfulness of the human being whose work you are taking upon yourself . . . If only you could take a leave. My dear, I am putting into these lines everything that the word "my great one" contains . . . I wish that it would come and carry you over the hesitations of these days and make you "buoyant" again . . . But be sure that everything that you decide is right . . . dear homesick child.

I think that you are sitting over there in the corner and that I am in front of you and speaking to you and doing for you what as a memory you have taken away from here with you, my great, noble friend . . .

Good night . . . write just *one* word to me . . .

I kiss your hand

Yours
Your G.

**157. A. S.**

[Günsbach]
Wednesday after Pentecost 1910 [May 15, 1910]

M. G.

How is the dear homesick child? I am always thinking of her when the air stirs gently and the sun shines. It is so beautiful in Günsbach.

The work is progressing quite well, although the American edition involves more writing that I had thought. But I hope to be finished with the main material for the first four volumes before Widor comes (Friday). A fair copy of the first page of the sermon is done. So fear cannot get a grip on me. I must confess that I have not been good in the matter of going to bed. In spite of all my good intentions, I never get to bed before twelve o'clock, and then . . . I still read about surgery. Please, dear friend, speak a word of authority and prescribe when I am to get to bed.

If I were in Strasbourg, I would write to you every day. But I don't dare to as it is because the postmark is bound to draw attention, and the letters from your friend do not look (on the outside) like those of your devoted mother.

How is it with my friend? . . . If your weariness becomes too great, you are to give everything up, without false pride, and come back.

Now there are the first leaves on the vines; when they grow red, you will be free and will come and sit on the little wall and tell Sülti about Bery, who is sweating out an exam in Strasbourg. Your card arrived, and everyone felt sorry for you . . . you were spoken of more than once.

The old lady from Strasbourg who saw you arriving with me that afternoon asked me who was the lady I was accompanying, and when I told her that it was you, she began to speak of you, how much she liked you, and I had to tell her about you.

Good evening. Sülti and I are taking this letter to the station so that you will get it tomorrow!

I kiss your hand

Yours
Your G.

**158. A. S.**

[On the return journey from Paris]
Monday morning
June 6th, 1910

M. G.

"The night is far spent, the day is at hand." [1] . . . It is seven in the morning; we have just left Avricourt. At first, I stood at the window for a few minutes to feel the air and to see the sun and the blue sky and to forget that I had been in Paris . . .

That is over now. Think of it, this journey that I had looked forward to with foreboding did not tire me out at all, but refreshed me! In spite of the work. Is old Bery growing young again? Just be careful: If it goes on like this, you may have to bring him up on a baby bottle!

[ . . . ]

Oh, how beautiful the fields are . . . and the meadows . . . and how happy I am to leap from the train into my work . . .

I am not worried about the *Bach* edition at all anymore. I only need slowly to make the final copy. The manuscript has been cut to size. Widor and I worked through all the preludes and fugues and agree about all the details. It will be something that lasts and is worth something.

Now that things have gotten to this stage, I am going on strike. I.e., I mean to raise the cost to the publisher to 3,000 francs exclusive of expenses! Let's see if that goes well! So little Bery will be a good match.

Oh, if only you could breathe this morning air with me . . . (First tunnel) . . .

Impossible to find a second in which to attempt the adventure of seeing Hélène [2] . . .

Heard the organ of St. Sulpice again. Its beauty does not pass away, and neither does my friend's . . .

I am almost afraid of my own premonitions. On the return journey, I saw workers on a curve on the stretch by Bar-le-Duc and was seized by fear that the foreman was not paying attention to the trains . . . A few minutes later a train came by in the opposite direction. I could not free myself of my

1. Romans 13:12.
2. Barrère.

fear . . . And on the following day, I read that it was this very train that crashed into the workers and crushed three of them . . . It was like that other time with the fire in Günsbach.

Good-bye.—I kiss your hand . . . and perhaps I will find a word from you when I get back . . .

Yours,

your G.

## 159. A. S.

[Strasbourg]
Thursday evening,
July 7th [1910]

M. G.

M. G. is to get a long letter because it is Thursday evening. But I have lost a lot of time over the last three days at the dentist's and am feeling very nervous . . .

And then masses of business letters have been lying about for weeks. Yesterday and today, apart from medicine and the lecture, I did nothing but work on them . . . and then to be able to work well on the Schirmer *Bach*, which is pressing.[1]

Yesterday I signed the contract. Your G. will get 3,500 Marks! And if the work is published in German in book format, 1,200M per sheet; if in English in book format, 100M. There are certainly twenty-five sheets!

How rich Bery is getting. And in the last three weeks, I have turned down at least four new publishers' contracts (music and theology)!

Now I am imagining that I might earn 5,000 Marks a year by writing and that we might live comfortably here . . . then I smile. It is nice to dream . . . but our life must be a different one . . . You understand me. So be glad with me.

Thanks for your good letter, which was waiting for me on Monday when I got back. I did not open it until I was lying in bed, before falling asleep. Oh, how prudent my friend is! She is just afraid of being put under

1. Schirmer was the publisher.

guardianship, hence her excellence in planning! We will give her credit for it. [ . . . ]

On Sunday, I will preach twice . . .

Yours, I kiss your hand,
Your G.

I am going to read your good letter again.

## 160. A. S.

[Strasbourg]
Saturday morning
[July 9, 1910]

M. G.

Just a little word for Sunday morning from your G. (from Madelung's[1] course on operations). Yesterday evening I finished early my sermon for Sunday, after practicing the organ at St. Thomas's for the concert that I am giving there on July 28th on the anniversary of Bach's death!

Miracles still happen. Official request to Monsieur Bery to play the organ for the subscription concert on February 1, 1911, under the direction of Herr Pfitzner! Then my friend can put on her ceremonial dress, if she is not still lingering in the blue south.

I already told you that I will play with Saint-Saëns, Widor, Gabriel Fauré in Munich on September 20th in the concert hall of the exhibition! (*Sinfonia Sacra* and *Requiem* of Fauré). And well paid (400 Marks!). Good news, isn't it?

In half an hour, back to the dentist. This afternoon the clinic group has an outing to Lichtenburg. [ . . . ] It appears that eight daughters of medical professors will be going along, to whom I will pay court assiduously, provided that they are offspring of my future examiners, in order to win myself the favor of the old gentlemen. I must be "sweet" to Annette Freund because Greda has told me to be. I am really looking forward to this excursion! It is so wonderful to have my sermon finished. Tomorrow I will preach for the last time before my exams.

---

1. Otto Wilhelm Madelung (1848–1926), professor of surgery.

In Paris, I met a young missionary from the Congo who had just come back on leave. He told me how eagerly I was awaited over there.

> So have a lovely, lovely Sunday, m. G. I kiss your hand, your G.

## 161. A. S.

[Strasbourg]
Thursday evening
July 28th, 1910

M. G.

My concert is over . . . I did not go for a glass of beer with my friends, for this hour belongs to you . . .

Last day of medical lectures! On October 28th at ten o'clock in the morning, it will be five years since I first started anatomy; it was a dark, cloudy day, and my heart was oppressed because of all the novelty and the work that was coming . . . and on July 28, 1910, at the same hour, I am crossing the same bridge under a blue sky and blazing sunshine on the way to the last lecture . . .

Is it possible that I have reached the end of this march? How did I manage not to fall by the wayside? And how much you helped me! Whenever I pick up my German *Bach*, I say to myself: This book would not yet be finished if my friend had not helped me . . .

That dear Bach, who has helped to support me! When I began to play this evening, I thanked him inwardly for everything he has given to me, spiritually and materially . . . How mysterious are things here on earth. My head is very tired, but I feel happy.

I am getting so forgetful! Every day I meant to send you a program . . . and every day I forget . . . And now I do not even have one here with me. Forgive me . . . but I can't help it. You know that it is not because I am not thinking of you.

Once again I play on the 28th of July.

Thank you for your good letter and the card. I got both on Tuesday morning when I came back. [ . . . ] This afternoon I paid your mother a visit. She was so fresh and charming that it was a pleasure to be with her . . .

Good night . . .

What a beautiful evening with you! And what a decisive evening.
I kiss your hand . . .

yours,<br>
your G.

## 162. H. B.

[Frankfurt]<br>
Saturday<br>
[August 6, 1910]

M. G., double congratulations—: for Sunday and for sending off of the
manuscript! One more thing, then there will be work enough for your return home with the *Paul* and the sermons—and Father Schweitzer with his
Alsatian stories must not be neglected either! I must hurry up and get to
sleep—

Farewell, no time. The boss has returned; the hours of cramming start
again on Monday, and the pastor's lectures start right away, too!

Happy Sunday!

From my heart,<br>
your G.

Absolutely between us, still a very deep secret: Our lad, our Hermann,[1]
is engaged—to a twenty-one-year-old girl, a stranger to us but apparently
very nice! And a person should not go crazy with such exciting correspondence in addition to the life here!—Mustn't give anything away when
you're told about it later—perhaps not for a long time—

## 163. A. S.

[Strasbourg]<br>
Thursday evening, September 1st, 1910

M. G.

I don't know why, but I can't go to sleep without writing you these few
words. I am already in bed after a long day's work. It will be midnight soon.

I think that it is the 1st of September that is having this effect on me

---

1. Helene's younger brother.

... The beginning of your last month . . . And afterward all bitterness will melt away in the blue October mist, for we two must never be bitter . . . Sleep well, m. G. . . .

I have spent the evening working in the Ruprechtsau. It is truly comfortable. I get there around eight o'clock, have a quick dinner, and then I sit in an armchair, take up my medical work (surgery), Frau Goehrs crochets, and I work in complete quiet until ten o'clock. The scent of the garden through the open window. That's how it was yesterday, that's how it was today. [ . . . ]

[ . . . ]

I kiss your hand

Yours<br>your G.

### 164. H. B.

[Frankfurt]<br>Saturday<br>[September 17, 1910]

M. G., I am sitting and writing my sample examination paper[1] and am stealing time from it and from myself for a Sunday greeting. A week from tomorrow my station work will be over—m. G., it is high time, you wouldn't believe how shaky my nerves have become. Two weeks from tomorrow I will be home, and then I will have survived everything. Farewell until then, and forgive your friend, who has not a single thought left in her head!

Your G.<br>[ . . . ]

### 165. A. S.

[Grand Hotel Grünwald, Munich]<br>Tuesday, September 20th, 1910

M. G.

I've just come from the full rehearsal for Widor's *Sinfonia Sacra* . . . it was wonderful . . . O, I need you . . . so as not to become vain . . . I am feted too much here.

---

1. Hospital report about patients.

No, do not write to me: I know that you are thinking of me . . . And you will tell me everything on the day you climb three flights of stairs and ring your friend's doorbell . . .

How will it be? Even in my dreams, I cannot see it all. Tomorrow I'll be playing Bach to a circle of invited guests. I'll come back Thursday morning. I will have all the famous people at the music festival sign a postcard for you.

Don't overexert yourself!

As for me, I'm living very reasonably; I accept hardly any invitations . . .

> Yours, I kiss your hand
> Your G.

The friendship between me and Widor is in danger: I introduced Frau Reinach[1] from Paris to him, and now he is paying court to her, kisses her hand, etc. . . . He doesn't need to go that far with my friends . . . especially not with the one I love so much because she resembles you externally and in spirit . . .

## 166. A. S.

> [Strasbourg]
> Christmas—
> Christmas Eve 1910

M. G.

The Christmas tree of the Curtius children is serving as a light in my room . . . It is on the oven and smells sweet . . . But I am quiet, thinking and dreaming. Sit down . . . and share the quiet with me . . . I'm thinking of two years from now, when there will be no tree burning in this room . . . the dear familiar room . . . and when it will be Christmas nonetheless. Things are so strange in my life . . . I wanted to complete it in a small circle that I created for myself . . . It was to run its course in the shadow of the seminary tree that proclaimed spring and autumn to me when I was young. Now everything has turned out so completely differently, from an inner necessity, not from external causes . . . I must carry the glow of the Christmas

---

1. Fanny Reinach (1870–1917), wife of Theodor Reinach, a member of the French Chamber of Deputies.

lights into the world . . . become simply human . . . in order to serve the one who was human and is my Lord, although as I stand in His presence I am inwardly free in ideas and views . . . but through my Lord, through His great, pure will, my life will become simple . . . The billows of the river were rushing by when I first dared to explain to you what this becoming "simply human" was to mean for my life. I still see the wonderful early summer that surrounded us . . . And you understood everything and found holy words to keep your friend steady on his way.

Now the years of weariness for you and me have passed away . . . We have grown older . . . but remained the same . . . You wish to travel with me on my way and have made great efforts to prepare yourself for it . . . Now it is time to catch our breath and to enjoy the hours of celebration that we have been missing for these five years. We will again, you and I, be as we were when we sat by the Rhine . . . and then we will carry the lighted tree out into the world . . . united through Him, the Master . . . His servants . . . That is the wonderful thing, that we are united in Him, and that we know that seeking how to live for Him brought us together . . . That is what is sacred in our friendship . . . And I thank you for understanding and wishing it . . .

Your G.

### 167. A. S.

[Günsbach]<br>On December 25th [December 26, 1910, evening]

M. G.

Yesterday while dining at Colmar, I thought a great deal of how you were among us two years ago, and I had to give you my arm for the journey from the station to the house.

My family always asks about you, and my parents are greatly attached to you.

The little goose from Strasbourg has arrived and was received with jubilation. You will get a letter.

Yesterday Madame Hadey came to set the day for the examination coffee party for Thursday.[1] And then she asked if Fräulein Bresslau would be in

---

1. To celebrate both Schweitzer's success in passing his medical examination and his brother Paul's in recently passing his engineering examination.

Günsbach on that day and if she would do her the honor of accompanying the gentlemen, Paul and Albert! I said that you would not be there, but that I would tell you about it and that you would regret being absent . . . I said that if, however, she thought it important, I could invite six to twelve young ladies from Strasbourg to this coffee party.

Rehearsal and concert in Münster today! I did not "warm up" (artistically) until I was playing. Really, I would have liked to sleep for the whole day before Christmas Eve. Got both your letters . . . I am writing to you immediately after returning from Münster, before going to bed . . . I can see you very clearly, lying prettily and poetically in your room with your beautiful braids around your head . . . That suits you so well . . . When will I get a letter telling me how you are?

I miss you so much, not running through the mountains with Sülti and you . . .

Yours, I kiss your hand
your G.

## 168. A. S.

[Günsbach]
December 31st, 1910 . . .

M. G.

My head hurts, but things are well inside my head, for I am leaving the old year, feeling quiet and self-possessed, and I thank it.

It gave me a great deal . . . the end of my studies, so that I became myself again after having been a student . . . and finally it took away the terrible fear for your health that was almost crushing me . . .

Now only one more New Year's Eve here after this one, and then, for the ones that follow I will not be writing to you, but you will read everything on my face as we wait far away to see if we can hear the stroke of the bell from the cathedral tower.

Can you imagine that?

I have put my pen down because it could not keep up with all the thoughts that were swimming about my head. The underlying thought is the one that you expressed in response to my Christmas letter . . . of things we have not spoken of for a long time.

You see, it is my fault. It is always present for me; in all the thoughts that go from me to you . . . that is the base of the chord. But then, because I consider it so obvious and present, I often say nothing about it . . . instead of letting the bell sound its note.

To the one who is sleeping in the Père Lachaise cemetery, I once said: I am the flint . . . one has to strike the flint to get the sparks that are in me . . . You know, if you are longing for a thought between us that I am not expressing, then strike the spark from the flint. Since I received your letter, I always feel as if I were hearing the fundamental chord of our being on the way to one another . . . the one that sets the key . . . that we were both searching for a purpose in life out of the longing of youth . . . and then found it with one another . . . in what the Great One said to us in the mighty words of His deep humanity . . .

That is why we are young as long as we live. Our life as we want it to be grew out of the youthful longing that became clearer . . . from the search for happiness . . . and we found happiness . . . and have only one wish . . . to remain healthy for a few years in order to let this happiness become a fact . . .

Life has taught us how to wait . . . We suffered when we were harried and weary and had no time to collect our thoughts. Sometimes I cannot believe that we survived . . . But it is behind us . . . Do you know that the quiet time is coming now, when we can breathe and compose ourselves again . . . and can be together in peace? I feel it wonderfully . . . I think of it all day long.

Now let the New Year come! We were afraid of the one that is passing. We smile as we turn to the one that is coming . . . *We shall call it the year of serenity* . . . and know that it will help us to find our beautiful youth again in something that is yet more perfect, the youth in which we had the strength to seek our path for ourselves—we did not know that the road would permit us to walk side by side— . . . I have a longing for our youth . . .

It is just striking twelve . . .

How do these two go together: youth and the passing of time?

Good morning, dear year of serenity! Good night, my friend, pure, noble being whom I was permitted to meet on my journey . . .

I see you in bed in your room . . . I kneel down and kiss your hand

Your G.

# *1 9 1 1*

## 169. A. S.

[Günsbach]
Thursday
January 5th, 1911

[ . . . ]

Now I have answered . . . so I do not need to think of it anymore and may rejoice from the depths of my soul in the progress of your back. You can imagine what reading those lines meant to me!

Now this is the doctor talking: no, don't go to the opera! Be careful . . . let *weeks* go by before you put any strain on your back at all! (by sewing, dinner invitations, etc.). I implore you! Don't give up halfway. Do you understand my pleas? We will go to the theater when you are quite strong, when I don't have to worry at all about how you are sitting. When that day comes, these terrible, terrible memories of coming to visit you and seeing you in pain will be erased.

I throw myself on my knees; I implore you on bended knee to lie down as if you were still in pain and not to change anything about the way you are living.

Thank you for your letter . . . am longing for our youth . . . I know that you feel as I do.

No, I do not find you changed . . . because we are both changing together.

O my dear little fool! Nietzsche's *Birth of Tragedy* is not worth much—and *Zarathustra* is insane. You must read *Beyond Good and Evil* and the *Genealogy of Morals*, which I will put into your dear hands . . .

The third volume[1] is almost done. I will arrive Saturday evening and will call that evening to ask you when I can see you on Sunday. I still don't know when I will be free. . . .

> I kiss your hand
> Your G.

## 170. A. S.

> [Strasbourg]
> Sunday evening, February 5th, 1911
> 11:00 P.M., in bed

M. G.

I made the whole journey with you; I knew where you were every hour, and every hour I asked myself whether you weren't feeling too tired. When I came down from the organ at six o'clock, I was relieved to be able to tell myself that you had arrived and soon found a nice little room with a view of the lake or the mountains. . . .

Then I saw you going down to dinner, beautifully dressed . . . now you have gone to bed. It is so peculiar to have to live someone else's life along with her, whether one wishes or not, and particularly if it is such a beautiful problem child as my friend. . . .

[ . . . ]

These lines will be mailed as soon as you send me your address.

> Yours, I kiss your hand
> Your G.

## 171. A. S.

> [Paris]
> Thursday evening in bed
> [May 4, 1911]

M. G.

My day. This morning, letters, etc., Père Lachaise (for you and me), errands, lunch Reinach. Driven to the rehearsal by Madame Reinach. After the rehearsal (met Mlle. De Loys, etc.) abducted by Tata. Walked home

---

1. Of Bach's organ works.

with her. Dinner Helene. Afterward half an hour with Tata. Walked home, to bed.

Morning. Widor, errands. Audition of a female singer, lunch at twelve at my uncle's. Then another singer. Visits, a ride in the Bois with Madame R. at three o'clock. She drops me off at the mission house. Conference. Home. Dinner. Concert.

Saturday morning meet René Baton (conductor), Tata . . . Leave for Strasbourg (11:30, arrive 9:00 P.M.).

These are my plans. This visit is pleasant; it always is. If you think that it is getting boring, it is good, and vice versa. Tata is very kind and affectionate when we speak of my plans, etc. I am not overexerting myself; I walk, I enjoy meeting people . . . And I always ask myself whether these will turn out to be friends to help my work . . .

What a good letter from you! I see you lying on the balcony . . . my great friend . . . But I am very, very homesick for trees, for work, for church, for you, you who are one with all my activities . . . my joy and my care . . .

I kiss your hand.

## 172. A. S.

[Paris]
Friday, May 5th, 1911

M. G.

It is 1:30 at night, but I know that you will not chide me if I write to you now. I must speak with you in this solemn hour . . . and it is as if you were with me in this room, which you do not know . . . Concert good, very good, party afterward; Madame Reinach took me home in her automobile, then I composed myself for an hour with folded hands . . . and listened to the heavenly music in my soul . . .

The conference (at the Paris mission) lasted from 4:30 to 6:30. In attendance: Boegner, Couve, Bianquis, and I. It was simple and beautiful.

So: (1) I am offering myself as an independent medical helper at the mission, which will provide me with accommodations. I will try to collect what I need every year. What I cannot raise will be provided by the mission.

(2) On the problem of nationality: I will remain German. They understand that. As regards the right to practice as a doctor without a French license, Monsieur Reinach (according to his wife) will smooth the way.

(3) Inventories of supplies (for ladies, too) will arrive one of these days (as a main question, I threw the leather sofa into the conversation. It can't come).

(4) The mission would welcome it if I were to find a nurse and would welcome it all the more if it can be arranged that a person with these skills was willing to bind herself to me in such a way as to bear my name. I said that at the moment I could express myself only theoretically on this point.

(5) Departure is set for the 25th of June or the 25th of July! This will mean arriving at the best season and having two months to acclimatize oneself before the rainy season . . . which would be especially important for a woman, I am told.

So! I am very moved. I think that now everything has been decided at last. . . . Good night . . . I kiss your hand. I will not leave until tomorrow evening at five o'clock and will arrive at one o'clock at night! What a magnificent train! And that will give me time to run errands and pay visits.

I kiss your hand

> Yours,
> your G.

## 173. H. B.

> Königsfeld spa
> Black Forest, Pension Waldeck
> May 30, 1911

M. G.

Thanks for your letters! Are you sure you're not working too hard? And you're going to bed on time? I am so happy that m. G. is making such magnificent progress; I am only surprised that you still need space to accommodate the bad books . . . can't they be disposed of quickly? I do so wish that you would soon get to the second, nicer part, the less scholarly one—will it take long? What period have you reached?

It's beautiful here, but it has been oppressive and sultry since yesterday, which isn't giving me any headaches now. Bery, things are really looking up; I can tell that by the fact that I overcome things more quickly. It was only on the first night that I slept badly; I hardly feel the lumbago now; I can stand up nice and straight and enjoyed walking for one and one-half hours yesterday. It is true that I am dreadfully cautious; I am careful to avoid catching cold and making improper movements; I will begin exercising as soon as I have felt nothing *at all* from my back for a couple of days. [ . . . ]

> Yours,
> Your G.

## 174. A. S.

> Günsbach
> Friday, June 9th, 1911
> rather late at night

M. G.

[ . . . ]

Today Widor and I finished the manuscript that we had to read through. He is enthusiastic about the work and satisfied with the transla-tion. I am looking forward to sitting down quietly with the *Paul* tomorrow; it also is making progress. I have a few images and metaphors, a few nasty remarks in my text, a few comparisons . . . and I'm afraid that a marten (to speak in images) will take the life from these colorful chickens! O dear marten . . . let just a few of them live when you get the manuscript . . . Marten, dear little marten! Schirmer[1] (who is really in Europe) paid for your coat and was delighted that it pleased you.

Will I really find you completely changed when I see you? . . . This let-ter will reach you on Sunday. Have a beautiful Sunday, my friend . . . I am going to bed, for I have earned my rest.

> I kiss your hand
> Your G.

[ . . . ]

1. Publisher.

## 175. A. S.

[Strasbourg]
Friday, midnight
July 28th, 1911

M. G.

The concert is over. It was wonderfully solemn and beautiful . . . Many, many people (I had sent tickets to your mother, too).

Now I am sitting at the table and have completed the final copy of the speech for Ziegler's[1] last lecture. Very brief, ten minutes. Because Mademoiselle Bresslau of course imagines what her friend will say on this occasion, she will get a copy of the manuscript in the mail.

Thank you for the long letter, which arrived this evening.

The inhuman heat is not affecting me. Tomorrow off to Günsbach with sixty-seven books for at least three weeks.

And all respect to whatever is worthy of respect in my friend's state of health.

During the time when you are taking baths, please take a thyroid pill only every third day because your metabolism is raised anyway.

So, the next news will be from the rock.

Good night, I must get my rest in order to be able to speak tomorrow.

Yours, I kiss your hand,
Your G.

## 176. A. S.

[Günsbach]
Saturday evening
[August 5, 1911]

M. G.

Let us put the manuscript aside then. It is almost seven o'clock. A little bit of a Sabbath is permissible, after all. In the course of the morning, I have sketched out the new chapter, after again reading through twelve large volumes yesterday. And I began to write at one o'clock; it is going very well.

---

1. Theobald Ziegler (1846–1918), professor of philosophy at the University of Strasbourg.

This evening I will get to a place where I can almost use whole pages of the old manuscript. By the end of the week, I hope to have finished this chapter and another one that is easier to write. Then two more, and the first volume will be done.[1] I have set August 20th as a deadline, and I am curious to see whether I get there on schedule.

I am waiting impatiently for your impression of the pages that you have received. Yesterday evening Sülti and I were on the rock, but it was too dark to write. Today I will go up after dinner, but if I don't write until then, this letter won't get mailed this evening. And it is meant to reach you Monday morning as a greeting for the new week.

Politics—thanks for the article—I find very sad. Probably "our Congo"[2] will go to Germany . . . the present missionaries must give way to others . . . or tensions will increase, and then my plan of founding a humanitarian effort with both nations will be impossible. Alas for the wretched nationalistic age! If one could not laugh about it, it would be horrible to live in it. But as it is, I laugh and know . . . that I will still be needed somewhere in the world. Good-bye, m. G. . . . I kiss your hand.

I think of you often, often, happily when the chapter is going well, sadly when it makes no progress.

[ . . . ]

I kiss your hand again. May one dare to send one's friend a box of candy? . . . Nothing to confess.

## 177. H. B.

Schwartau, Fürstenhof
August 8th, 1911

M. G.

Just a little *bonjour* today and *merci* for your last two letters—so that you will see that I am still alive and thinking of you—very, very, very much, in fact. [ . . . ] So far I have found so little to correct in the manuscript that I am quite anxious about whether I am working thoroughly enough. I have only one objection, as I did in the *Reimarus,* that it often does not become clear until very late whether you are presenting your own view or that of

---

1. The book on the history of research on Paul.
2. Occupied by the French at that time.

the author whom you are discussing at the moment. I understand that it can hardly be avoided if one does not want to speak constantly in the clumsy and unnatural-sounding subjunctive, but it makes it harder to read.—I wonder if I will finish reading it over this week? I hope so.

With reference to politics, I do not agree with you—if "our Congo" really does become German, you must go there immediately and make sure that the French mission is not deprived of the fruit of its labors. Even on the other side, one can show that one stands above the nations. Please keep me informed.

> From the bottom of my heart
> Your G.

If one is good, one may send me anything one wants to. (Being good means being reasonable and not writing too far into the night!)

## 178. H. B.

> Schwartau,
> August 12th [1911]

*I*

M. G.

Thanks for your little note, which I received Thursday evening when I got back from a wonderful outing on the sea.

How beautiful it all is—I cannot say how happy I was to know that you are so happy . . . Is it still that way? Tomorrow is August 13th; are you thinking of that?

Fate has arranged it that my cousin from Hamburg will be here today, my favorite cousin[1] [ . . . ] We probably will spend the day at the sea.

I am returning the speech for Ziegler; it is very fine. But I could not refrain from noting the slips of the pen, and I ask you to read it through again before you put it into other people's hands.

I also am enclosing a note; I leave it up to you whether to send it to Mme. Reinach or not. It strikes me as so stiff and formal, but on the other hand it seems impossible not to write to this woman, particularly in French, in the most deferential terms. Tell me what you decide. [ . . . ]

---

1. Jacques Loeb.

The report on Carmen Silva[1] to my parents has been done—am I not a well-behaved friend?

My parents are in Strasbourg again, by the way—just so that you know to whom you can give pleasure if you happen to come to the city again! By the way, are you now conducting a tender correspondence with my sister-in-law?

Farewell, m. G.; this will not arrive on Sunday, but I will still think of you very much.

> With all my heart,
> your G.

II

Where is my lesson, i.e., the request for answers to my questions? I am reading the new manuscript and am painfully aware of my stupidity because it is getting too difficult for me to grasp the connections in these hair-splitting disputes, and I am only reading sentences. Why does d. G. not write a single word about whether he agreed to and accepted the few corrections?—

7:00 P.M.

I have ten more pages done and am determined to finish it tonight and tomorrow and to send it back immediately because I am too afraid to leave it here in the hotel.

At least d. G. cannot complain that I am keeping him waiting too long!

Good night, this is to be mailed this evening.—

## 179. A. S.

> [Günsbach]
> Wednesday evening
> August 23rd, 1911

M. G.

It has just struck ten. I held my head in my hands, and all my worries about politics and all my bitterness against country-devouring patriotism

---

1. No details available on this person.

were carried out by the bells into the distant valleys, and you came and laid your hands into mine . . .

God be with you . . .

Now I must get back to work so that most of the chapter will be finished tonight. The hours with Mme. Reinach were truly solemn. What a pure soul. We spoke much of you. I showed her your portrait (the big one in the table drawer). She finds you pretty and likes you; she thinks that there is something sad about your mouth . . . When I told her that I sometimes ask myself if I have the right to take you somewhere where disease and perhaps death are waiting, she said: "No, let her be; it is her right . . . and tell her that I understand and that I envy her for such a life." Perhaps she will go back from Wiesbaden via Strasbourg (October?), and then she would really like to meet you.

Good night . . . Paul is waiting . . . I have nearly reached the Weier im Tal station (i.e., I have almost finished) in this work . . .

> I kiss your hand
> Your G.

Addendum: 3:00 A.M. Chapter finished. Thirty-three pages! And I did it in five days, including one Sunday and two Reinach days. Thank you for your very good letters. . . . How are breathing, sleep, etc.?

## 180. H. B.

> [Schwartau]
> Saturday evening
> August 26th, 1911

M. G.

When I got back from Travemünde yesterday, I found your note announcing the end of the chapter: congratulations! I am so glad that you have survived it, survived it well—and that you had some good days with Mme. Reinach. Yes, it would be good to see her in October!

Your Friday greetings have just been brought to me, *merci*, m. G. I will take care of one of the chapters as soon as I get it; if you could send me the other two so that I could have them by midweek, I would be very grateful; if you can't manage both, please send just one. I would like to finish by Saturday and be able to return it because I am going to Hamburg on the 3/IX (a week from tomorrow) for one day to be together with Hermann one more time before the wedding; he can't come here anymore. And I would be un-easy if I knew that the manuscript was here in the hotel during my absence. If you send the last chapter a week from today, I will get it Monday and can look through it immediately. It wouldn't be practical to leave the whole thing for that week because I do not yet know whether I might not be leav-ing Schwartau soon after that. [ . . . ]

I will address this to Strasbourg, and you will get it earlier than the greetings I sent yesterday from Travemünde, which will be waiting for you when you get home.

Yes, m. G., I am breathing well, even breathing more deeply in the wa-ters in order to breathe in the invigorating brine. [ . . . ]

One more word on politics, for your bitter observation in yesterday's letter has kept running through my head. Don't you see, the "devourers of countries" are the French this time; they are not satisfied with what the Al-geciras agreements granted them and think they can get what they want because they feel England's jealously behind them. But Morocco means such a colossal increase in power for France that Germany may indeed feel uneasy at such a shift in the balance, and because it has genuine interests of German subjects to protect—which were threatened already in the previ-ous situation—, it probably is justified in demanding reparations. France definitely wants Morocco, but both nations wish to avoid war (only En-gland wants that!), and so the idea of compensation for the Congo does not seem so improbable to me. And I—first without thinking of the two of us!—would be happy to see it (although as a colony it cannot make up even remotely for Morocco) because it is just through a really significant increase in France's power that England's ever-watchful suspicion of us, which is constantly stirring up intrigues, can be diverted.

But for us, what would it mean if the Congo were to become German? If I call to mind your reasons for choosing to go there, there are three of them: (1) to rescue the intelligent and educable natives there from the burgeoning influence of Islam; (2) to help the French Protestant mission, *which needs people*; (3) to prove that human labor can and should rise above all the na-tional differences that separate us. *As long as the Fr. mission remains in the country*, all these reasons are independent of the nationality of the region it-self. Now if the Congo were really to become German, it seems to me that it is a worthy task for anyone who desires peace and the labors of peace (and then to work with the mission itself) to make it stay in the country. In the interests of the country, but in its own interest, too, for I think that it cannot lightly give up a field of labor into which it has put so much.

You wouldn't believe how I long to speak with you about all these questions; that is why I have told you how I think about it and what I meant when I said that fate itself will perhaps make our path clear to us (for if it turned out like that, it would have removed the greatest difficulty for us). I would be so grateful to you if you would tell me in a little more detail what you think, not only in a couple of disconnected catchwords.

Farewell—and if you must consider me a complete baby politically, keep on loving me a little bit anyway!

From my heart,
your G.

## 181. A. S.

Monday
[August 28, 1911]
[ . . . ]
6:00 P.M., on the train to Colmar

[ . . . ]

On your letter: I am far from thinking you a baby politically. On the contrary. But this one time you do not see what lies behind it all. The treaties of Algeciras were not a solution, but only a source of further disputes . . . the reason being that Germany wanted to put the thing off so that (1) France would get a lot of trouble; (2) the Mannesmann brothers[1] would buy lots of mines and lots of land; (3) it could arm its own fleet to be able to fight England if need arises. Here under heading number 3 is the fly in the ointment! What Germany wants above all is an Atlantic harbor so that it can make an enormous military harbor out of it, maintain an Atlantic fleet, and thus threaten England from east and west because England now only has to defend itself against the North Sea. An Atlantic German fleet is impossible because it would have no ports for coal, etc. But in England's case, it is not envy but the purest self-preservation that it can never permit Germany to have a military port on the northern coast of Africa near the ocean. The fact that the only object of Germany's world policies is

1. Important German industrialists.

to get the upper hand over England and threaten it with invasion by a German army is as clear as daylight . . . And that is the nasty part. Germany has to acknowledge the current state of ownership . . . but it still wants to triumph over England; then it can take as many colonies as it wants. Hence the coalition against Germany. (Thank God!) Hence the danger of war, whether now or in a year makes no difference. In the long run, Germany cannot survive this insane rearmament and is bound to collapse. That is why it must risk everything before that happens, a life-or-death risk . . . only because of insane plans for greatness . . . That is the one truth . . . By the way, I developed the theory of the war harbor for you two years ago . . . You see how right I was.

And with regard to our Congo, if it becomes German, the German God, who made iron grow,[1] will have to come in at the same time. The French missionaries will have to move out of the area at once and leave it to a German society. Then the children will have to learn "Hail to the victor's crown,"[2] etc., in German right away. By the way, France would do just the same if it took over a German colony. It is the insane nationalism that always comes first. Then there is no place for me. I do not wish to torment myself to pieces in such senseless periods of transition! But we will find something somewhere else. Perhaps the missionary society will settle somewhere else . . . or, as is more probable, Germany will strike a milder chord and will not get the Congo. As things are, it would have to fight against France and England; Italy can't say a word, or the fleet just concentrated in the Mediterranean by the excellent Declassé will set sail (France has assembled all its squadrons in the Mediterranean and is leaving the fight in the North Sea to England) . . . You know that I do not hate Germany; I honor it. But this delusion of grandeur, to which decency, honesty, morality, etc., are no more than empty concepts, is unworthy of this people . . . Is this a political letter, my little baby? My ink even ran out along the way . . .

I hope to be able to send you a chapter of the manuscript tomorrow evening or early Wednesday. I will send off the next-to-last chapter on Saturday so that you get it Monday.

[ . . . ]

1. Alluding to a German patriotic poem by E. M. Arndt (1769–1860).
2. German national anthem before 1914.

**182. A. S.**

[Günsbach, August 30, 1911]
Wednesday evening . . . late

M. G.

I am busy with the next-to-last chapter—the revision—and the "cramming in" of the literature that has not yet been included. It is horrible and boring. But I hope to be finished by noon tomorrow . . .

At ten o'clock, I hung your portrait on its nail in the window niche, and I looked at you from time to time . . . Then I suddenly had the oddest feeling that a day will come when it is not the picture but the person who is near to me and can approach me in the middle of the night and ask about the end of working . . . and will express wishes and commands about it . . . And I did not know, it came over me so strangely, whether I should rejoice (I trembled inwardly!) or be afraid of this new situation that necessarily will limit my freedom (and thus also to some degree my work and my night work) . . .

Here I sit with a weary head at the end of this heavy task; it is two o'clock, and I think of all these things, the serious part and a couple of silly things (e.g., whether someone appearing to admonish me will be wearing a beautiful kimono? . . . ) and on politics, Congo and all . . . Life appears so strange to me . . . and yet at bottom everything is beautiful.

I enclose the view of LaMotte Savoy,[1] which I can send without qualms because the text is quite impersonal . . . A little letter from the other Hélène, which suggests a rendezvous in Switzerland . . . I do not know whether I will stretch out my hands for this delicious meal.[2] I would like to, all right, because I feel that soon I will know what the word "rendezvous" means only by looking it up in the dictionary . . .

And so good night. The manuscript arrived today. I will look through it tomorrow evening.

I kiss your hand

yours
your G.

1. A castle in France where Schweitzer had gone for a rest.
2. Reference to a meal in Homer's *Odyssey*.

**183. H. B.**

["Fürstenhof," Bad Schwartau]
September 2nd, 1911

[ . . . ]

Thanks for your Wednesday night letter! Tell me, Bery, do you really believe in a limitation of your freedom, and are you afraid of it? Don't you know that you are always, always free and would be completely free, yes, m. G., utterly and completely free the moment you might wish to be? You *do* know it, and I understand what you meant. But consider that this image of someone coming up to you during the night and interrupting you has never risen before me—I don't think I ever would dare interrupt you, and I never would do anything but what I am already doing now: beg you in advance to consider your health and not to let it get too late.

When I read what you had written, I thought: "He felt how I was feeling on that evening, and that gave him that 'strange' mood in thinking of me." Tell me, can it really be true—that people *feel* together like that? It would be such a comfort to me, particularly in view of the realization—which does not trouble me anymore, but is like a scar that one must not touch—that there is something on which our thinking is fundamentally different. We will speak no more about politics, and may Heaven grant that it has no role to play in our lives.

Today the weather is beautiful, and now I want to go to the woods to walk a little: but first I must post this.

Will I get a few words today?

When and where will the rendezvous with Hélène Barrère be? I can't quite believe in this lack of familiarity with "rendezvous," after all those recent meetings with sweet and pretty ladies! But I would be happy if you saw her and could tell me about her: She has so little to say to me. Then please urge her to come along with me to Ringgenberg;[1] it would be the last time that we could be together.

My last week here has begun, and I am happy about it. Four more baths in the next few days, and Friday evening I am thinking of going to Hamburg for a few days. Then rendezvous and convalescence with my parents in Denmark and then to the wedding[2] with them.

1. In Switzerland.
2. Hermann's wedding.

Farewell, m. G. The "little note" has now turned into a great long let-ter—is anyone angry about that?

> From my heart,
> your G.

[ . . . ]

## 184. A. S.

> [Strasbourg]
> Sunday night
> September 3rd, 1911

Now come and let me kneel before you and kiss your hands, my dear one, my great one . . .

I have just written the last sentence of the last chapter. How I was able to sketch it out yesterday in six hours and write it all down in final form today in half an afternoon, weary from a sermon and the journey and half a night, is a mystery to me! I felt that I had wings. And I was so afraid of this final summing up. It could just as easily have cost me three weeks as one day.

. . . I imagine that you are bending over me and taking my head in your hands. I am not seeking fame in this work, although I feel that I could have founded a "school," like Baur.[1] But I know that it will force people into thinking and into tranquil truthfulness, not now, but for a later generation that will read this judgment on modern theology when it has been fulfilled.

I still have enough strength to read through all ten pages (ten!) and make improvements in style and elegance so that the chapter will go out to-morrow, with the sermon.

Thanks for the long letter. Oh no, m. G., there must be nothing we cannot say to each other . . . But you always have to keep in mind that we cannot look at things with ordinary feeling, but only from the desire for the kingdom of God, which the ten o'clock bell wants to sing out over the fields and which we want to carry to a far-off land . . . For us there is nothing but this . . . All other bonds have been loosened . . . and this creates the strongest bonds between us two, which makes us so peaceful and . . . proud. Now I stand up and kiss your eyes . . . yours

> your G.

1. See p. 109n.

A quiet interval, in which I sit quietly and look at your picture . . . and then begin again on the first page with erasing, crossing out, correcting . . .

Yours

your G.

Later. Finished reading over. I will read your letter once more and go to sleep! Good night.

## 185. A. S.

[On the train]
Tuesday
December 19th, 1911

M. G.

The train is moving . . . Paris again! And I hope you are home again and that as you are falling asleep, you are thinking of your friend, who is traveling into the dark night and hoping to sleep soon, too. How can I tell you what those solemn ten minutes that we spent together meant to me? I needed them, for they formed the grand chord that has been sounding within me for several days and making me tranquil. To feel with you the whole depth of our friendship and what has led us since we dared to grow closer to one another: What is sacred between the two of us and lifts us up above everything. My friend! To feel that, to know that is possible with you.—Later, after I had written this, I closed my eyes and dreamed for a long time . . . How seriously our life and how deep our happiness.

But now you have been awake long enough: Go to sleep. Good night.

I kiss your hand
Your G.

## 186. A. S.

[Paris, 80 boulevard Malesherbes]
December 22nd, 1911

I am still in bed, obeying you and getting a good rest . . . It is nine o'clock. . . . My stay here is sad; it is raining the whole time, no carriages, no automobiles (because of the strike), almost no streetcars because of construction on the streets . . . Yesterday I had to run all my errands on foot and became dreadfully wet . . . No Christmas mood to make Christmas music . . .

Your letter has just arrived . . . such a letter as only you could write . . . Yes, there is something like an undertone of melancholy when I think of binding you to my uncertain life, but with you everything is possible, and blessings will come from all this.

I am constantly thinking about announcing our decision, but I have not yet become clear about it.

But that is not essential . . . in our great undertaking clarity and light prevail . . .

Oh, those short minutes of holiday on Tuesday, how good they were! And that is how it will always be in our life . . .

I kiss your hand

Yours,
Your G.

## 187. A. S.

Paris, 80 boulevard Malesherbes
December 22nd, 1911

Dear Professor Bresslau, dear Mrs. Bresslau,

I come to ask your permission to call on you next Sunday between ten and eleven o'clock—because I have services at other times—to discuss with you a matter that is of great concern to you and me. You will not be inordinately surprised when I tell you that it concerns your daughter and that I venture to ask you to permit your daughter to accept my name and to accompany me to the Congo. I am aware of the severity of this request. Ever since this plan became a reality in me, I have felt a pain when I look at you and know about the sacrifice I have to ask from you. It is a heavy burden for me. I come to you and ask you to let your daughter go with me, without being able to promise her a secure existence for her future and with the intention of moving to a place where the sun may cause many dangers to our health.

But I have a large circle of faithful and well-to-do friends who will support my overseas work, whom I can trust, and who will not abandon me. And if I should be forced, for reasons of health, to give up my activities, there are always opportunities for church positions in Alsace. This is a reassuring thought. As far as the health issue is concerned, all those who work in the Congo have assured me that one can avoid the dangers if one observes the correct precautions and especially if one returns every two to three years for several months in the northern climate, which is my intention.

I know that all these considerations cannot ease my heavy responsibility or your worries about your daughter when she becomes my companion . . . and yet I dare to come to you with my request and hope that you will not reject it. The thought of joining our lives in common work grew steadily in your daughter and in me, and in the course of time and events became a firm resolution. We have thought about this, considered everything carefully, and finally found that we both have the right to make this decision and that through everything we have thought, worked, and experienced together, we belong together.

I beg you, esteemed professor, to have confidence in me. Even if I cannot offer your daughter a brilliant existence or even a steadily secure one, I will strive with all I have to make her happy and—for the great sacrifice she brings me—to be hers in deep gratitude to my last breath.

I have told my parents and my sister and brothers about my plans. They love your daughter very much and would be happy to receive her into our family.

I am barely able to express myself adequately and clearly because I am writing these lines with deep emotion. Please do understand what I cannot express quite as I would like. In case you want to receive me on Sunday between ten and eleven, it is not necessary to leave a message at Thomasstaden. I return home on Saturday evening.

With feelings of deep respect,
Your Albert Schweitzer

**188. A. S.**

Günsbach
Wednesday morning
[December 27, 1911]

M. G.

I am sitting here at my desk, writing letters to my friends and telling them about our decision. And the whole time I am thinking of my terrible worries last year at the same time . . . and I cannot believe that everything has taken such a happy turn.

Your portrait is hanging in the window niche . . . now in daylight, too—and last night when I came home, I spoke to it for more than an hour and finally kissed the glass . . . Forgive me . . . It is almost as good that I am alone to gather myself together a little with all these emotions, and I am very exhausted.

It was so beautiful yesterday to see the complete accordance between our families. And what my mother said to you was so beautiful!

[ . . . ]

Such times . . . How strange your friend is . . . He feels it as a pang that our secret does not belong to us any more and that now all the world will talk about it . . . But he soon regains his composure at the thought that this will be the path to our new seclusion, far away from the world.

Yours, I kiss your hand

your G.

Are you resting well?

# *1 9 1 2*

**189. A. S.**

[Strasbourg]
January 1st, 1912

Day has just begun . . . I was standing at the window when the twelve strokes sounded from the cathedral . . . and I trembled . . . Now "our year" is here . . . how will we be when it has run its course? Oh, my great friend . . . I feel your thinking about me, your great, your holy thinking . . . How privileged we are that we can work together, that we have carried out what we had planned . . . Oh, how different this is from last year, when I was full of fear, full of fear . . . Will you ever know what I suffered for you?

The year is already rushing by . . . the first quarter is just striking . . . What does it hold for us?

Oh, see, my great one, it can bring us what is destined for us . . . but one thing it must do: leave us what is noble. We must be "noble" with one another, more and more, and keep this always in our consciousness . . .

And we never want to forget this either: that we are together to serve *the* Great One and that every happiness that we may be permitted to partake of is only a magnificent extra gift . . .

Oh, the sun tomorrow, my great, great friend! And thank you for everything that you are for me . . . for everything. . . . I kiss your hand

Your G.

**190. H. B.**

[Strasbourg, January 30, 1912]

M. G.

Thank you for your little note! When will you arrive? It bothered me when I left that I did not even know when you would be there, when the poor weary G. would get to sleep? Was he able to sleep? and properly? I went to bed at eleven and slept well.—"Very well?"—very well, my friend, thank you!

This morning I had an idea. Because you are in Tübingen for once, you can make direct contact with Siebeck and Mohr while you are there and ask (1) whether the second part of the *Paul* will be set in type all at the same time and if the composition can remain for a few weeks until the corrections have been returned? And (2), about the English translation. Perhaps they will agree to give up the translation rights for a fixed sum so that you don't have to share the honorarium with Black every time: I find it so unjust if you aren't to get anymore than they do. It is better to discuss these matters orally, and it saves writing.

Farewell, Mother is waiting to go into town.

Yours,
Your G.

**191. A. S.**

Tübingen
February 2nd, 1912

M. G.

My friend is the best and the cleverest one that can be imagined. Now for the answer to your suggestions: (1) spoke to Mohr, and this is how it will be arranged: The books (to be *our* books in the future) will be set in type as a whole and will be corrected in central Africa.

(2) I already have arranged in my contract that I have the right to dispose of my *Paul* in any way that I wish in exchange for a reimbursement of 100M.

(3) I arrived around 1:30 in the morning.

My organ concert was an *enormous* success. Mohr has only one more copy of the *Reimarus!* So the new edition must come out soon. Poor Bery.

This evening, Friday, St. Matthew's Passion. I am planning to leave after the concert at one o'clock in the morning with Wendling[1] and to be in Strasbourg at five o'clock! So when you wake up tomorrow morning, your friend will be sleeping in Strasbourg. Half of the sermon is already written, and the rest will be done this afternoon . . .

I dream of my friend arriving Saturday evening and encouraging me with her kind eyes . . . I also have something to tell her about the Paris concert.

I kiss her hand<br>Her G.

**192. A. S.**

[Beaulieu]<br>March 10th, 1912

I have been here in the house of Fanny Reinach for two days now, and it is simply marvelous. The house is very beautiful and at the same time comfortable. It has only one drawback: I am constantly getting lost in it, for it is large, and all the rooms look alike. I sleep and sleep and find that I already am more rested, much less nervous, and I do not feel the pains in my head anymore. We have just dined, and I am sitting across from Madame Reinach, who asks me to leave some space for her so that she can add a word. She is so kind to me and looks much healthier than at our last meeting.

The days go by too quickly. Yesterday I did not come down until eleven o'clock and walked till noon. In the afternoon, I slept again, wrote a few letters, studied the Mass, and began to give Madame Reinach a summary of the second half of my lecture. This morning I went on presenting the main ideas of the lecture; this afternoon I worked out the program for the 25th of April,[2] and it was decided that Fräulein Bresslau will sit in Madame Reinach's box at the concert.

I did not go out today because it is very windy, and I do not want to risk my cold hanging on longer now that it is on the way to recovery.

1. Violinist Carl Wendling (1875–1962).
2. A concert to raise funds for his mission to the Congo.

I leave you and kiss your hand in order to write anther Congo letter with which I wish to prepare for certain visits in Le Havre.

I hear the wind and the waves. It is a beautiful music.

What are you doing? Are you living reasonably? Did you receive the few words that your friend wrote in the train shortly before he arrived? I hope to have a brief greeting from you tomorrow . . .

Good-bye . . . How long it lasts this time . . .

Yours<br>Your G.

## 193. H. B.

March 18th, 1912

M. G. the 18th! Blue flowers—sunshine—a tree trunk in the Neuhüfler Forest—is my dear friend thinking of that?

But I don't want him to feel homesick—think of it, there are only one and one-half weeks now before we are together again!—Oh, Bery, can you imagine that? And even if it is only for one day,—still, it means that after fourteen more days the last great separation will be over—can it be true? . . . become reality?—*Mon cher* G., in such thoughts it is easy to celebrate the day of the blue flowers even alone, isn't it? And perhaps even the 22nd without the Rhine—probably I won't be able to come out,[1] there's much still to be done. But I am not sad any more, but truly cheerful and glad within. Berylein, my dear, you are getting a healthy wife who will be able to endure things once more. And even if I had learned nothing at all in the clinic—but you learn heaps of things there every day—I would have been happy to have gone there simply because I see how well I am taking it. I am there in the morning at 8:00, 8:15 at the latest, and on my feet until 1:00 or 1:30 and am getting on famously. They let you get at something right away, giving injections, catheterizing; today I applied bandages and was in charge of the instruments in a minor case. And the sister shows me everything very charmingly and gives me good advice on the care and maintenance of the instruments and of everything else. And today she also told me that I was the most envied girl in Strasbourg. Can you guess why? Don't rack your brains over it, my dear, I will tell you: because I—am getting such a famous

1. To Günsbach.

husband! I really have to laugh. If I were to be envied only because of his fame!—

I'm already on the fourth page, and there's so much more to tell you. And they are big sheets, too!

I have something to confess, too: Your friend, in league with Frau Wölpert, has pounded the books in the attic, cleaned them (is someone very angry? Frau Wölpert was so happy!), and packed them nicely sorted into the two boxes. Now theology, history, philosophy, music, etc., are arranged separately and are easy to get at (when you come on the 30th, I will go up with you and show you how conveniently everything is arranged); I took all the works of literature downstairs and set them up on the spinet in good order so that they won't get in your way. But *Hutten's Last Days* was not among them—don't you still have the first book that your friend gave you and that was the occasion of our becoming better acquainted, or do you have it somewhere else? I also didn't find the *Faust* that I gave you once. [ . . . ]

My head is gradually feeling empty, to the same degree that the things I have to worry about make progress, and that is a comforting feeling. The whole dressmaking question will be taken care of soon (except for the wedding dress); but along with everything else, I have had the dressmaker here for four days, and she will be here for two more, and I also have fittings with two in town. All the linen is almost ordered, too. Now there are only the cooking utensils . . .

It is five minutes of ten. My letter must get off. Where should I send it? M. G. doesn't write to tell me when he will leave Spain? I will address it to Paris so that you will find it waiting for you in case you didn't get my Sunday card in Barcelona and will remember to give birthday wishes to your father on the 21st and to mine on the 22nd.

And say Hello to Paris and the Parisians for me and tell them that I am looking forward to getting to know them soon.

I embrace you, m. G.

> With all my heart,
> your G.

**194. A. S.**

[Paris]
March 21st, 1912

M. G.

And now the 22nd is coming, and we will not be together! This time we will not look at the sky together when we get up to see whether J and B[1] can take us to the river . . . but it is still a beautiful 22nd, isn't it, m. G., the last 22nd in the "old covenant" . . . How much I think again of everything, of this wonderful enchantment of things that brought us together and is leading us to a far land . . . and over everything a breath of spring, of newly budding branches, of little blue and yellow flowers . . .

And it is as though all this matched our friendship, all that is serious and beautiful in it. If you had dreamed where this question "whether friendship existed" would lead you . . . that those minutes when we walked along together beside our bicycles contained the deciding moment of your life . . .

And we forget all the years that lie between, the years in which you had to struggle, you were sad, you were ill . . . and think straight back to what our friendship has given us . . . Of the rest, we keep only the memory of the great and beautiful things. And I will never forget how noble and great you were in all those afflictions . . . When I think of it, I am touched . . . that my friend was so true to her friend, and it seems to me like a beautiful poem that I am reading, but not like natural history.

[ . . . ]

Tomorrow, when the evening bells ring, I will be sitting at the organ to begin the Passion . . . and in thought I will be far from Paris . . . with you . . . , will be holding your hand and listening to the bells with you . . . and thinking ahead of smaller bells, in a smaller church—which will soon ring out for us over blossoming trees.[2] . . .

Yours, I kiss your hand
Your G.

---

1. Their bicycles.
2. Church at Günsbach where their wedding will take place on June 18.

## 195. H. B.

[Grand Hotel Brissagno]
April 2nd, 1912

M. G.

Now I am settled in my very peaceful room, in which you can hear nothing but the music of the powerful wind making the trees sing and groan with its force; and from here you see nothing but the green and blue waves of the lake with little whitecaps, and behind them the brown-green mountains, their peaks still covered with snow. And blue sky and brilliant sun— could anyone wish for more?

At the moment, there are only twenty people in the hotel (Frau Dehio will not arrive until tomorrow, my uncle and my aunt the day after tomorrow), and my parents and I are quite alone on our floor and thus the absolute masters and possessors of a wonderful terrace that runs along the whole front. I have just fought my way back and forth a couple of times facing the storm for exercise, my head firmly wrapped in a veil.

The journey yesterday was not pleasant; the trains were crammed, sheets of rain after Lucerne, a snowstorm in Airolo. I got a violent headache, but slept last night, in spite of the frenzy of the storm, only interrupted by waking up a few times. And I always had G.'s picture before me, not only in his really very good photographs, but within—the picture of my good, caring, loving friend as he took his leave of me on Palm Sunday, and the silent rejoicing that was in us both: The fact that this is the last separation always echoes within me.

[ . . . ]

I found my parents very contented here when I arrived, and I already have informed my father that there must not be more than three courses at our wedding. He does not agree, and I gave him permission to have those three as exquisite as he pleases. Is m. G. satisfied with his friend?

I hope that I will hear from him very shortly and in the meantime I send him many heartfelt good thoughts.

I embrace you with all my heart.

Your G.

My parents send best wishes.

**196. A. S.**

April 6th, 1912, at night

M. G.

The Faustian night that will vanish on Easter morning when the Easter bells will ring it to its grave. If I did not have to preach tomorrow morning, I would stay awake and work, like my dear cousin in universality, whom our great Goethe describes so magnificently . . . Now, however, I go to bed— not a poetic act, admittedly, but I comfort myself with the realization that I do not have to be like Faust in all aspects, and I don't want to be. I would rather take my Gretchen[1] with me to Africa than leave her behind. This is (1) more pleasant, (2) more honorable, (3) more profitable. And there must not be a poodle either, but a wire-haired dog, as large as possible.

I do not have to confess how late it is. My work is progressing well.

> With Faustian greetings and a kiss on your hand
> (but with proper intentions)
> your G.

**197. A. S.**

[On the train]
Sunday morning
[April 14, 1912]

M. G.

From Strasbourg to Paris for the last time . . . writing to my friend for the last time on the journey where the forest of August 13th beckons to me . . . How many memories, what suns and shadows of parting . . . But it is good that everything is now being fulfilled . . . And never again will I write to you on this journey . . . Never again undertake this trip as I do now . . .

Business matters. Go to my house immediately. On the bookshelves upstairs, where the sermons are, there is an envelope from Breitkopf[2] on the right among the sermons with your address on it, with 1,000 Marks for the Congo, to be invested immediately! Colmar was good and is still promising.

1. A character from Goethe's play.
2. Publisher.

(2) My address: 29 boulevard de Courcelles, care of Monsieur Paul Harth.

(3) I will take care of lodgings immediately.

(4) Give me your address in Frankfurt and the dates.

(5) I implore you, do not arrive exhausted!

The sun is laughing . . . I am seeing this country like this for the last time.

I am going to have to restructure my dissertation fundamentally.[1] Pfersdorff found it too literary generally and not medical enough. But we did quite thorough outlines together. He wants to keep it much simpler than I wanted it to be. I was sad for a few days because I had thought I was almost finished with it. But Bery always lifts himself out of sadness immediately and begins again from the beginning. That is why he is Bery and the friend of his friend.

> I kiss your hand
> Your G.
>
> [ . . . ]

**198. H. B.**

> Frankfurt A.M.
> April 17th, 1912
> c/o Fr. Isay-Michaelis, Hansa-Allee 20/I

Thank you for this morning's note! But now I have caused you trouble for the last time, poor thing, and now you must not write to me anymore, unless you really have a little time and want to come to me for rest.

You need not worry about me; I don't have anything at all to do here. The weather is most magnificent, and I am being lovingly looked after and go for walks. Mama is in Hamburg, Father in Berlin, Luise and her child in Darmstadt. I would have had to go back and forth between the Hoffs and Fr. Fischer—judge for yourself whether that would have been less exhausting. And here I am really giving pleasure to my relatives, who can have me for a little bit longer—so I think you understand, don't you?

A thousand thanks for looking for lodgings; I can't judge if it's expensive because I don't know if it is full room and board or only the room . . .

---

1. *The Psychiatric Study of Jesus*, Schweitzer's medical school doctoral dissertation.

But that doesn't matter at all now; if there is no other choice, the money must be paid. So I will arrive in Paris on the evening of the 23rd at 9:20 and will take the 2:14 train from Strasbourg, which is the best. I asked Papa to get the connection via Strasbourg on the return journey because it would be no shorter directly from here than from here via Strasbourg, and this way I can divide the journey in two parts and spend one more night in Strasbourg. Besides, this way I don't have to haul all my Paris *élégance* to Frankfurt, and last but not least I am now happy because I also can take care of the question of the wedding banns that only caught up with me here. *Voilà.* (I will write immediately after Stettin!)

We just saw the solar eclipse very well through a black piece of glass—you see how seriously I am spending my time here! My cousins are giving me the individual spoons that we are still missing, so that the silver is now complete. In general, I should list many more wedding presents—I only know that people are too good to us! Do you think that we should take a Goethe along, too? If so, I would like one in the nice thin paper edition, like the Schiller I have—what do you think?

I am really worried about Bery. I think the man is letting himself be harried too much, and I also find that he should set aside his begging for the Congo and have a little more trust in the good Lord, who will continue to help. If he lets himself be kept up until all hours of the night by everybody for the sake of Congo conferences and has all his work and travel arrangements tossed aside, he will ruin his health. Don't you think so? And wouldn't you, too, be afraid to enter into a new life and new circumstances alone with such a weary man? I am sure that you agree with me that he must spare himself a little more, if only for my sake and for the sake of what we desire for the future. So please try to obtain a little influence over him in this direction! Just now practical and theoretical medicine are quite enough for him, and if he has even a spark of common sense, he will begin to limit himself energetically.

[ . . . ]

*Between the letters of April 16 and May 26, 1912, lies the crisis that came close to putting a stop to Albert Schweitzer's work in Africa. It spans the time between May 9 and 13. Schweitzer categorically refused to sign a contract submitted by the directors of the Paris mission, according to which he would have to follow the instructions of the committee while in Lambaréné. In consequence, the commit-*

tee wanted to break off relations with him. In the decisive meeting of May 13, the mission director, Jean Bianquis, succeeded in reversing this decision. The committee contented itself with Schweitzer's promise to respect the discipline of the mission and to "be as mute as a carp" on theological questions.

Schweitzer played down this conflict in his 1930 autobiography and mentioned only the outcome.

The great nervous strain of these days, in conjunction with an angina, led Schweitzer to a physical and psychic breakdown that lasted several months. He suffered from queasiness, nausea, fevers, and heart problems. At his wedding on June 18, 1912, he was only partially recovered. Their departure for Africa, which had been scheduled for June or July, had to be postponed. It was not until January 1913 that he felt strong enough to undertake the voyage, which they did in March.

**199. A. S.**

[Strasbourg]
Whitsun evening
[May 26, 1912]

I have thought of you often today and have to tell you how much I like you because you are so good. Our past life passed before my eyes in the silence of this holiday, and there you stood before me, surrounded by rivers of light and purity, and I would have liked to kiss your hands to thank you for being as you are and going your way as you did without thinking of yourself. Between us, we are rich in shared spiritual possessions, which we gathered in youthful, great, and difficult times. We shall always think of these treasures so that we will not stand before one another in wretched everyday clothing, but with the adornments that each of us wears in the presence of the other.

Oh you noble, great friend. Now the night is coming, and when the sun shines again, you will come to me . . . do you know how much I look forward to it?

This is a little note for tomorrow night.

Yours,
your G.

**200. A. S.**

[Strasbourg]
Thursday evening
August 21st [22nd], 1912

The literature of the last two years is so extensive that I am making slower progress than I had thought. Although the library is closed in the afternoon, I crept in from 3:30 to 6:00 today to put together lists, and as I left I decided to stay here to be able to toss my order slips into the box this evening. I'll finish the lists tomorrow, to arrange for some important books that are missing to be obtained for me, to check at Schmidt's to see if I can find the others so as to look through them without buying them . . . and get home tomorrow evening (I have permission to go to the library again tomorrow afternoon) at eight o'clock when I have finished everything. I dined with your parents; they were very pleased. Your mother wishes very much to see you. Afterward I met the Lenels. I had already had a room at Frau Fischer's[1] put in order; she has given me standing permission to make use of her house when she is away (and I had not intended to claim that right so soon). After dinner, I will write seventy more book slips! And then submit them. One box with books is already full. Do not forget to change Sülti's bandages tomorrow morning! (if it is not unpleasant for you: a little wick in the wound and nothing more.)

Give my regards to everyone. I am writing to you in haste, in order to finish the book slips and to look through my list one more time.

Yours, I embrace you.
Your G.

Sleep well.

**201. A. S.**

[Strasbourg]
Monday, September 9th, 1912
evening

It is striking ten. I feel that you must hear it. I am in the process of reading the revised chapter. I like it. I made music for one and one-half hours *without tiring myself out!* What progress. It seemed to me that you must be

1. Annie Fischer-Stinnes, a friend and contributor.

Albert Schweitzer and Helene Bresslau's wedding, June 1912. *Courtesy of the Albert Schweitzer Archive, Günsbach.*

hearing the improvisation. It was like a song with five stanzas, and the text was dark in my thoughts, but in reality it was an expression of gratitude for the nobility and the purity of your soul . . . You stand so distinguished and with such calm assurance in my life . . . that is magnificent, magnificent . . . I kiss your hand

Your G.

*Night*

Since you are the soul of discretion, you will not ask me at what time these lines are being written. It will be enough for you to learn that my pen has filled many pages cheerfully today and that the chapter has been read over almost completely and many parts have been revised! And I am very happy. I can still do something after all!

Good night, I kiss your hand. I had lit the oven . . . and your lamp! At first, the chimney was sooty, but afterward it was white as snow again! Only I was afraid of being scolded . . .

Your G.

*After a civil marriage ceremony on June 12, 1912, Helene Bresslau and Albert Schweitzer were married in the church at Günsbach on June 18.*

# INDEX